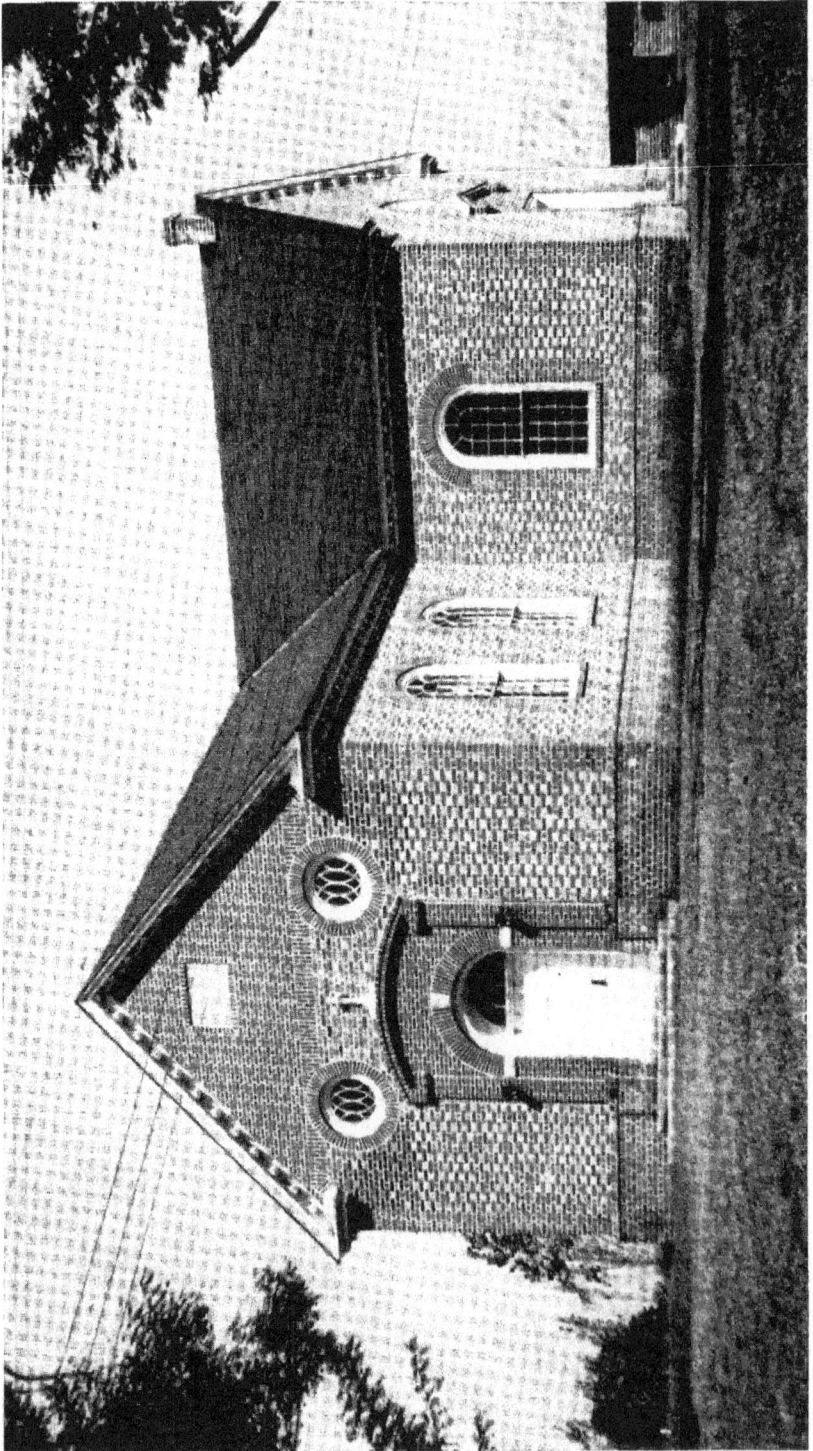

NORTH FARNHAM PARISH CHURCH
BUILT 1737

THE REGISTERS
OF
NORTH FARNHAM PARISH
1663 - 1814
AND
LUNENBURG PARISH
1783 - 1800
RICHMOND COUNTY
VIRGINIA

* * * * *
* * * *
* * *
* *
*

Compiled by:
George Harrison Sanford King

Southern Historical Press, Inc.
Greenville, South Carolina

Please direct all correspondence and orders to:

www.southernhistoricalpress.com
or
SOUTHERN HISTORICAL PRESS, Inc.
PO BOX 1267
Greenville, SC   29601
southernhistoricalpress@gmail.com

ISBN #0-89308-580-4

Printed in the United States of America

IN MEMORIUM

EARL GREGG SWEM, Litt.D., LL.D.

1870 ——— 1965

LIBRARIAN - HISTORIAN - BIBLIOGRAPHER

A sincere friend and advisor
for over thirty years.

Those who knew him best,
loved him most.

NORTH FARNHAM PARISH COMMUNION SILVER - 1720

CHURCH SILVER OF NORTH FARNHAM AND LUNENBURG PARISHES [1]

Farnham Parish, Richmond County, Virginia; founded about 1693. [2]

A plain cylindrical silver flagon on a wide splayed base, having a flat topped cover, a scrolled thumb-piece and a scrolled handle. The sacred trigram in a glory is engraved on the body

Pharnham Parish.

Height: 11 1/2"; diameter of the mouth, 4"; and of the base, 7 1/8".

London date-letter for 1720-1721. Maker's mark: F.A., with a fleur-de-lis above and a mullet below, in a shaped shield, for Thomas Farren.

The plain chalice has a bell-shaped body on a thick stem, encircled by a moulding, and a moulded base. The sacred trigram is engraved on one side with

Pharnham Parish.

Height: 8 3/4"; diameter of the mouth, 4 1/8"; and of the base, 3 7/8".

The date-letter and the maker's mark are the same as those on the flagon.

Both of these vessels are inscribed as follows:

Presented to St. John's Church
Washington City
By
Col. John Tayloe
Dec. 16, 1816

Lunenburg Parish (St.John's Church), Richmond County, Virginia; founded about 1693. [2]

A plain silver flagon in this church is a duplicate of one belonging to Farnham Parish described on page 179. It was restored to this parish by the vestry of St. John's Church, Washington City, having been purchased and presented to that church in 1816 by Colonel John Tayloe after the War of 1812, when all the communion vessels of unoccupied Episcopal churches were confiscated and sold by a statue which had been passed by the legislature of Virginia.

---

1 - The picture of the North Farnham Parish communion silver on the opposite page and the description of it above are adopted from Edward Alfred Jones, The Old Silver Of American Churches [(1913) NK-7215, U-5, J-7], pages 179, 186, 252.

2 - 1693 is incorrect; see page xiii.

REFLECTIONS

Enquire, I pray thee,
  of the former Age,
And prepare thyself
  to the search of their Fathers;
For we are but of yesterday.

VIII Job 8:9

. . . "At the very base of family spirit is found the respect for the
past, for that which a family has best are the souvenirs held in common.
Intangible, indivisible, inalienable, capital, these souvenirs constitute
a sacred deposit. Each member of the family ought to consider them as his
most precious possession. They exist in a double form, in idea and in fact.
One finds them in language, the ruts of thought, the sentiments, instincts
even. And under a material form we see them represented by portraits, fur-
niture, constructions, costumes and songs. To profane eyes this is nothing;
to the eyes of those who know how to appreciate these things of the family
life, they are relics which should not be abandoned at any price."

[Charles Wagner, The Simple Life (New York, 1904, from
the original French edition), page 132.]

"It is wise occasionally to recur to the sentiments and to the character
of those from whom we are descended. Men who are regardless of their ancestry
and their posterity are very apt to be regardless of themselves. . . . The
contemplation of our ancestors and of our descendants ought ever to be within
the group of our thoughts and affections. The past belongs to us by affectionate retrospect, while the future belongs to us no less by affectionate
anticipation of those who are to come after us. And then only do we do our-
selves justice when we are true to the blood we inherit, and true to those to
whom we have been the means of transmitting that blood."

[The Honorable Daniel Webster (1782-1852)]

"People who never look backward to their ancestors, will never look for-
ward to posterity."

[The Right Honorable Edmund Burke, M.P., (1729-1797)]

C O N T E N T S

I L L U S T R A T I O N S

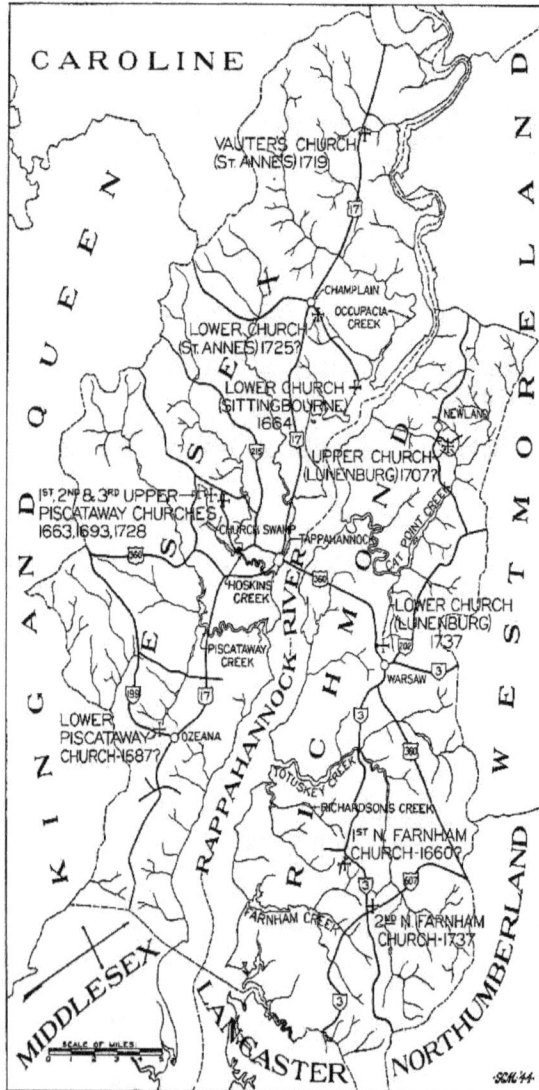

CAROLINE

QUEEN

ESSEX

RICHMOND

KING

WESTMORELAND

NORTHUMBERLAND

MIDDLESEX

LANCASTER

VAUTER'S CHURCH
(ST. ANNE'S) 1719

CHAMPLAIN

OCCUPACIA
CREEK

LOWER CHURCH
(ST. ANNE'S) 1725?

LOWER CHURCH
(SITTINGBOURNE)
1664

NEWLAND

UPPER CHURCH
(LUNENBURG) 1707?

1ST, 2ND & 3RD UPPER
PISCATAWAY CHURCHES
1663, 1693, 1728

CHURCH SWAMP

ST. POINT CREEK

TAPPAHANNOCK

HOSKINS
CREEK

LOWER CHURCH
(LUNENBURG)
1737

PISCATAWAY
CREEK

WARSAW

LOWER
PISCATAWAY
CHURCH-1587?

OZEANA

TOTUSKEY CREEK

RICHARDSONS CREEK

1ST N. FARNHAM
CHURCH-1660?

FARNHAM CREEK

2ND N. FARNHAM
CHURCH-1737

RAPPAHANNOCK RIVER

SCALE OF MILES

-SCH. '44-

PLATE 1. MAP OF ESSEX AND RICHMOND
COUNTIES, SHOWING OLD CHURCHES

THE ORIGINAL PARISH REGISTERS of North Farnham and Lunenburg are not known to be in existence. Instead we have two alphabetical arrangements which are of Eighteenth Century origin and these have been referred to at times as the "original registers," but they obviously are not. A few late Eighteenth and Nineteenth Century entries have been made in the North Farnham Parish Register (1663-1814).

It is obvious that in transcribing the presently preserved alphabetized volumes, various errors were made and some of these will be apparent in the present arrangement. However, with certain reservations, I feel we can trust these transcripts for the most part.

As neither of these parish registers have been published heretofore and the North Farnham Parish Register is the only known unpublished colonial parish register of the Northern Neck of Virginia, I hope many may find items of interest. The present volume should be used in close conjunction with Marriages of Richmond County, Virginia, 1668-1853, compiled and published by me in 1964.

The surviving North Farnham Parish Register volume is approximately two hundred years old and some of the pages have disintegrated in places, one of the leather bound covers is missing and many pages separated from the binding spine. Unfortunately, several persons at varying times have numbered the pages haphazardly with ink, lead pencil and blue crayon and these paginations are not always identical. Recently the volume was restored by the lamination process at the Virginia State Library and as some of the pages were obviously out of place, a few pages were again shuffled before the volume was rebound - all of which has forced me to dispare of citing the page number for the entries here as my data cards were made before the volume was rebound.

The page numbers will be given for entries in the Lunenburg Parish Register (1783-1800) which is a relatively small volume of only birth and baptismal entries. There are no marriage or death entries in the Lunenburg Parish Register but an unfortunate abundance of Negro slave birth recordings. All entries not designated as recorded in the Lunenburg Parish Register, thus L: (followed by the page number), are to be found in the North Farnham Parish Register [NFPR].

In order not to completely neglect the many Negro slave birth recordings in both of these parish registers, I am including on pages 209-216 an alphabetical arrangement of the Negro slave owners. Attention is called to the two paragraphs on page 209 preceeding the listing of the Negro slave owners.

Most persons are familiar with the complications wrought by the duplexity of dates in the Julian calendar, commonly called the "old style" calendar, which was in use in England and its colonies prior to 1752. According to the Julian calendar, the year began on 25 March and ended on the 24 March, however, in 1752 England and its colonies adoped the Gregorian calendar and thereafter the year began on 1 January and ended on 31 December. But various clerks did not always use the proper double date prior to 1752 and this neglect sometimes leaves us in doubt as to the exact date intended. Therefore, if the months of January, February or March are involved prior to 1752, the double date must be taken into consideration even though it may not be given. If, for instance, the parish register records the death of a man in November 1741 and the court records indicate his will was admitted to probate in February 1741 the only logicial conclusion is that the will was probated in February 1741/2 and for some unknown reason the court clerk neglected to enter the double date. Most often by paging the court record books and carefully noting the sequence of the recordings, these discrepancies can be resolved. Likewise, if the original North Farnham Parish Register with its chronological arrangement had been preserved, there would be no doubt as to the exact date intended for recordings in the months of January, February and March prior to 1752 even if the parish clerk neglected to enter the double date.

While the "old style" double dating prior to 1752 in the months of January, February and March serves to explain some irregularities, there are others which cannot be explained through the complications of the Julian calendar. A case in point: I see a couple were married 13 July 1730 and their son Benjamin was born 25 December 1730. If Benjamin's birth had been entered as, say, 25 January 1731 then it is possible he might have been born 25 January 1731/2 which would have been a more appropriate time than he was - 5 months after his parents were married

The following table may prove helpful as sometimes prior to 1752 a document is dated, as was the will of James Dempster, the 15th of X^{ber} 1676 and proved 6 June 1677 in Rappahannock County, Virginia, court. This means that Dempster's will was dated the 15th of the 10th month [i.e., December 15, 1676] and proved 6 June 1677.

OLD STYLE Prior to 1752, the year began March 25		NEW STYLE The year 1752 began with January 1	
March	1st month	January	1st month
April	2nd month	February	2nd month
May	3rd month	March	3rd month
June	4th month	April	4th month
July	5th month	May	5th month
August	6th month	June	6th month
September	7th month	July	7th month
October	8th month	August	8th month
November	9th month	September	9th month
December	10th month	October	10th month
January	11th month	November	11th month
February	12th month	December	12th month

Therefore, prior to 1752 New Year's Day was March 25th but by virtue of an Act of Parliament of 1751 adopting the Gregorian calendar throughout Great Britain and her colonies, New Year's Day fell on the 1st of January 1752.

When the North Farnham Parish Register (1663-1814) opens, there was no such parish; it was simply Farnham Parish and covered both sides of the Rappahannock River in Old Rappahannock County. In 1684 Farnham Parish was subdivided into North Farnham Parish and South Farnham Parish and the Rappahannock River served as a natural boundary. In 1692 when Old Rappahannock County became defunct and became the parent of two new counties, South Farnham Parish fell into Essex County and North Farnham Parish fell into Richmond County. For further detail in regard to the formation and history of the parishes in these two counties, I refer those interested to the scholarly article by the late George Carrington Mason (1885-1955), Historiographer of the Diocese of Southern Virginia, entitled "The Colonial Churches of Essex and Richmond Counties," in The Virginia Magazine of History and Biography, Volume 53, pages 3-20.

No history of Richmond County has been published but a number of works afford considerable data in regard to its civil and ecclesiastical affairs. Bishop William Meade in his masterly work, Old Churches and Families of Virginia, Volume II, pages 172-182, has recorded some interesting facts. On page 425 he indicates that Farnham Parish doubtless derived its name from a town in Surrey, England, in which the castle of the Bishop of Winchester was located. Lunenburg Parish seemingly took its name from one of the several titles of England's Hanoverian kings, H.R.H. King George II (1683-1760), Duke of Brunswick - Lüneburg, having been on the throne five years when the parish of Lunenburg was formed in 1732.

Dr. George MacLaren Brydon has left us some interesting detail in regard to Richmond County and its parishes in Virginia's Mother Church (two volumes, Richmond, 1947 and 1952) but this gentleman of cloth spares us much of the detail in regard to the great dissatisfaction in Lunenburg Parish during the tenure of the Reverend Mr. William Kay from 1745 to 1752. If we can believe all the Rev. Mr. Kay related to the Lord Bishop of London in his letter written from Williamsburg on the 14th of June 1752 as to conditions in Lunenburg Parish, then there is little wonder that a colonial register of the parish did not survive the turmoil. By some mischance shortly after he took charge of Lunenburg Parish in 1745, the Rev. Mr. Kay says he "found to my sorrow, that I had one wealthy, Great, powerful Colonel named Landon Carter, a leading Man in my Vestry, whom I could not reasonably please or oblige, very proud, haughty, imperious and fickle." . . . "He drew over six of the Vestry to him and most of these his kindred relations, or such as were subject unto him," and they signed an order to discharge me and "lock up the doors and Nail up the pulpits, Reading desks and windows of both Churches, which they did; and he himself with the other six vestrymen the next Sabbath Day forbad me and the Congregation to enter the Church; but at one of my Churches, where were many of my friends, they forced him and his six away, broke open the doors, pulpits and desks, and conducted me in. This Church, I had free liberty of, while I stayed in the parish. But at the other Church I preached out of doors in the yard two years and a half. These Seven let out my Glebe, Rent free, to three Men poor and wicked enough not to stick at anything." . . . "The names of these Men are William Degge, George Russell and Thomas Russell." [See the original full text of the Rev. Mr. William Kay's letter to the Lord Bishop of London in W.S. Perry, Historical Collections of the Protestant Episcopal Church, Volume I (1650-1776), pages 389-393; privately printed, 1870.]

James Scott Rawlings in <u>Virginia's Colonial Churches: An Architectural Guide</u> (Richmond, 1963), pages 145-147, gives an excellent technical description of North Farnham Parish Church and it is likely many may find this volume interesting and informative. Appendix II contains a list of all the colonial Virginia vestry books and parish registers, where they are deposited, which have been published and by whom.

The many years of experience of Mr. Thomas Hoskins Warner as a surveyor in the area and his fervent study of the court records, has enabled him to add a unique touch to his <u>History of Old Rappahannock County, Virginia, 1656 - 1692</u> (Tappahannock, Va., 1965) that we do not usually find in county histories. Since Richmond County was formed in 1692 from that portion of Old Rappahannock County which lies on the north side of the Rappahannock River, the records in regard to persons in the Richmond County area prior to 1692 are to be found in the Old Rappahannock County court record books which are kept in the clerk's office of Essex County at Tappahannock. Likewise, for this same reason, the late William Montgomery Sweeny's carefully compiled and indexed <u>Wills of Rappahannock County, Virginia, 1656 - 1692</u> (Lynchburg, Va., 1947) is an indispensable reference volume.

<u>The Diary of Colonel Landon Carter of Sabine Hall 1752 - 1778</u> (Richmond, 1965) serves to throw a most interesting light on the life of an aristocratic family in colonial Virginia and as Colonel Landon Carter (1710-1778) built handsome Sabine Hall and resided there during the entire period of his published diary, there is much mention of various persons resident in the Richmond County neighborhood.

The late Henry Ragland Eubank, Esquire, has left us some interesting lore in regard to the old homes, churches and families of Richmond County in his work, <u>Historic Northern Neck of Virginia</u> (Richmond, 1934), pages 82-89. Currently, the <u>Northern Neck of Virginia Historical Magazine</u> is publishing family sketches, tombstone inscriptions, Bible records, diaries and other source material of prime interest to the genealogist and historian.

The Hereditary Order of Descendants of Colonial Governors restored and bound the North Farnham Parish Register in 1965 and it has been placed in the office of the clerk of the court of Richmond County where there is also a 1902 transcript of this register. The Virginia State Library has photocopies of both of these volumes as well as the Lunenburg Parish Register.

I wish to express my appreciation to John Melville Jennings, Esquire, director of the Virginia Historical Society, for granting permission to use as illustrations in this volume the picture of North Farnham Parish Church which appears as the frontispiece and the Map of Essex and Richmond Counties on page x; both originally appeared in <u>The Virginia Magazine of History and Biography</u>, Volume 53.

Geo: H.S. King

George Harrison Sanford King

1303 Prince Edward Street
Fredericksburg
Virginia   22401
1 February 1966

KEY TO ABBREVIATIONS OF TITLES AND SYMBOLS

--   Torn and/or mutilated

?   --   Questionable

_____   --   Not entered

AP&P(2) -- Adventurers of Purse and Person, Virginia, 1607-1625 by Annie Lash Jester and Martha Woodroof Hiden (Princeton, N.J., 1964, Second Edition)

c.   --   circa - about

Hayden   --   Virginia Genealogies by the Rev. Horace Edwin Hayden (Wilkes-Barre, Pa., 1891)

L: --   Lunenburg Parish Register 1783-1800, Richmond County, Virginia

MRC   --   Marriages of Richmond County, Virginia, 1668-1853 compiled and published by George H.S. King (Ann Arbor, Michigan, 1964)

Meade   --   Old Churches, Ministers and Families of Virginia, in two volumes, by the Rt. Rev. William Meade, Bishop of P.E.C. of Virginia (Philadelphia, Pa., 1889)

+NFPR   --   North Farnham Parish Register 1663-1814, Richmond County, Virginia

OPR   --   The Register of Overwharton Parish, Stafford County, Virginia, 1723-1758, compiled and published by George H.S. King (Ann Arbor, Michigan, 1961)

SPR   --   The Register of Saint Paul's Parish 1715-1798, Stafford County, Virginia, 1715-1776; King George County, Virginia, 1777-1798, compiled and published by George H.S. King (Ann Arbor, Michigan, 1960)

Sweeny -- Wills of Rappahannock County, Virginia, 1656-1692 by William Montgomery Sweeny (Lynchburg, Va., 1947)

T   --   Tyler's Quarterly Historical and Genealogical Magazine, citing the volume ante and the page post,T

V   --   Virginia Magazine of History and Biography, citing the volume ante and the page post, V

VSL:AD -- Virginia State Library, Archives Division, Richmond, Virginia

"I have gon, and rid, and wrote, and sought and
search'd with my own and friends' Eyes, to make what
Discoveries I could therein. . . . I stand ready
with a pencel in one hand, and a Spunge in the other,
to add, alter, insert, expunge, enlarge, and delete,
according to better information. And if these my
pains shall be found worthy to passe a second Impress-
ion, my faults I will confess with shame, and amend
with thankfulnesse, to such as will contribute clearer
Intelligence unto me."

                              Fuller, _Worthies of England_ (1662)

                         ——————

       Since the above paragraph appeared more than
three hundred years ago, the art of genealogical re-
search has progressed considerably. It is, therefore,
reasonable to request that those persons who choose to
submit corrections, alterations and other relevant material, cite their sources to the original recordings in
the civil and parochial manuscripts rather than to printed sources as some of these are known to be erroneous.
For this consideration and the information submitted,
the compiler will be forever grateful.

A

B. A___#___, ANNE daughter of John and ___#___ .

M. ABSHONE, WILLIAM and Eleanor Starks, 15 October 1729.

B. ADAMS, CATHARINE daughter of John and Mary Adams, 30 April 1684.

B. ADAMS, ALEXANDER son of John and Mary Adams, 10 May 1686.

D. ADAMS, MARY 30 December 1726.

B. ADAMS, WILLIAM free child of Molley, formerly the property of Col. William Fauntleroy, 28 December 1792 [L:22].

B. ADKINS, MARTHA daughter of William and Eliz.[a] Adkins, 12 October 1730.

B. AGNEFEALD, WILLIAM son of William and Payson Angefeald, 24 May 1_#_ .

D. ALDERSON, ___#___ 19 February 1729.

M. ALDERSON, JOHN and Jane Starks, 4 July 1729.

B. ALDERSON, JAMES son of John and Jane Alderson, 18 May 1730.

B. ALDERSON, REUBIN son of James and Sarah Alderson, 22 January 1755.

B. ALDERSON, JENNY daughter of James and Sarah Ann Alderson, 22 September 1756.

B. ALDERSON, SARAH ANN daughter of James and Sarah Ann Alderson, 14 June 1759.

B. ALDERSON, ANN daughter of James and Sarah Ann Alderson, 5 January 1762.

B. ALDERSON, JAMES son of James and Sarah Ann Alderson, 28 February 1764.

B. ALDERSON, JOHN son of James and Sarah Ann Alderson, 18 November 1766.

B. ALDERSON, WILLIAM son of James and Sarah Ann Alderson, 11 June 1769.

B. ALDERSON, JEREMIAH son of James and Sarah Ann Alderson, 31 May 1774.

B. ALDERSON, NANCEY daughter of John and Rachel Alderson, 21 January 1790.

B. ALDERSON, REDMAN COWARD son of Tieliff Alderson, 3 July 1792 [L:1].

B. ALDERSON, JOHN son of Jerry and Katey Alderson, 3 May 1793 [L:2].

B. ALDERSON, WILLIAM son of Jerry and Katey Alderson, 27 September 1794 [L:1].

B. ALDERSON, JERY son of John and Rachel Alderson, 15 November 1797.

1

B. ALDERSON, FORTUNATUS DAVENPORT son of John and Rachel Alderson, 29 October 1798.

B. ALDERSON, LUCEY ROUT daughter of John and Betsey Alderson, 7 October 1804.

B. ALDERSON, RICHARD COELMAN son of John and Betsey Alderson, 25 March 1806.

B. ALDERSON, SARAH WALKER daughter of John and Elizabeth Alderson 4 November 1808.

B. ALDERSON, BENJAMIN son of John and Betsey Alderson, 3 April 1811.

ALGAR   SEE: AYLGAR PAGE 7

B. ALGAR, MARY daughter of Thomas and Alicia Algar, 2 August 1692.

B. ALGAR, ANNE daughter of Thomas and Alicia Algar, __ December 1694.

B. ALGAR, ELIZABETH daughter of Thomas and Alicia Algar, 1 December 1694.

B. ALGAR, THOMAS son of Samuel and Mary Algar, 5 February 1721/2.

B. ALGAR, ALICIA daughter of Samuel and Mary Algar, 7 June 1724.

B. ALGAR, SAMUEL and MARY son and daughter of Samuel and Mary Algar, 31 March 1730.

B. ALGAR, BETTIE daughter of Samuel and Mary Algar, 10 February 1731.

B. ALGAR, MARY daughter of Samuel and Mary Algar, 26 May 1736.

D. ALGAR, MARY 26 May 1736.

B. ALGAR, SUKEY daughter of Samuel and Mary Algar, 10 August 1739.

B. ALGAR, WINNY daughter of Samuel and Mary Algar, 13 October 1740.

B. ALGAR, SAMUEL and SARAH twins of Samuel and Mary Algar, 15 April 1743.

B. ALGAR, SUSANNA daughter of Samuel and Mary Algar, 25 November 1745.

B. ALGAR, WILLIAM son of Samuel and Mary Algar, 4 January 1747.

B. ALGAR, JOHN and ANN twins of Samuel and Mary Algar, 9 February 1749.

D. ALGAR, ANN daughter of Samuel and Mary Algar, 11 February 1749.

D. ALGAR, SAMUEL 28 February 1749.

M. ALLARD, HENRY and Grace Davis, 15 February 1730/1.

B. ALLARD, MARGARET daughter of Henry and Grace Allard, 5 January 1733.

ALLEN : ALLIN

M. ALLIN, ANNE and William Creswell, 18 June 1677.

M. ALLEN, ANNE and Francis Elmore, 2 December 1677.

M. ALLEN, JOHN and Catherine Major, 15 November 1678.

B. ALLEN, ANNE daughter of Richard and Elizabeth Allen, 4 October 1712.

ALGOOD : ALLGOOD

B. ALLGOOD, JOHN son of Edward and Elizabeth Allgood, 30 November 1724.

B. ALGOOD, EDWARD son of Edward and Elizabeth Algood, 23 December 1730.

B. ALGOOD, SARAH daughter of Ann Algood, 28 September 1735.

B. ALLGOOD, EDWARD son of William and Mary Ann Allgood, 19 October 1741.

B. ALLGOOD, JOHN son of William and Mary Ann Allgood, 27 July 1743.

B. ALLGOOD, ELIZABETH daughter of William and Mary Ann Allgood, 26 August 1745.

B. ALLGOOD, ANN daughter of John and Mary Ann Allgood, 3 October 1745.

B. ALLGOOD, WINNY daughter of William and Mary Ann Allgood, 17 March 1747.

B. ALLGOOD, MANDLAY son of John and Mary Ann Allgood, 18 June 1748.

B. ALGOOD, HANNAH daughter of John and Mary Ann Algood, 26 January 1750.

B. ALLGOOD, JOHN son of William and Mary Ann Allgood, 12 May 1751.

B. ALLGOOD, ISHMAEL son of William and Sarah Allgood, 17 June 1756.

B. ALLGOOD, VINCENT JACKSON son of Elizabeth Allgood, ___ November 1781.

B. ALLGOOD, BETSY JACKSON "a bastard of Elizabeth Allgood," 30 September 1788.

B. ALLGOOD, TOMME JACKSON "bastard son of Elizabeth Allgood," 26 September 1790.

B. ALLOWAY, GABRIEL son of John and Dorothy Alloway, 28 May 1672.

B. ALLOWAY, PRISCILLA daughter of John and Dorothy Alloway, 28 May 1678.

B. ALLOWAY, JOHN son of Gabriel and Eliz.^{a} Alloway, 29 April 1695.

B. ALLOWAY, JUDETH daughter of Gabriel and Eliz.^{a} Alloway, 10 November 1703.

B. ALLOWAY, ALEXANDER son of Gabriel Alloway, 5 November 1706.

B. ALLOWAY, GABRIEL son of Gabriel and Eliz.^{a} Alloway, 13 December 1713.

D. ALLOWAY, MATTHEW 15 December 1718.

B. ALLOWAY, JOHN son of Alexander and Judith Alloway, 24 March 1735.

D. ALLOWAY, JUDITH 29 March 1736.

B. ALLOWAY, GABRIEL son of Alexander and Eliz.^{a} Alloway, 13 February 1738.

B. ALLOWAY, JUDITH daughter of Gabriel and Kathrine Alloway, 28 October 1738.

B. ALLOWAY, ELIZABETH daughter of Gabriel and Kathrine Alloway, 30 November 1740

D. ALLOWAY, GABRIEL 31 January 1745.

D. ALLOWAY, ELIZABETH 8 November 1747.

D. ALLOWAY, ELIZABETH 10 December 1750.

B. ALLOWAY, NANCY daughter of Isaac and Mary Alloway, 17 October 1765.

B. ALLOWAY, CATY daughter of Isaac and Mary Alloway, 26 December 1766.

B. ALLOWAY, JOHN son of Isaac and Mary Alloway, 2 December 1768.

B. ALLOWAY, MARY daughter of Isaac and Mary Alloway, 13 March 1771.

B. ALLOWAY, JUDITH daughter of Isaac and Mary Alloway, 3 November 1773.

B. ALLOWAY, BETTY daughter of Isaac and Mary Alloway, 23 May 1776.

B. ALLOWAY, SUSANNA daughter of Isaac Alloway, 30 September 1782.

B. ALVERSON, ELEANOR daughter of John and Eleanor Alverson, 22 December 1711.

B. ALVERSON, BETTY daughter of John and Eleanor Alverson, 29 January 1713.

B. ALVERSON, SARAH daughter of Teliph and Rebeccah Alverson, 5 April 1715.

B. ALVERSON, JOHN son of John and Eleanor Alverson, 13 June 1716.

D. ALVERSON, TILIPH 26 December 1718.

B. ALVERSON, MARTHA daughter of John and Eleanor Alverson, 16 July 1719.

B. ALVERSON, SARAH daughter of George and Susanna Alverson, 7 February 1723.

B. ALVERSON, ARCHIBALD son of John and Eleanor Alverson, 17 October 1724.

M. ALVERSON, REBECCA and Peter Oldham, 17 February 1728/7 (sic).

M. ALVERSON, ANN and Herbert Maxwell, 7 October 1729.

M. ALVERSON, MARY and John Watts, 9 January 1729/30.

B. ALVERSON, MARY daughter of Teilief and Eleanor Alverson, 30 October 1734.

B. ALVERSON, ELEANOR daughter of Telief and Eleanor Alverson, 9 November 1736.

B. ALVERSON, JOHN son of Tuliph and Eleanor Alverson, 26 March 1740.

B. ALVERSON, MARY ANN daughter of Tuliph and Eleanor Alverson, 19 December 1742.

D. ALVERSON, ELEANOR 15 January 1749.

D, ANDERSON, MARGARET 20 July 171#.

B. ANDERSON, WILLIAM son of George and Susanna Anderson, 7 December 1710.

B. ANDERSON, RICHARD son of Richard and Anne Anderson, 11 September 1711.

B. ANDERSON, GEORGE son of George and Susanna Anderson, 12 March 1711/12.

B. ANDERSON, SUSANNA daughter of George and Susanna Anderson, 15 November 1714.

B. ANDERSON, GEORGE son of Richard and Anne Anderson, 21 May 1715.

B. ANDERSON, MARGARET daughter of George and Susanna Anderson, 15 August 1718.

D. ANDERSON, SUSANNA 29 July 1719.

B. ANDERSON, JOHN son of George and Susanna Anderson, 23 June 1720.

M. ANDERSON, EDWARD and Margaret Conor, 18 October 1725.

B. ANDERSON, SARAH daughter of Andrew and Charity Anderson, 2 October 1750.

B. ANDERSON, JOHN son of Andrew and Charity Anderson, 22 August 1757.

D. ANGUISH,   #   24 April 1730.

M. ANSWORTH, JOHN and Sarah Bridger, 15 July 1678.

APLEBY : APPLEBE : APPLEBY &c.

M. APLEBY, RICHARD and Anne Arnolds, 4 July 1680.

B. APPLEBY, RICHARD son of Richard and Anne Appleby, 14 June 168#.

B. APPLEBY, THOMAS son of Richard and Mary Appleby, 1 October 1724.

D. APPLEBE, MARY 12 January 1726.

M. APPLEBY, RICHARD and Elizabeth Pression, 17 November 1728.

B. APPLBY, ANN daughter of Richard and Sarah Applby, 5 June 1777.

ARESKIN   SEE: ERSKINE PAGE 60

D. ARESKIN, WILLIAM 11 March 1749.

B. ARMISTEAD, ELIZABETH daughter of Francis and Sarah Armistead, 28 March 1716.

B. ARMISTEAD, JOHN son of Francis and Sarah Armistead, 26 February 1718.

D. ARMISTEAD, FRANCIS 4 April 1719.

B. ARMISTEAD, WILLIAM BURGESS son of Henry and Winifred Armistead, 10 November 1775.

B. ARNOLDS, JOHN son of John and Anne Arnolds, 25 December 1677.

B. ARNOLDS, ANNE daughter of John and Anne Arnolds, 17 December 168#.

M. ARNOLDS, ANNE and Richard Apleby, 4 July 1680.

B. ARS GRIFFIN, CATHARINE daughter of William and Jane ArsGriffin, 22 December 1721.

B. ARS GRIFFIN, THOMAS son of William and Jane ArsGriffin, 27 September 1724.

B. ARS GRIFFIN, ANN daughter of William and Jane ArsGriffin, 21 October 1731.

B. ARS GRIFFIN, BETTIE daughter of William and Jane ArsGriffin, 11 Oct. 1734.

B. ARS GRIFFIN, ALICE daughter of William and Jane ArsGriffin, 7 December 1741.

B. ARS GRIFFIN, WILLIAM son of William and Sally ArsGriffin, 3 October 1762.

B. ASBURY, JAMES HENRY son of Thomas and Molly Asbury, 18 November 1794 [L:1].

B. ASCOUGH, CHRISTOPHER son of Thomas and Eliz.^{a} Ascough, 17 February 1699.

B. ASHES, ISAAC son of a servant belonging to Samuel Peachey, 22 December 1702.

M. ASKINS, WILLIAM and Elizabeth Morgan, 23 December 1729.

B. ASPALL, JOHN son of John and Helena Aspall, 4 February 1687.

B. ATON, HETHTHRY daughter of Robert and Ann Aton, 7 April 1774.

B. ATWILL, LUCEY daughter of Francis and Fanny Atwill, 31 March 1798 [L:1].

M. AUDLEY, SARAH and Thomas Williams, 2 October 1726.

AYLGAR   SEE: ALGAR PAGE 2

D. AYLGAR, ___#___ , 10 April 1730.

D. AYLGAR, ___#___ , 20 April 1730.

B. AYLOFF, MARY daughter of Thomas and Mary Ayloff, 12 August 1756.

B. AYRES, SUSANNA daughter of Robert and Catharine Ayres, 15 December 1699.

B. AYRES, ELIZABETH daughter of Robert and Catharine Ayres, 21 December 1713.

B. AYRES, JOANNA daughter of Robert and Catharine Ayres, 12 July 1716.

D. AYRES, JOANNA 2 January 1718.

D. AYRES, CATHARINE 5 January 1718.

D. AYRES, ANNE 27 March 1718.

B

B. BAGLY or BAGBY, ANNE daughter of Samuel and Elizabeth Bagly or Bagby, 26 December 1727.

BAILEY : BAYLEY   SEE: BAYLIS PAGE 12

B. BAILEY, JOYCE daughter of Samuel and Joyce Bailey, 17 January 1677.

B. BAYLEY, SAMUEL son of Samuel and Sarah Bayley, 20 March 1691.

B. BAYLEY, FRANCES daughter of Robert and Ellin Bayley, 28 September 1717.

M. BAILEY, SAMUEL and Elizabeth Metcalfe, 2 December 1725.

D. BAILEY, SAMUEL 30 November 1727.

B. BAILEY, JOHN son of Samuel and Ann Bailey, 29 September 1746.

D. BAILEY, ANN 8 January 1750.

D. BAILEY, JOHN 30 January 1750.

B. BAILEY, WILLIAM son of Samuel and Ann Bailey, 29 September 1750.

B. BAILEY, BETTY daughter of Samuel and Caty Bailey, 31 March 1754.

B. BAILEY, LEROY son of Samuel and Caty Bailey, 4 May 1756.

B. BAILEY, CHARLES son of Samuel and Caty Bailey, 28 February 1758.

B. BAKER, ELIZABETH daughter of John and Jane Baker, 8 October 1696.[See, BARBER p. 9]

B. BAKER, WILLIAM son of Bartholomew and Elizabeth Baker, 9 September 1703.

B. BAKER, CONSTANCE daughter of Bartholomew and Elizabeth Baker, 11 January 1705

B. BAKER, PATIENCE daughter of Bartholomew and Elizabeth Baker, 1 May 1708.

B. BAKER, ELIZABETH daughter of Samuel and Mary Baker, 13 May 1709.

B. BAKER, ELIZABETH daughter of Bartholomew and Elizabeth Baker, 30 May 1710.

B. BAKER, SAMUEL son of Bartholomew and Elizabeth Baker, 13 July 1711.

B. BAKER, MARY ANN daughter of Samuel and Mary Baker, 18 July 1711.

B. BAKER, ELIZABETH daughter of William Baker, 12 November 1718.

B. BAKER, JOHN son of William and Lucy Baker, 25 February 1719.

B. BAKER, JOHN son of William and Lucy Baker, 25 February 1720/1.

B. BAKER, WILLIAM son of William and Lucy Baker, 24 February 1724/5.

B. BAKER, LUCY daughter of William and Lucy Baker, 1 August 1727.

B. BAKER, BARBARA daughter of William and Lucy Baker, 26 September 1731.

D. BAKER, LUCY 1 March 1733.

D. BAKER, ELIZABETH 3 May 1743.

D. BAKER, DORCAS wife of William Baker, 4 October 1745.

B. BAKER, MARY daughter of William and Elizabeth Baker, 19 February 1746.

B. BAKER, JOHN son of William and Ann Baker, 28 March 1748.

B. BAKER, LUCY daughter of William and Ann Baker, 27 December 1752.

B. BAKER, WILLIAM son of William and Ann Baker, 27 January 1754.

B. BAKER, SAMUEL son of William and Ann Baker, 28 January 1758.

B. BAKER, CATY daughter of William and Ann Baker, 22 April 1760.

B. BALDERSON, LUCY daughter of Ebenezer and Ann Balderson, 15 May 1798 [L:3].

D. BALL, MARY __ January 1718.

D. BALL, ANNE ___ February 1718.

M. BALL, SARAH and William Harding, 14 February 1730/1 ; see page 87.

B. BANISTER, ISAAC son of Mary Banister, 2 April 1731.

B. BARBER, ELIZABETH daughter of William and Mary Barber, 11 January 1665 (sic). [This should probably be 1675; see the following entries.]

B. BARBER, CHARLES son of William and Mary Barber, 19 June 1676.

B. BARBER, THOMAS son of William and Mary Barber, 19 January 1678.

B. BARBER, WILLIAM son of William and Mary Barber, 7 August 1679.

B. BARBER, LUCY daughter of William and Mary Barber, 16 January 1681.

B. BARBER, WILLIAM son of John and Jane Barber, 6 January 1698. [Although the surname is plainly BARBER it probably should be BAKER; see page 8.]

B. BARBER, THOMAS son of Charles and Frances Barber, 16 March 1701.

B. BARBER, CHARLES son of Charles and Frances Barber, 11 August 1704.

B. BARBER, MARY daughter of Charles and Frances Barber, 26 December 1706.

B. BARBER, ANNE daughter of Charles and Frances Barber, 16 August 1709.

B. BARBER, ELIZABETH daughter of Charles and Frances Barber, 4 March 1711.

B. BARBER, JOYCE daughter of William and Joyce Barber, 9 June 1712.

B. BARBER, WILLIAM son of Charles and Frances Barber, 17 November 1714.

D. BARBER, CHARLES JUN.^R 24 November 1726.

D. BARBER, CHARLES 27 November 1726.

M. BARBER, SAMUEL and Ann Foster, 30 November 1727.

B. BARBER, WILLIAM son of Samuel and Ann Barber, 27 August 1728.

M. BARBER, MARY and James Samford, 20 September 1728.

B. BARBER, THOMAS son of Thomas and Anne Barber, 28 February 1729.

M. BARBER, THOMAS and Ann Nash, 28 January 1729/30.

M. BARBER, ELIZABETH and George Hunt, 5 June 1730.

B. BARBER, SAMUEL son of Samuel and Anne Barber, 16 January 1730/1.

B. BARBER, CHARLES son of Thomas and Ann Barber, 27 October 1731.

D. BARBER, WILLIAM 21 November 1731.

M. BARBER, ANN and Billington McCarty, 16 June 1732.

B. BARBER, FRANCES KENYON daughter of Charles and Mary Barber, 12 July 1768.

B. BARBER, FRANCES daughter of Charles and Mary Barber, 6 August 1774.

B. BARBER, JOHN son of William and Elizabeth Barber, 11 December 1776.

B. BARBER, LUCI daughter of William and Betty Barber, 14 April 1780.

B. BARICK, BECKA THORNTON daughter of George and Esabeth Barick, 28 February
    1788. [See, BARRICK, p. 11.]

B. BARNS, WILLIAM son of John and Mary Barns, 24 May 1720.

M. BARNS, PENILOPY and William Ersking, 27 May 1726.

B. BARNS, VIOLATO daughter of Samuel and Winifred Barns, 18 February 1734.

B. BARNS, GEORGE son of Samuel and Winifred Barns, 14 August 1735.

B. BARNS, CHARLES son of Samuel and Winifred Barns, 16 January 1739.

B. BARNS, MERRYMAN son of Samuel and Winifred Barns, 17 September 1741.

B. BARNS, WINNY daughter of Samuel and Winifred Barns, 11 April 1743.

B. BARNS, AMNAH daughter of Samuel and Winifred Barns, 24 June 1745.

B. BARNS, MILLION daughter of Samuel and Winifred Barns, 30 December 1747.

B. BARNS, SAMUEL son of Samuel and Winifred Barns, 6 December 1748.

B. BARNS, SAMUEL son of Charles and Ann Barns, 10 March 1764.

B. BARNS, TRAVERSE son of Charles and Ann Barns, 15 February 1766.

B. BARNS, CATY daughter of Charles and Ann Barns, 25 July 1768.

B. BARNS, THADDEUS son of George and Betty Barns, 27 July 1768.

B. BARNS, NEWMAN son of Newman B. and Lucy Butler Barns, 14 April 1769.

B. BARNS, EDWARD son of Samuel and Betty Barns, 26 August 1770.

B. BARNS, MORTON son of Newman B. and Lucy Butler Barns, [not entered] 1771.

B. BARNS, NANCY daughter of Samuel and Elizabeth Barns, 28 October 1781.

B. BARNS, NELLY daughter of Charles and Ellison Barns, 24 December 1781.

B. BARNS, BROCKENBROUGH GWIN son of Travis Barns and Betsy Mitchell, 15 February 1788.

B. BARNS, NEWMAN son of Samuel and Bettey Barns, 12 J_#__ 1789.

B. BARNS, EPAPHRODITUS TUNE son of Peter and Winneyfred Barns, 20 October 1790.

B. BARNES, MARIA REBECCA ROANE daughter of Richard and Rebecca Barnes, 3 April 1795 [L:3].

M. BAROH, AGNES and William Smith, 15 March 1731/2.

BARRICK   SEE: BARICK PAGE 10

B. BARRICK, SARAH daughter of David and Charity Barrick, 18 June 1688.

B. BARRICK, SARAH daughter of David and Charity Barrick, 5 August 1688 [! (sic)].

B. BARRICK, ELIZABETH daughter of David and Charity Barrick, ___ January 1690.

B. BARRICK, ANNE daughter of David and Charity Barrick, 11 November 1694.

B. BARROW, JOHN son of Edward and Elizabeth Barrow, 20 February 1729.

B. BARTLET, JAMES son of Thomas and Elizabeth Bartlet, 6 January 1726.

D. BARTLETT, FRANCES 25 May 1727.

B. BARTLETT, ANIS daughter of Thomas and Elizabeth Bartlett, 24 May 1729.

B. BARTLETT, JEHU son of Elisha and Leah Bartlett, 18 November 1791 [L:3].

B. BARTLETT, ELIZABETH daughter of John and Elizabeth Bartlett, 14 March 1792 [L:3].

B. BARTLETT, JOANNA daughter of Elisha and Leah Bartlett, 2 March 1794 [L:3].

B. BARTLETT, PENELOPE WILLSON, daughter of John and Elizabeth Bartlett, 13 July 1794 [L:3].

B. BARTLETT, JOEL son of Elisha and Leah Bartlett, 28 January 1796 [L:3].

B. BARTLETT, JOHN son of John and Elizabeth Bartlett, 28 November 1796 [L:3].

M. BARTON, SARAH and Charles Elmore 11 October 1728.

B. BATES, WINNIFRED daughter of Kathrine Bates, 20 January 1723/4.

M. BATES, EDWARD and Jane Peck, 16 January 1729/30.

B. BATES, MARY daughter of Edward and Jane Bates, 4 December 1730.

B. BATES, MARGARET daughter of Edward and Jane Bates, 31 March 1732.

D. BATES, MARGARET 1 September 1732.

B. BATES, ELIZABETH daughter of Edward and Jane Bates, 17 June 1733.

B. BATES, JOHN and JANE, son and daughter of Edward and Jane Bates, 15 April 1735.

B. BATES, EDWARD son of Edward and Jane Bates, 20 June 1737.

B. BATES, SARAH daughter of Edward and Jane Bates, 26 May 1741.

B. BATES, FRANCES daughter of Edward and Jane Bates, 24 January 1742.

B. BATES, MARGARET daughter of Edward and Jane Bates, 6 November 1745.

B. BATES, THOMAS son of Edward and Jane Bates, 12 September 1748.

BATTIN   SEE: BOOK PAGE 17 AND BOWLES : BOWLS PAGE 18

B. BATTIN, PHILLIS daughter of John and Mary Battin, 7 September 1680.

B. BATTIN, JOHN son of Charles and Phillis Battin, 21 January 1722/3.

BAYLEY   SEE: BAILEY : BAYLEY PAGE 7 AND BAYLIS PAGE 12

BAYLIS   SEE: BAILEY : BAYLEY PAGE 7

B. BAYLIS, AMADINE daughter of Thomas and Catharine Baylis, 18 January 1684.

B. BAYLIS, WILLIAM son of Robert and Jane Baylis, 16 September 1684.

B. BAYLIS, ROBERT son of Thomas and Catharine Baylis, 7 September 168#.

B. BAYLIS, FRANCES daughter of Thomas and Catharine Baylis, 23 September 1686.

B. BAYLIS, CATHARINE daughter of Thomas and Catharine Baylis, 28 March 1691.

B. BAYLIS, THOMAS son of Thomas and Catharine Baylis, 3 February 1696.

B. BAYLIS, ELIZABETH daughter of Robert and Eleanor Baylis, 29 September 1712.

B. BAYLIS, THOMAS son of Robert and Eleanor Baylis, 9 July 1715.

B. BAYLIS, FRANCES daughter of Robert and Ellin Baylis, 12 October 1719.

D. BAYLIS, ELLIN 9 November 1721.

D. BAYLIS, KATHRINE 6 December 1721.

D. BAYLIS, ELIZABETH 1 January 1724/5.

B. BAUGH, SANDS son of Jon.[a] and Elizabeth Baugh, 28 February 1736.

B. BEACHMAN, ELLIPHELETT WEST son of John W. and Ann Beachman, 14 March 1787 or 14 March 1788 [?].

M. BEAGES, WILLIAM and Katherine Hopper, 5 May 1728.

B. BEALE, ANNE daughter of Thomas and Anne Beale, 10 August 1672.

B. BEALE, THOMAS son of Thomas and Anne Beale, 29 January 1675.

B. BEALE, CHARLES son of Thomas and Anne Beale, 20 October 1678.

B. BEALE, ANNE daughter of Thomas and Elizabeth Beale, 3 September 1711.

B. BEALE, RICHARD son of Thomas and Elizabeth Beale, 19 December 1723.

B. BEALE, REUBIN son of Thomas and Elizabeth Beale, 19 December 1725.

M. BEALE, THOMAS and Sarah McCarty, 27 April 1728.

D. BEALE, THOMAS 24 February 1728/9.

D. BEALE, ELIZABETH 21 March 1728/9.

M. BEALE, WILLIAM and Haruear Haruear, 29 April 1729.

B. BEALE, THOMAS son of Thomas and Sarah Beale, 17 May 1729.

D. BEALE, THOMAS JUNIOR 9 October 1732.

M. BEALE, ANN and Gilbert Hamilton, 4 November 1732.

Baptized, BEALE, CHARLES son of Thomas and Sinai Beale, 19 April 1792 [L:3].

B. BECKWITH, TARPLEY son of Marmaduke and Elizabeth Beckwith, 2 October 1718.

B. BECKWITH, JONATHAN son of Marmaduke and Elizabeth Beckwith, 14 November 1720.

B. BECKWITH, BETTY daughter of Marmaduke and Elizabeth Beckwith, 15 August 1723.

B. BECKWITH, MARGARET daughter of Marmaduke and Elizabeth Beckwith, 29 July 1725.

D. BECKWITH, BETTY 7 April 1726.

B. BECKWITH, MARY, daughter of Marmaduke and Elizabeth Beckwith, 12 June 1727.

Baptized, BECKWITH, ISAAC EDMUND JENNINGS son of Jennings and Katey Beckwith, 29 March 1793 [L:3].

B. BEDDO, BETHIAH daughter of Laurence and Elizabeth Beddo, 1 August 1793 [L:3].

B. BEDDO, ANGILICO daughter of Laurence and Elizabeth Beddo, 14 Novr 1796 [L:3].

M. BEDWELL, MARY and Isaac Webb, 6 April 1678.

B. BELFIELD, JOSEPH son of Thomas and Nancey Belfield, 3 May 1792 [L:3].

    BENDALL : BENDOLL

B. BENDALL, ELIZABETH daughter of William and Elizabeth Bendall, _____ A.D. 1671.

B. BENDALL, JANE daughter of William and Elizabeth Bendall, _____ A.D. 1674.

B. BENDOLL, JOHN son of William and Elizabeth Bendoll, 10 May 1677.

B. BENGER, KATHRINE daughter of John and Mary Benger, 10 October 1723.

D. BENGER, KATHRINE 5 February 1723/4.

D. BENGER, MARY 6 May 1724.

D. BENGER, JOHN 31 October 1725.

M. BENJAMIN, DOROTHY and John Green, 24 October 1673.

    BENNEHAM : BENNEHAN : BEANHAM : BENNIHAM   SEE: BRANHAM PAGE 20

B. BEANHAM, ELIZABETH daughter of Dominick and Elizabeth Beanham, 29 March 1692.

B. BEANHAM, ALEXANDER son of Dominick and Elizabeth Beanham, 29 June 1695.

B. BEANHAM, FRANCES daughter of Dominick and Elizabeth Beanham, 4 December 1697.

B. BEANHAM, MARY daughter of Dominick and Elizabeth Beanham, 5 September 1700.

B. BENEHAM, DUDLEY son of Dominick and Elizabeth Beneham, 22 October 1713.

D. BENNEHAM, DOMINICK 27 April 1716.

D. BENNEHAM, ALEXANDER 18 March 1719.

B. BENNEHAM, DOMINICK son of Dudley and Rachel Benneham, 25 August 1734.

B. BENNEHAM, ALEXANDER son of Dudley and Rachel Benneham, 22 April 1736.

B. BENNEHAM, WILLIAM son of Dudley and Rachel Benneham, 10 July 1738.

B. BENNEHAM, DUDLEY son of Dudley and Rachel Benneham, 29 December 1740.

B. BENNEHAM, RICHARD son of Dudley and Rachel Benneham, 15 April 1743.

B. BENNEHAN, BETTY daughter of Dudley and Rachel Bennehan, 3 November 1745.

B. BENNEHAN, GEORGE son of Dudley and Rachel Bennehan, 2 February 1747.

D. BENNEHAM, DUDLEY 12 March 1749.

B. BENNEHAM, WILLIAM son of Alexander and Ann Benneham, 17 March 1768.

B. BENNEHAM, RICHARD son of Dominick and Ann Benneham, 8 May 1769.

B. BENNETT, MARY daughter of John and Elizabeth Bennett, 5 April 1682.

B. BENNETT, ELIZABETH daughter of John and Elizabeth Bennett, 12 February 1683.

B. BENNETT, JOHN son of John and Elizabeth Bennett, 2 April 1689.

B. BENNETT, WILLIAM son of John and Elizabeth Bennett, 16 October 1691.

B. BENNETT, MARGERY daughter of John and Elizabeth Bennett, 11 May 1694.

B. BENNETT, JOHN son of William and Elizabeth Bennett, 2 February 1718.

B. BENNET , SARAH daughter of Thomas and Judith Bennet, [not entered] 1779.

B. BENTLEY, ANN daughter of Daniel and Ann Bentley, 2 November 1717.

B. BENTLEY, SAMUEL son of Daniel and Ann Bentley, 30 December 1719.

B. BENTLEY, WILLIAM son of Daniel and Ann Bentley, 13 March 1720; [i.e.,1720/1].

B. BENTLEY, ALICE daughter of Daniel and Elizabeth Bentley, 13 April 1724.

B. BENTLEY, DANIEL son of Daniel and Elizabeth Bentley, 28 February 1726.

B. BENTLEY, ANN daughter of Samuel and Mary Bentley, born 30 November 1741.

B. BENTLEY, DANIEL son of John and Mary Bentley, 5 February 1743.

B. BENTLEY, MARY daughter of Samuel and Mary Bentley, 24 September 1746.

B. BERWICK, GRIFFIN son of Charles and Elizabeth Berwick, 5 January 1796 [L:3].

D. BEWFORD, JOHN 5 October 1725.

B. BIGBIE, ARCHIBALD son of George and Mary Bigbie, 15 December 1734.

B. BIGBEE, GEORGE son of George and Mary Bigbee, 26 December 1736.

B. BILLINGS, ELIZABETH daughter of Thomas and Elizabeth Billings, 24 March 1727.

M. BILLINGTON, ALICIA and John Russell, 11 September 1673.

D. BIRD, ELIZABETH   8 September 1715.

M. BIRD, PHILEMAN and Mary Mackgyar,   25 February 1727/8.

B. BIRD, SARAH daughter of Phellimon and Mary Bird, 20 November 1728.

B. BIRD, MARY ANN daughter of Phillemon and Mary Bird, 9 January 1730.

B. BIRD, BETTY daughter of Phlleman and Mary Bird, 28 December 1732.

B. BIRD, ABNER son of Phillemon and Mary Bird, 5 July 1735.

B. BIRD, DAMARIAS daughter of Philemon and Mary Bird, 20 November 1737.

B. BIRD, JOHN son of Phillemon and Mary Bird, 4 February 1739.

B. BIRD, JOANNA daughter of Phillemon and Mary Bird, 21 July 1743.

D. BIRD, DEMARIUS 15 December 1743.

B. BIRD, PHILEMON son of Philemon and Mary Bird, 19 December 1745.

D. BIRD, ABNER son of Philemon Bird, 21 March 1750.

D. BIRD, PHILEMON   7 January 1752.

BLACKERBY : BLACKERLY : BLACKEBY

B. BLACKEBY, WILLIAM son of James Blackeby, 30 August 1715.

B. BLACKERLY, JAMES son of James and Frances Blackerly, 12 January 1716.

B. BLACKARBY, THOMAS son of James and Frances Blackarby, 17 February 1719.

B. BLACKARBY, JOHN son of James and Frances Blackarby, 18 November 1722.

B. BLACKARBY, WINNIFRED daughter of James and Frances Blackarby, 8 February 1723

B. BLACKARBY, LEANNA daughter of James and Frances Blackarby, 8 January 1726.

D. BLACKERBY, LEANNA 24 December 1727.

B. BLACKERBY, JOSEPH son of James and Frances Blackerby, 12 December 1728.

B. BLACKERBY, HANNAH daughter of James and Frances Blackerby, 20 February 1730.

B. BLACKERBY, THOMAS son of Thomas and Leannah Blackerby, 4 July 1750.

B. BLACKERBY, GEORGE son of James and Ann Blackerby, 17 August 1755.

M. BLACKMORE, GEORGE and Christian Shaw, 13 September 1729.

B. BLEWFORD, CANNADAY son of George and Mary Blewford, 1 September 1702.

B. BLEWFORD, GEORGE son of George and Mary Blewford, 23 June 1705.

B. BLEWFORD, WINNY daughter of Elizabeth Blewford, 13 November 1730.

M. BLEWFORD, GEORGE and Janey Palmer, 26 January 1730/1.

B. BLEWFORD, MARY ANN daughter of George and Janey Blewford, 2 July 1731.

B. BLUETT, MARTHA daughter of Thomas and Eleanor Bluett, 1 April 1739.

B. BOARER, HENRY son of Henry and Mary Boarer, 17 May 1706.

B. BOARER, JOHN son of Henry and Mary Boarer, 19 January 1708.

M.[?] BODKIN, ANNE and George Green: Isaac Green son of George Green and Anne Bodkin was born 12 August 1688.

M. BOGGES, BENNETT and Elizabeth Samford, 27 December 1727.

B. BOLTIZER, HENRY son of Peter and Mary Boltizer, 7 April 1709. [The surname is also rendered JAMESBOLTIZER.]

B. BONEWALL, ANNE daughter of John and Elizabeth Bonewall, 8 October 1724.

B. BONNER, CATHARINE daughter of John and Elizabeth Bonner, 22 August 1686.

B. BONNER, ELIZABETH daughter of Thomas and Priscilla Bonner, 20 September 1751.

D. BONNIVAL, ELIZABETH 2 December 1739.

BOOK   SEE: BATTIN PAGE 12 AND BOWLES : BOWLS PAGE 18

B. BOOK, WILLIAM son of Charles and Phillis Book, 28 September 1726.

D. BOON, SAMUEL 28 January 1735.

BOOTH : BOOTHE

B. BOOTH, ADAM son of John and Phebe Booth, 23 October 1711.

B. BOOTH, WILLIAM son of John and Phebe Booth, 22 June 1715.

B. BOOTH, RICHARD son of John and Phebe Booth, 28 March 1720.

D. BOOTH, JOHN JUNIOR 9 June 1722.

D. BOOTH, JOHN 15 July 1722.

M. BOOTH, JAMES and Frances Dale, 5 November 1727.

B. BOOTH, ELIZABETH daughter of James and Frances Booth, 31 August 1728.

B. BOOTH, SARAH daughter of James and Frances Booth, 8 May 1731.

B. BOOTHE, JOHN son of James and Frances Boothe, 25 June 1734.

D. BOOTH, SARAH 25 January 1735.

B. BOOTHE, JAMES son of James and Frances Boothe, 28 February 1736.

B. BOOTH, JOSEPH son of James and Frances Booth, 8 September 1740.

B. BOOTH, ANN OLDHAM daughter of John and Sarah Booth, 13 December 1760.

B. BOOTH, THADDEUS son of John and Winnefred Booth, 21 June 1783.

M. BOSTON, ROBERT and Margaret Thornton, 14 September 1727.

    BOWIN : BOIN

B. BOIN, MATTHEW son of John and Elizabeth Boin, 23 March 1799 [L.13].

    BOWLES : BOWLS   SEE: BATTIN PAGE 12   and   BOOK PAGE 17

B. BOWLS, JANE daughter of John and Jane Bowls, 25 February 1675.

B. BOWLS, JOHN son of John and Jane Bowls, 15 April 1680.

B. BOWLS, THOMAS son of John and Jane Bowls, 1 February 1681/2.

B. BOWLS, CHARLES son of John and Jane Bowls, 5 January 1683/4.

B. BOWLS, HENRY son of John and Jane Bowls, 6 July 1687.

B. BOWLS, MARY daughter of Charles and Phillis Bowls, 12 July 1725.

D. BOWLS, MARY 12 October 1725.

D. BOWLS, WILLIAM 9 December 1729.

D. BOWLS, CHARLES 22 August 1744.

D. BOWLES, CHARLES 10 January 1749.

D. BRABLIN, MARY 6 November 1722.

B. BRAD, JOSEPH son of Thomas and Catharine Brad, 10 August 1679.

B. BRADLEY, THOMAS son of Thomas and Isabella Bradley, 11 December 1687.

B. BRADLEY, ELEANOR daughter of Robert and Elizabeth Bradley, 8 April 1710.

B.   BRADLEY, JOHN son of Robert and Elizabeth Bradley, 15 December 1712.

B.   BRADY, ELIZABETH daughter of Patrick and Mary Brady, 5 September 1712.

B.   BRADY, OWEN son of Patrick and Mary Brady, ___ September 1713.

B.   BRADY, MARY daughter of Patrick and Mary Brady, 31 March 1716.

B.   BRADY, RACHAL daughter of Patrick and Mary Brady, 27 October 1724.

D.   BRADY, PATRICK   23 December 1726.

B.   BRADY, ANN daughter of Owen and Betty Brady, 9 November 1745.

B.   BRADEY, MARY daughter of Owen and Elizabeth Bradey, 19 December 1747.

B.   BRADY, BETTY ANN daughter of Owen and Betty Brady, 17 February 1749.

B.   BRADY, LEANAH daughter of Owin and Elizabeth Brady, 25 January 1753.

B.   BRADY, CATY daughter of Owen and Elizabeth Brady, 1 February 1755.

B.   BRADY, OWEN son of Owen and Elizabeth Brady, 5 March 1756.

B.   BRAGG, JOSEPH son of Joseph and Mary Bragg, 1 October 1719.

B.   BRAGG, THOMAS son of Joseph and Mary Bragg, 7 February 1721.

D.   BRAGG, MARY   16 January 1726.

B.   BRAGG, BETTY daughter of Joseph and Mary Bragg, 16 April 1726.

M.   BRAGG, CHARLES and Elizabeth Packet, 11 June 1728.

B.   BRAGG, WILLIAM son of Charles and Elizabeth Bragg, 30 March 1729.

B.   BRAGG, WILLIAM son of Joseph and Elizabeth Bragg, 22 May 1731.

B.   BRAGG, JOSEPH son of Charles and Elizabeth Bragg, 3 August 1731.

D.   BRAGG, MARY   10 September 1731.

B.   BRAGG, THOMAS MOORE son of William and Ruth Bragg, 19 July 1791 [L:3].

B.   BRAGG, BETSEY daughter of William and Ruth Bragg, 26 July 1796 [L:3].

B.   BRAGG, JAMES son of John and Rachel Bragg, 2 July 1799 [L:3].

BRAMHAM : BRANHAM   SEE: BENNEHAM &c. PAGES 14 - 15

B.   BRAMHAM, JOHN son of Richard and Deborah Bramham, born 20 September 1690.

B. BRAMHAM, JOHN son of Richard and Alce Bramham, 5 March 1712.

B. BRAMHAM, RICHARD son of Richard and Alce Bramham, 28 November 1714.

B. BRAMHAM, WILLIAM son of Richard and Alce Bramham, 29 March 1716.

D. BRAMHAM, JEREMIAH 4 September 1721.

D. BRAMHAM, ANNE 27 December 1726.

M. BRANHAM, JOHN and Rachel Gower, 16 March 1726/7.

B. BRANHAM, JOHN son of John and Rachel Gower, 5 March 1727/8.

B. BRANHAM, BENJAMIN son of Richard and Eles Branham, 1 December 1728.

B. BRANHAM, JOSEPH son of Caron and Margaret Branham, 27 April 1729.

B. BRANHAM, SPENCER THADDEUS son of John and Rachael Branham, 22 October 1729.

B. BRANHAM, BETTY daughter of John and Rachel Branham, 21 December 1730.

B. BRANHAM, SUSANNA daughter of John and Rachel Branham, 4 April 1732.

B. BRANHAN, THOMAS and ELEANOR twins of Karon and Susanna Branham, 5 Oct. 1750.

B. BRANHAM, BARBARA daughter of Karon and Susanna Branham, 16 April 1753.

B. BRANHAM, WILLIAM and CATY, twins of Karon and Susanna Branham, 26 Sept. 1756.

B. BRANHAM, ANN daughter of Karon and Susanna Branham, 28 August 1758.

B. BRANHAM, SARAH daughter of Karon and Susanna Branham, 16 September 1760.

B. BRANHAM, JAMES son of Karon and Susanna Branham, 19 November 1766.

B. BRANHAM, SPENCER son of Karon and Susanna Branham, 27 November 1769.

BRANAN   SEE: BRAMHAM : BRANHAM PAGE 20

B. BRANAN, JOHN son of Caron and Margaret Branan, 22 July 1718.

B. BRANAN, JAMES son of Caren and Margaret Branan, 13 October 1720.

B. BRANAN, THOMAS son of Caran and Margaret Branan, 10 April 1723.

B. BRANAN, CAREN son of Caren and Margaret Branan, 11 June 1726.

B. BRANAN, JAMES son of Thomas and Kathrine Branan, 29 November 1742.

B. BRANAN, MARY daughter of James and Wilmoth Branan, 8 October 1743.

B. BRANAN, NANNY daughter of Thomas and Kathrine Branan, 8 April 1745.

B. BRANAN, WILLIAM son of James and Wilmoth Branan, 21 June 1745.

B. BRANAN, SARAH daughter of Thomas and Kathrine Branan, 29 July 1747.

B. BRANAN, BETTY daughter of James and Wilmoth Branan, 27 February 1748.

M. BRASSER, RICHARD and Elizabeth How, 7 July 1678.

M. BRIAN, MARGARET and William Nash, 30 May 1729.

B. BRICKEY, ANNE daughter of John and Sarah Brickey, 10 February 1726 (sic).

B. BRICKEY, ANNE daughter of John and Sarah Brickey, 19 February 1726 (sic).

B. BRICKEY, SARAH daughter of John and Sarah Brickey, 19 February 1728/9.

B. BRICKEY, BETTY daughter of John and Sarah Brickey, 19 February 1731/2.

D. BRICKEY, JOHN 19 December 1732.

M. BRIDGER, SARAH and John Answorth, 15 July 1678.

BRIDHAM   SEE: PRIDHAM PAGE 151

D. BRIDHAM, KATHRINE 20 November 1726.

D. BRIDHAM, THOMAS 27 November 1726.

BRISTO : BRISTOW

D. BRISTOW, JOHN 19 November 1726.

B. BRISTOW, KATHRINE daughter of Thomas and Kathrine Bristow, 26 January 1728.

B. BRISTO , MICHELL son of Thomas and Kathrine Bristo, 9 November 1731.

B. BROCKENBROUGH, WILLIAM son of William and Mary Brockenbrough, 10 November 1687.

B. BROCKENBROUGH, WINNIFRED daughter of Newman and Kathrine Brockenbrough, 21 March 1723/4.

B. BROCKENBROUGH, WINIFRED daughter of Newman and Kathrine Brockenbrough, 21 March 1726 (sic).

D. BROCKENBROUGH, WILLIAM 25 January 1733.

D. BROCKENBROUGH, NEWMAN 15 May 1742.

B. BROMBLO, EDWARD son of Edward and Mary Bromblo, 13 November 1710.

B. BROMBLO, ELIZABETH daughter of Edward and Mary Bromblo, 23 September 1713.

B. BROMBLO, SARAH daughter of Edward and Mary Bromblo, 8 July 1716.

B. BROME, ELIZABETH daughter of John and Ann Brome, 13 August 1711; [See,BROWN].

B. BROOKE, ELIZA ALLEN daughter of Edmund and Catharine Brooke, 3 Feb.1793 [L:1].

M. BROOKS , ANNE and Jeremiah Phillips, 3 June 1678.

B. BROOKS, JOHN a mulatto belonging to Michell Connell, 8 February 1713.

B. BROUGHTON, JOHN son of Willoughby and Elizabeth Broughton, 24 June 1750.

D. BROWN, SARAH 15 July 1711.

B. BROWN, ELIZABETH daughter of John and Anne Brown, 13 August 1711; [See,BROME].

D. BROWN, ELIZABETH 5 January 1713.

B. BROWN, WILLIAM son of John and Anne Brown, 6 August 1713.

B. BROWN, CHRISTIAN daughter of John and Anne Brown, 17 September 1715.

B. BROWN, ANNE daughter of John and Anne Brown, 23 October 1717.

D. BROWN, MARGARET 26 February 1718.

B. BROWN, JEREMIAH son of John and Anne Brown, 13 November 1719.

(sic)

B. BROWN, JEREMIAH son of John and Anne Brown, 13 November 1720.

B. BROWN, SUSANNA daughter of John and Anne Brown, 2 April 1722.

B. BROWN, WINIFRED daughter of Richard and Elizabeth Brown, 3 April 1723.

B. BROWN, JOHN son of John and Anne Brown, 29 April 1724.

B. BROWN, SARAH ANN daughter of Richard and Elizabeth Brown, 12 July 1725.

D. BROWN, ANNE 16 February 1727.

B. BROWN, MARY daughter of John and Anne Brown, 27 October 1727.

B. BROWN, RICHARD son of Richard and Elizabeth Brown, 19 December 1727.

D. BROWN, SARAH ANN 13 May 1728.

D. BROWN, MARY 16 March 1729.

M. BROWN, FRANCES and John Carpenter, 9 June 1729.

B.   BROWN, JOHN son of Richard and Elizabeth Brown, 28 June 1730.

B.   BROWN, NANNY daughter of John and Ann Brown, 11 August 1731.

D.   BROWN, ELIZABETH 6 January 1733.

B.   BROWN, GEORGE son of Richard and Elizabeth Brown, 2 May 1733.

D.   BROWN, ELIZABETH 17 September 1734.

. B.   BROWN, JAMES son of Manly and Mary Brown, 27 September 1741.

B.   BROWN, RICHARD son of Manly and Mary Brown, 13 July 1745.

B.   BROWN, PETER son of Thomas and Kathrine Brown, 22 February 1747.

D.   BROWN, RICHARD 10 May 1750.

B.   BROWN, HANNAH daughter of Manly and Mary Brown, 13 April 1751.

B.   BROWN, DANIEL son of Thomas and Catharine Brown, 2 January 1752.

B.   BROWN, WILLIAM son of George and Lettice Brown, 15 November 1753.

B.   BROWN, CHARLES son of George and Ann Brown, 17 September 1754.

B.   BROWN, RICHARD son of Richard and Wilmoth Brown, 3 November 1755.

B.   BROWN, ELIZABETH daughter of George and Lettice Brown, 5 February 1756.

B.   BROWN, SARAH daughter of Richard and Wilmoth Brown, 29 September 1757.

B.   BROWN, GEORGE son of George and Lettice Brown, 10 March 1760.

B.   BROWN, JAMES son of Thomas and Eleanor Brown, 22 June 1771.

B.   BROWN, ELIZABETH daughter of John and Elizabeth Brown, 8 August 1776.

B.   BROWN, CATY daughter of Daniel and Lucy Brown, 12 November 1776.

B.   BROWN, SUSANNAH daughter of Charles and Susannah Brown, 30 January 1778.

. B.   BROWN, NANCY HARRIS daughter of John and Nancy Brown, 1 February 1778.

B.   BROWN, JOHN son of Charles and Susannah Brown, 5 April 1778.

B.   BROWN, POLLY daughter of John Brown, 16 February 1779.

B.   BROWN, CATY daughter of John Brown, 16 July 1779.

B.   BROWN, JOHN OLDHAM son of Charles Brown, 5 April 1780.

B. BROWN, BETSY daughter of John Brown, 22 July 1783.

B. BROWN, HUDSON son of Thomas and Nancy Brown, 8 March 1792 [L:3].

B. BROWN, JOHN TAYLOR son of Daniel and Hannaranne Brown, 4 June 1793 [L:1].

B. BROWN, CHRISTOPHER DIGMAN son of Thomas and Nancy Brown, 6 Oct. 1795 [L:3].

B. BROWN, SIMON MORRIS son of Thomas and Nancy Brown, 14 February 1798 [L:3].

B. BROWN, THOMAS son of Thomas and Nancy Brown, 22 May 1800 [L:3].

    BRUCE : BRUSE

B. BRUCE, WILLIAM son of Henry and Mary Bruce, 31 October 1689. [Depositions of said Henry Bruce, aged 48, and his wife Mary Bruce, aged 47, taken 7 May 1712 and recorded in Richmond County Miscellaneous Record Book 1699-1724, page 69.]

B. BRUSE, MARY daughter of Henry and Mary Bruse, 3 April 1692.

B. BRUCE, BETTY daughter of Hencefield and Sarah Bruce, 11 July 1725.

B. BRUCE, WILLIAM son of Hencefield and Sarah Bruce, 29 December 1727.

M. BRUCE, JOSEPH and Katherine Taylor, 30 April 1728.

B. BRUCE, SARAH daughter of Hencefield and Sarah Bruce, 10 May 1730.

D. BRUCE, JOHN 4 December 1731.

B. BRUCE, MARY daughter of Hencefield and Sarah Bruce, 2 July 1732.

B. BRUCE, BETTY daughter of Thomas and Sarah Bruce, 10 May 1754.

B. BRUCE, LUCEY MARKS daughter of Benjamin and Hannah Bruce, 25 January 1790. [L:3]

B. BRUCE, LEROY son of Benjamin and Hannah Bruce, 23 January 1792, [L:3].

B. BRUCE, NANCEY daughter of Benjamin and Hannah Bruce, 1 October 1795 [L:3].

B. BRUCE, WILLIAM son of Benjamin and Hannah Bruce, 16 March 1798 [L:3].

B. BRUER, JAMES son of James Bruer, 14 February 1706.

B. BRUMBELOE, JESSE son of Isaac and Mary Brumbeloe, 2 November 1742.

B. BRIMBELOE, ISAAC son of Isaac and Mary Brimbeloe, 13 January 1744.

B. BRUMBELOE, EDWARD son of Isaac and Mary Brumbeloe, 13 September 1747.

B. BRUMBELOE, DAVID son of Isaac and Mary Brumbeloe, 15 December 1750.

B. BRUMBELOE, SOLOMON son of Isaac and Mary Brumbeloe, 18 June 1753.

B. BRUMBELOE, ELIZABETH daughter of Isaac and Mary Brumbeloe, 7 January 1755.

BRUSE   SEE: BRUCE : BRUSE PAGE 24

B. BRYANT, THOMAS son of Thomas and Elizabeth Bryant, 12 July 1688.

B. BRYANT, MARGARET daughter of Thomas and Ellinor Bryant, 22 July 1693.

B. BRYANT, MARY daughter of Thomas and Elizabeth Bryant, 28 May 1695.

B. BRYANT, GEORGE son of Thomas and Eleanor Bryant, 12 May 1699.

B. BRYANT, WILLIAM son of Thomas and Mary Bryant, 14 March 1715.

B. BRYANT, JAMES son of James and Mary Bryant, 29 July 1719.

B. BRYANT, CHARLES son of Thomas and Elizabeth Bryant, 16 December 1719.

D. BRYANT, BARBARA 2 July 1721.

B. BRYANT, ELMORE son of Patience Bryant, 28 October 1722.

B. BRYANT, LEROY son of Willfree and Elizabeth Bryant, 28 October 1722.

B. BRYANT, ANNE daughter of John and Anne Bryant, 6 March 1723/4.

B. BRYANT, THOMAS son of Wilphree and Elizabeth Bryant, 10 December 1724.

B. BRYANT, WILLIAM son of Jeremiah and Anne Bryant, 10 November 1725.

D. BRYANT, THOMAS 10 February 1726.

D. BRYANT, JOHN 18 February 1726.

M. BRYANT, JOHN and Mary Hinds, 3 August 1726.

D. BRYANT, TIMOTHY 30 October 1726.

B. BRYANT, JANE daughter of John and Jane Bryant, 21 November 1726.

M. BRYANT, EDWARD and Frances Smith, 6 April 1727.

B. BRYANT, CHARLES son of Patience Bryant, 30 April 1727.

B. BRYANT, SARAH daughter of Wilifry and Elizabeth Bryant, 27 June 1727.

B. BRYANT, JANE daughter of John and Anne Bryant, 18 November 1727.

B. BRYANT, SAMFORD son of Patiance Bryant, 19 March 1728.

M. BRYANT, MARY and Thomas Hammond, 23 September 1728.

B. BRYANT, THOMAS son of John and Anne Bryant, 23 January 1729.

M. BRYANT, THOMAS and Elizabeth Fowler, 27 June 1729.

B. BRYANT, ALCE daughter of Willfree and Elizabeth Bryant, 9 April 1730.

B. BRYANT, WILLFREE son of Thomas and Elizabeth Bryant, 2 June 1731.

B. BRYANT, KATHRINE daughter of William and Onnor Bryant, 24 August 1731.

B. BRYANT, ELEANOR daughter of John and Anne Bryant, 25 March 1732.

B. BRYANT, WILLFREE son of Willfree and Elizabeth Bryant, 12 February 1733.

B. BRYANT, PETER son of John and Anne Bryant, 7 February 1734.

B. BRYANT, BETTY daughter of Patience Bryant, 8 June 1734.

B. BRYANT, JESSE son of Joseph and Rebeccah Bryant, 10 March 1736.

B. BRYANT, THOMAS son of Thomas and Elizabeth Bryant, 8 December 1736.

B. BRYANT, WINIFRED daughter of Willfree and Elizabeth Bryant, 12 June 1737.

D. BRYANT, THOMAS 28 September 1737.

B. BRYANT, MILLION daughter of Fauntleroy and Elizabeth Bryant, 25 October 1737.

B. BRYANT, BETTY daughter of Thomas and Elizabeth Bryant, 23 January 1738.

B. BRYANT, ALICE daughter of Peter and Elizabeth Bryant, 13 October 1738.

M. BRYANT, WILMOTH and Joshua Stone, 22 November 1738.

M. BRYANT, CHARLES and Margaret Jeoffrey, 30 November 1738.

B. BRYANT, BETTY daughter of Peter and Betty Bryant, 13 February 1740.

B. BRYANT, WINIFRED daughter of Fauntleroy and Elizabeth Bryant, 16 January 1741.

D. BRYANT, THOMAS 18 February 1741.

B. BRYANT, THOMAS son of Charles and Margaret Bryant, 1 April 1742.

B. BRYANT, RAWLEIGH son of Joseph and Dorcas Bryant, 8 September 1742.

B. BRYANT, CATY daughter of Alexander and Hannah Bryant, 6 August 1743.

B. BRYANT, JEREMIAH son of Joseph and Dorcas Bryant, 28 November 1743.

B. BRYANT, ANN daughter of Charles and Margaret Bryant, 8 October 1744.

D. BRYANT, CATY daughter of Alexander and Hannah Bryant, 1 March 1746.

B. BRYANT, MERRYMAN son of Fauntleroy and Elizabeth Bryant, 27 November 1746.

B. BRYANT, CATY ANN daughter of Alexander and Hannah Bryant, 10 October 1747.

D. BRYANT, MARGARET 22 January 1749.

B. BRYANT, ALEXANDER son of Alexander and Hannah Bryant, 4 March 1749.

B. BRYANT, JONATHAN son of Joseph and Judith Bryant, 30 September 1749.

B. BRYANT, REBECCAH daughter of Joseph and Judith Bryant, 8 February 1750.

B. BRYANT, MOSES son of Fauntleroy and Elizabeth Bryant, 31 December 1751.

B. BRYANT, AGA daughter of Joseph and Judith Bryant, 28 January 1753.

D. BRYANT, CHARLES 29 January 1753.

B. BRYANT, RACHEL daughter of Joseph and Judith Bryant, 18 March 1755.

B. BRYANT, ROBERT son of Joseph and Judith Bryant, 13 February 1759.

B. BRYANT, LETTICE daughter of Joseph and Judith Bryant, 11 March 1762.

D. BRYANT, JOSEPH 6 October 1763.

B. BRYANT, NATUS son of Reubin and Sarah Ann Bryant, 19 March 1767.

B. BRYANT, MARY daughter of Alexander and Lisha Bryant, 13 January 1771.

B. BRYANT, WILLIAM SMOOT son of John and Sarah Bryant, 17 March 1777.

B. BRYANT, JOHN son of Jonathan and Elizabeth Bryant, 15 May 1777.

B. BRYANT, RICHARD son of Jesse and Hannah Bryant, 7 May 1778.

B. BRYANT, THOMAS bastard child of Rachel Bryant, 1 July 1783.

B. BRYANT, JAMES ROBERTSON son of Tarpley and Sarah Bryant, 8 May 1796 [L:3].

B. BRYANT, LUCY T. daughter of Alexander and Betty Bryant, 3 January 1802.

D. BRYER, GEORGE 8 November 1726.

B. BUCKLEY, REUBIN BRUCE son of Reubin and Molley Buckley, 18 April 1792 [L:3].

B. BUCKNOLL, SUSANNAH a bastard child [no mother recorded], 22 November 1735.

D. BUFIRD, MARY 10 October 1718.

B. BUFORD, ROBERT son of John and Elizabeth Buford, 18 July 1721.

D. BUFORD, JOHN 2 December 1721.

D. BUFORD, GEORGE 25 November 1722.

B. BUFORD, JOHN son of Betty Buford, 13 August 1732.

D. BUFORD, ROBERT 10 February 1744.

B. BURCH, ELIZER daughter of Jilson B. and Lucey Burch, 21 March 1798.

B. BURGES, ELIZABETH daughter of John and Sarah Burges, 3 June 1716.

B. BURGIS, ELIZABETH daughter of John and Sarah Burgis, 21 July 1723.

BURK   SEE: BURT PAGE 29

D. BURK, KATHRINE 15 April 1721.

D. BURK, ELIZABETH 3 December 1726.

B. BURN, THOMAS son of Thomas and Sarah Burn, 4 March 1728.

M. BURN, JOSEPH and Eleanor Flowers, 3 April 1728.

M. BURN, CHRISTOPHER and Alice Gwien, 2 August 1728.

B. BURN, JOHN son of Thomas and Sarah Burn, 18 October 1732.

B. BURNAM, WILLIAM son of Alexander and Elizabeth Burnam, 1 April 1739.

B. BURNHAM, ALEXANDER son of Eliz.^{a} Burnham, 6 May 1716.

B. BURNS, MARY ANN bastard child of Ann Burns, 14 September 1750.

BURREL ; BURRELL

B. BURRELL, LUCY daughter of Susanna Burrell, 25 March 1737.

B. BURREL, SAM "a free Negro son of Susanna Burrel," 25 May 1739.

B. BURREL, WINIFRED "a free Molatto of Barbara Burrel," 7 December 1740.

B. BURRELL, SAM son of Sue "a free Molatto," 15 August 1742.

B. BURREL, SUSANNA daughter of Susanna Burrell, "a free Negro," 26 January 1753.

B. BURRIS, SUSANNA daughter of William and Jane Burris, 23 December 1767.

BURT   SEE: BURK PAGE 28

M. BURT, DAVID and Mary Read, 19 October 1673.

B. BURT, DAVID son of David and Mary Burt, 7 March 1673 (sic) [? 1673/4 ?].

B. BUTLER, JAMES ESKRIDGE son of William and Jenny Butler, 21 January 1783 [L:3].

B. BUTLER, WILLIAM RANSDELL son of William and Jane Butler, 13 Oct. 1792 [L:3].

B. BUTTERY, ANNE daughter of William and Mary Buttery, 4 April 1714.

M. BUXSTON, JOHN and Anne Hais, 18 February 1730/1.

C

M. CALL, ELIZABETH and John Gibson, 7 August 1729.

B. CALVERT, REUBIN son of Christopher and Anne Calvert, 5 November 168#.

M. CAMEL, KATHERINE and Abraham Harper, 8 January 1729/30.

D. CAMPBELL, ELLEN 27 July 1721.

M. CAMRON, DENNIS and Ann Preseon, 1 December 1728.

M. CANES, ANNE and John Marsy, 11 July 1680.

B. CANNADAY, SARAH daughter of John and Sarah Cannaday, 3 October 1673.

B. CANNADAY, JOANNA daughter of John and Sarah Cannaday, 15 October 1678.

B. CANNADAY, MARY daughter of John and Sarah Cannaday, 11 October 1680.

B. CANNADAY, SAMUEL son of John and Sarah Cannaday, 16 September 1684.

M. CANTERBERY, MARGARET and John Smith, 9 February 1725/6.

D. CAREL, SARAH 17 November 1726.

B. CAREY, JUDITH HIGGINS daughter of John and Katherine Carey, 15 February 1722.

M. CARILL, DANIEL and Ann Lase, 26 February 1726/7.

D. CARPENTER, MARY 29 December 1721.

M. CARPENTER, JOHN and Frances Brown, 9 June 1729.

B. CARPENTER, SAMUEL son of John and Frances Carpenter, 8 November 1730.

B. CARPENTER, THOMAS son of John and Frances Carpenter, 11 February 1734.

B. CARPENTER, ABSOLOM son of John and Frances Carpenter, 15 September 1737.

B. CARPENTER, PATTEY daughter of William and Nelley Carpenter, 26 May 1791 [L:5].

B. CARPENTER, JAMES son of William and Nelly Carpenter, 24 June 1793 [L:5].

B. CARRY, SARAH DOWTEN "a bastard child of Cathrine Carry's," 3 November 1750.

B. CARTER, THOMAS son of William and Frances Carter, 3 May 1739.

B. CARTER, ROBERT WORMELEY son of Landon and Katharine Carter, 2 January 1792;
    baptized 19 March 1792 [L:5].
    [Robert Wormeley Carter (1792-1861) was the son of Landon and Catherine
    (Tayloe) Carter and great-grandson of Colonel Landon Carter (1710-1778) of
    "Sabine Hall," Richmond County. The Diary of Colonel Landon Carter 1752-1778
    (Charlottesville, Va., 1965) was published by the Virginia Historical Society
    in two handsome volumes and convey an interesting picture of the life of an
    aristocratic family in colonial Richmond County, Virginia.]

B. CARTER, SAMUEL STOWERS son of George and Letty Carter, 15 March 1795 [L:5].

M. CARY, MARY and John Jacobs, 8 November 1680.

B. CARY, JUDITH HIGGINS daughter of John and Katherine Cary, 15 February 1722.
    [This child's birth is also entered as Judith Higgins Carey; see page 29.]

D. CAUERNOR or CAVERNOR, FRANCES 20 February 1721.

M. CEARRON, WILLIAM and Ann Dammurell, 27 August 1730.

D. CEEF, ELIZABETH 5 October 1722.

M. CHANDLER, FRANCIS and Margaret Mozingo, 18 July 1731.

M. CHANLER, JOHN and Sarah Mozingo, 25 August 1729.

B. CHAPMAN, JOHN son of Richard and Mary Chapman, [not entered] A.D. 1702.

B. CHAPMAN, JUDITH daughter of Richard and Mary Chapman [not entered] A.D.
    September 1705.

B. CHAPMAN, SARAH daughter of Richard and Mary Chapman, 1 October 1711.

B. CHAPMAN, GEORGE son of John and Eleanor Chapman, 5 February 1732.

    CHARLETON   SEE: CHORTON PAGE 31

B. CHARLETON, WILLSON son of Thomas and Hester Charleton, 2 January 1710.

B. CHARLETON, THOMAS son of Thomas and Hester Charleton, 16 January 1713.

B. CHILTON, THO [?] son of John Steward and Mary Chilton, 15 March 1761.

CHORTON   SEE: CHARLETON PAGE 30

B. CHORTON, ELIZABETH daughter of Thomas and Esther Chorton, 10 December 1716.

B. CHRISTIAN, RAWLEIGH CHINN son of Francis H. Christian, 7 September 1757.

B. CHRISTIAN, FRANCIS son of Francis H. Christian, 14 July 1759.

B. CHRISTIAN, MARY daughter of Francis H. Christian, 20 October 1760.

B. CHRISTIAN, NANCEY daughter of Francis H. Christian, 3 April 1761.

B. CHRISTIAN, DAVID son of Francis Humphrey Christian, 2 October 1763.

B. CHRISTIAN, EDWARD son of Francis and Ann Christian, [not entered] 1772.

M. CHRISTIE, ROBERT and Elizabeth Lambeart, 23 April 1731.

B. CHRISTER (sic), WILLIAM son of Robert and Elizabeth Christer, 1 April 1733.

B. CHRISTIE, JOHN son of Robert and Elizabeth Christie, 1 September 1735.

D. CHRISTIE, JOHN 13 September 1736.

B. CHRISTIE, JOHN son of Robert and Elizabeth Christie, 21 September 1741.

D. CHRISTIE, JOHN son of Robert Christie, 2 December 1742.

M. CHURCHWELL, ELIZABETH and ISAAC DOGGETT, 11 December 1729.

M. CHURCHWELL, SIMON and Darks [Darcas] Starks, 4 March 1730/1.

B. CHURCHWELL, SIMON son of Simon and Ann (sic) Churchwell, 17 May 1734.

D. CHURCHWELL, SAMUEL 13 February 1735.

B. CHURCHWELL, ANN daughter of Simon and Dorcas Churchwell, 24 February 1735.

B. CHURCHWELL, JAMES son of Simon and Dorcas Churchwell, 15 June 1738.

B. CHURCHWELL, SARAH ANN daughter of Simon and Dorcas Churchwell, 10 July 1750.

CLARK : CLARKE

B. CLARK, JOHN son of Henry and Jane Clark, 13 February 1666.

B. CLARK, HENRY son of William and Mary Clark, 19 September 1713.

B. CLARK ALCE [ALICE] daughter of William and Mary Clark, 17 August 1716.

D. CLARK, WILLIAM 23 April 1726.

M. CLARK, MARY and George Hill, 20 October 1726.

B. CLARK, MARY daughter of John and Elizabeth Clark, 21 August 1732.

D. CLARK, WILLIAM 28 May 1734.

B. CLARK, GEORGE son of Henry and Emparnell Clark, 8 May 1739.

B. CLARK, WILLIAM son of Henry and Emparnell Clark, 8 December 1741.

B. CLARK, DUDLEY son of Henry and Amparnel Clark, 29 January 1743.

B. CLARK, ALEXANDER son of William and Winifred Clark, 7 June 1747.

B. CLARK, GEORGE son of George and Mary Clark, 13 March 1750.

B. CLARK, WILLIAM son of John Clark and Rebecca Rhymer, 5 October 1750.

B. CLARK, FRANKY daughter of George and Mary Clark, 31 March 1751.

B. CLARK, ROBERT son of John and Rebecca Clark, 2 March 1752.

B. CLARK, RODHAM son of Thomas and Elizabeth Clark, 21 May 1753.

B. CLARK, KATHRINE daughter of Thomas and Elizabeth Clark, 30 December 1754.

B. CLARK, WILLIAM son of Thomas and Elizabeth Clark, 22 May 1757.

B. CLARKE, HANNAH daughter of John and Elizabeth Clarke, 16 July 1778.

B. CLERK, BETTY daughter of William and Caty Clerk [Clark], 16 May 1783.

B. CLARK, SUSANNA daughter of William Clark, 20 January 1788.

B. CLARK, EPAFREDITUS son of Presley and Winefret Clark, 23 January 1788.

B. CLARK, THOMAS son of Rodham and Elizabeth Clark, 23 April 1788.

B. CLARK, SAHARY daughter of Thomas and Susanna Clark, 26 April 1788.

B. CLARKE, RICHARD son of Thomas and Susanna Clarke, 15 April 1791 [L:5].

B. CLARK, NANCE daughter of William and Catherine Clark, 28 June 1791.

B. CLARK, ELIZABETH daughter of Thomas and Susanna Clark, 28 February 1795 [L:5].

B. CLARK, THOMAS son of Thomas and Susaner Clark, 9 June 1800 [L:5].

B. CLATER, PEGGY HUDSON daughter of Richard and Nancy Clater, 16 Nov.1796 [L:5].

B. CLAYTOR, WILLIAM RANDALL son of Richard and Anne Claytor, 10 September 1794 [L:5].

B. COATES, JAMES son of Rachel Coates, 7 February 1770.

B. COATS, FANNY daughter of Edney and Jemima Coats, 19 March 1792. [L:5].

B. COATS, REBECCA daughter of James and Eleanor Coats, 8 May 1793 [L:5].

B. COATS, JOSEPH BARTLETT son of Thomas and Molley Coats, 1 October 1793 [L:5].

B. COATS, EDNEY son of Edney and Jemima Coats, 7 April 1794 [L:5].

B. COATS, JAMES son of Edney and Jemima Coats, 7 [not entered] 1796 [L:5].

B. COATS, NANCEY daughter of Thomas and Molley Coats, 11 Sept. 1796 [L:5].

B. COATS, SALLEY DAVIS daughter of Thomas and Molley Coats, 18 Jany 1798 [L:5].

B. COCKRELL, ASTEN son of Presly Cockrell, 1 February 1778.

B. COCKRELL, MOLLEY daughter of Presly Cockrell, 1 February 1778.

M. COEAR, JANE and William Crawley 30 November 1728.

B. COLE, WALTER son of Giles and Elizabeth Cole, 5 March 1677.

B. COLE, ROBERT son of Robert and Mary Cole, 30 September 1677.

COLEMAN : COELMAN [See MRC, p.41 and Fleet, Northumberland County, Va., Births 1661-1810, p.32,34,36,131 which duplicates the entries below in NFPR and also records the death of Betty Coelman 14 December 1788 in her 49th year.]

B. COELMAN, LUCY daughter of Thomas and Betty Coelman, 1 March 1759.

B. COELMAN, RICHARD son of Thomas and Betty Coelman, 22 April 1761.

B. COELMAN, BETTY daughter of Thomas and Betty Coelman, 26 January 1763.

B. COELMAN, THOMAS son of Thomas and Betty Coelman, 30 June 1770.

B. COELMAN, ROBERT son of Thomas and Betty Coelman, 15 August 1772.

B. COELMAN, SARAH daughter of Thomas and Betty Coelman, 19 May 1775.

B. COELMAN, JAMES son of Thomas and Betty Coelman, 4 January 1778.

B. COELMAN, MOLLEY daughter of Thomas and Betty Coelman, 23 April 1780.

B. COELMAN, THADDEUS son of Thomas and Ann Coelman, 21 May 1791.

M. COLLEE, THOMAS and Anne Fann, 13 July 1673.

COLLIN : COLLINGS : COLLINS

B. COLLIN, SARAH daughter of James and Elizabeth Collin, 9 November 1697.

B. COLLIN, ELIZABETH daughter of James and Elizabeth Collin, 26 June 1700.

D. COLLINGS, EDWARD 16 February 1726.

D. COLLINS, SARAH 20 October 1726.

M. COLLINS, MARY ANN and Henry Webster, 15 September 1730.

B. COLLINS, THOMAS son of John and Ann Collins, 18 February 1754.

B. COLSTON, SUSANNA daughter of William and Anne Colston, 8 December 1686.

B. COLSTON, CHARLES son of William and Anne Colston, 17 April 1691.

B. COLSTON, WILLIAM son of William and Mary Colston, 1 August 1713.

B. COLSTON, TRAVERSE son of Charles and Rebeccah Colston, 4 January 1714.

D. COLSTON, ELIZABETH 18 January 1726.

D. COLSTON, CHARLES 25 January 1726.

D. COLSTON, WINIFRED 29 January 1726.

D. COLSTON, REBECCAH 29 December 1726.

COLVERT SEE: CALVERT PAGE 29

B. COLWICK, MARY daughter of Hezekiah and Mary Colwick, 27 November 1681.

B. COMAN, THOMAS born of a servant belonging to Samuel Peachey, 13 Nov. 1702.

CONNALLY : CONNELLY : CONNOLLY : CONNELLEE &c:

D. CONALLY, FELIX 20 April 1720.

M. CONNELLY, PATRICK and Mary Widdilow, 28 July 1728.

M. CONNELLY, JOHN and Margaret Oldham, 26 February 1729/30.

D. CONNALLY, ANN 11 June 1735.

B. CONNELLY, THOMAS son of John and Margaret Connelly, 12 September 1738.

D. CONNALLY, OLDHAM son of John and Margaret Connally, 25 January 1739.

D. CONNALLY, MARGARET 29 January 1739.

M. CONNELLY, MARGARET and James Robinson, 29 July 1739.

D. CONNALLY, YANNY 27 February 1749.

D. CONNALLY, [#] 24 February 1754. [Probably John Connally as the inventory of the estate of John Connelly was filed in Richmond County in 1754.]

B. CONNALLY, CHARLOTTE daughter of James and Mary Connally, 10 December 1772.

B. CONNOLLY, WILLIAM MORRIS son of George and Sally Connolly, 8 Aug. 1792 [L:5].

B. CONNOLLY, MOLLY ANN JENKINS daughter of George and Sally Connolly, 29 August 1794 [L:5].

B. CONNOLLY, MOLLEY EIDSON daughter of George and Sally Connolly, 18 April 1796 [L:5].

B. CONNELLEE, SALLEY MORRIS daughter of George and Salley Connellee, 12 June 1798 [L:5].

B. CONNELLEE, FAIR SABRA daughter of George and Salley Connellee, 17 January 1800 [L:5].

M. CONNELL, MICHAEL and Mary Jesper, 8 September 1727.

B. CONNELL, ELIZABETH daughter of Michael and Mary Connell, 18 June 1729.

B. CONNEL, DAVIS son of Michal and Mary Connel, 3 April 1736.

D. CONNEL, ANNE 4 October 1737.

B. CONNELL, THOMAS son of Michael and Mary Connell, 23 September 1738.

B. CONNELL, ANN daughter of Michael and Mary Connell, 10 January 1740.

B. CONNELL, SARAH daughter of Michael and Mary Connell, 2 September 1743.

B. CONNELL, WINNY daughter of Michael and Mary Connell, 20 February 1745.

B. CONNELL, CATY daughter of Michael and Mary Connell, 19 August 1748.

B. CONNELL, MICHAEL son of Michael and Mary Connell, 5 August 1750.

D. CONNELL, MICHAEL son of Michael and Mary Connell, 19 April 1751.

B. CONNER, ELIZABETH daughter of William and Susanna Conner, __ August 1766.

B. CONNER, ANN daughter of William and Susanna Conner, 17 January 1769.

B. CONNER, SALLEY daughter of William and Susanna Conner, 16 October 1771.

B. CONNER, JAMES son of William and Susanna Conner, 11 March 1774.

M. CONOR, MARGARET and Edward Anderson, 18 October 1725.

M. CONSERVE, EMANUEL and Elizabeth Killingsby,   22 January 1675.

B. CONWAY, MARY daughter of Charles and Honour Conway, 19 August 1693.

B. COOK, ELEANOR daughter of Sarah Cook, 20 September 1736.

    COOKMAN   SEE: KOOKMAN PAGES 111 - 112

B. COOPER, RICHARD son of William and Elizabeth Cooper, 3 September 1680.

B. COPE, ANNE daughter of Richard and Mary Cope, 3 January 1710.

B. CORNELIUS, JANE daughter of Josiah and Jane Cornelius, 2 January 1782.

B. CORNWALL, JOHN son of Edward and Jane Cornwall, 2 August 1697.

M. COWARD, MARGARET and Stephen Gupton,   23 January 1728/9.

B. CRASK, ELIZABETH HALL daughter of John and Martha Brask, 24 June 17___ [not
    entered but circa 1791; L:5].

B. CRASK, JAMES WALKER son of John and Martha Crask, 19 October 1793 [L:5].

B. CRASK, WILLIAM CREWDSON son of Jesse and Peggy Crask, 14 Feby 1794 [L:5].

B. CRASK, SUSANNA daughter of Jesse and Peggey Crask, 27 August 1796 [L:5].

B. CRAWFORD, THOMAS son of Presley and Elizabeth Crawford, 25 May 1772.

M. CRAWLEY, WILLIAM and Jane Coear, 30 November 1728.

D. CRAWSBY, MARY 29 April 1730.

D. CREEL, THOMAS 23 April 1727.

M. CREEL, WILLIAM and Ales [Alice] Dodson, 25 November 1729.

B. CREEL, JOHN son of William and Alice Creel, 28 February 1732.

B. CRENTHEAN, SALLY daughter of David Crenthean, 8 June 1787. [David Crenshaw
    is upon the 1787 Richmond County tax lists, but no person named Crenthean.]

B. CRESWELL, ANNE daughter of Joseph and Frances Creswell, 18 February 1675.

M. CRESWELL, WILLIAM and Anne Allin, 18 June 1677.

M. CRESWELL, FRANCES and John Partridge 6 April 1678.

D. CRIBIN, THOMAS 27 April 1727.

M. CRIBIN, ELIZABETH and John Spendergrass, 2 December 1728.

M. CROLORIR, THOMAS and Alice King, 13 October 1729.

D. CROMELL, JANE 9 April 1732.

CROOSBY   SEE: CRAWSBY PAGE 36

B. CROSWELL, GILBURD son of Gilburd and Margaret Croswell, 8 December 1716.

D. CROSWELL, ELIZABETH daughter of Gilburd and Mary Croswell, 2 September 1717.

D. CROSWELL, GILBERT 9 February 1726.

M. CROSWELL, GILBERT and Eleanor Hill, 9 December 1728.

B. CROUCHER, Caty daughter of William and Ann Croucher, 24 September 1748.

B. CROUCHER, CATY daughter of William and Eleanor Croucher, 24 January 1752.

B. CROWDER, JEREMIAH son of Elizabeth Crowder, 6 June 1783.

B. CROWSON, FANNY daughter of James and Elizabeth Crowson, 29 May 1772.

D. CRUSE, JOHN 10 April 1726.

B. CRUTCHER, JOHN son of John and Jane Crutcher, 3 October 1682.

B. CRUTCHER, JANE daughter of John and Jane Crutcher, 15 June 1686.

B. CRUTCHER, CICELY daughter of John and Jane Crutcher, 17 July 1692.

D. CURTIS, ANNE 8 October 1723.

B. CURTIS, HENRY COX son of James and Nancey Curtis, 2 January 1797 [L:5].

D

DAGOD   SEE: DOGGETT : DOGGITT : DOGED PAGE 50

M. DAGOD, MARGARET and George Dodson, 30 April 1726.

DALE   SEE: DELLEWAR [!] PAGE 44

B. DALE, ALEXANDER son of Thomas and Frances Dale, 25 September 1720.

B. DALE, FRANCES [parents not entered], 18 March 1721.

B. DALE, RUBIN son of Abraham and Winnifred Dale, 21 September 1721.

B.   DALE, BETTY daughter of Thomas and Frances Dale, 19 April 1722.

D.   DALE, BETTY 5 August 1722.

D.   DALE, ALEXANDER 22 November 1722.

B.   DALE, THOMAS son of Thomas and Frances Dale, 12 August 1723.

B.   DALE, ABRAHAM son of Abraham and Winnefred Dale, 4 April 1724.

B.   DALE, ALEXANDER son of Thomas and Frances Dale, 3 February 1726.

M.   DALE, FRANCES and James Booth, 5 November 1727.

B.   DALE, ISAAC son of Abraham and Winnifred Dale, 15 November 1727.

B.   DALE, ROBERT son of Abraham and Winifritt Dale, 27 March 1730 (sic).

B.   DALE, THOMAS son of Abraham and Winifritt Dale, 20 April 1730.

B.   DALE, WILLIAM son of William and Frances Dale, 1 September 1737.

B.   DALE, PETER son of William and Frances Dale, 5 October 1739.

B.   DALE, REUBIN son of William and Frances Dale, 24 January 1741.

B.   DALE, ELIZABETH daughter of William and Frances Dale, 31 March 1745.

B.   DALE, ISAAC son of William and Frances Dale, 8 September 1747.

B.   DALE, ISAAC son of Reubin and Hannah Dale, 17 June 1751.

B.   DALE, AGA daughter of Alexander and Lettice Dale, 29 June 1751.

B.   DALE, DUDLEY son of Thomas and Joice Dale, 18 August 1752.

B.   DALE, WINIFRED daughter of Thomas and Alice Dale, 17 September 1752.

B.   DALE, SARAH daughter of Alexander and Lettice Dale, 21 February 1753.

B.   DALE, FRANCES daughter of William and Frances Dale, 11 March 1753.

B.   DALE, ABRAHAM son of Reubin and Hannah Dale, 30 July 1753.

B.   DALE, NANNY daughter of Thomas and Joice Dale, 20 April 1754.

B.   DALE, JAMES son of William and Frances Dale, 29 December 1754.

B.   DALE, NANNY daughter of Thomas and Alice Dale, 5 March 1755.

B.   DALE, FRANCES daughter of Alexander and Lettice Dale, [not entered] 1757.

B. DALE, WILLIAM son of Reubin and Hannah Dale, 29 November 1757.

B. DALE, RICHARD son of William and Frances Dale, 1 December 1757.

D. DALE, WILLIAM [not entered] January 1758.

B. DALE, ELIZABETH daughter of Thomas and Alice Dale, 6 January 1758.

B. DALE, RAWLEIGH son of Thomas and Alice Dale, 10 February 1760.

B. DALE, ROBERT son of Reubin and Hannah Dale, 14 March 1760.

B. DALE, BETTY daughter of Reubin and Hannah Dale, 15 June 1764.

B. DALE, NATUS son of Thomas and Alice Dale, 9 October 1767.

B. DALE, ELIZABETH daughter of Joseph and Million Dale, 22 June 1772.

B. DALE, JAMES son of John and Lucy Dale, 7 November 1772.

B. DALE, ARCHELUS son of Joseph and Million Dale, 22 April 1774.

B. DALE, BETSY daughter of George and Hannah Dale, 1 January 1777.

B. DALE, REUBIN son of John and Lucy Dale, 19 April 1778.

B. DALE, POLLY daughter of Joseph and Million Dale, 12 March 1781.

B. DALE, ALESY daughter of Alexander and Sarah Dale, 28 April 1783.

B. DALE, HANNAH daughter of George Dale, 14 November 1783.

B. DALE, JOHN STONEHAM son of Lucy Dale, 12 November 1789.

D. DALLIAN or DILLIAN, MATTHEW 2 October 1737.

D. DALPHEN, ROBERT [day not entered] November 1722.

B. DALTON, DEREMIAH (sic), son of Derimiah (sic) and Joan Dalton, 9 July 1693.

B. DALTON, ROBERT (a Bastard child), 22 September 1722.

D. DALTON, MARY 12 December 1734.

B. DAMERON, WILLIAM son of Roger Dameron, 17 August 1777.

M. DAMMURELL, ANN and William Cearron, 27 August 1730.

B. DANIEL, SARAH daughter of Elizabeth Daniel, 1 January 1777.

B. DARBEY, JAMES son of Peter and Mary Darbey, 23 February 1705.

B. DARBEY, PETER son of Peter and Mary Darbey, 3 April 1710.

B. DARBEY, JOHN son of Peter and Mary Darbey, 16 June 1711.

B. DARBEY, WINNEFRED daughter of Peter and Mary Darbey, 22 August 1712.

B. DARBEY, WILLIAM son of Peter and Mary Darbey, 30 July 1715.

B. DARBY, DARBY (a Bastard), 10 June 1732 (sic).

D. DARBEY, JAMES 10 November 1747.

M. DASEY, WILLIAM and Mary Mills, 8 January 1727/8.

M. DAVENPORT, WILLIAM and Elizabeth Heale, 26 November 1728.

B. DEAVENPORT, WILLIAM son of William and Elizabeth Deavenport, 6 February 1735.

B. DAVENPORT, FORTUNATUS son of William and Elizabeth Davenport, 12 June 1738.

B. DAVENPORT, RAWLEIGH son of William and Elizabeth Davenport, 28 September 1741.

B. DAVENPORT, LINDSY son of William and Elizabeth Davenport, 22 April 1744.

B. DAVENPORT, JUDITH daughter of William and Elizabeth Davenport, 4 April 1747.

B. DAVENPORT, ELIZABETH daughter of William and Elizabeth Davenport, 27 Dec.1749.

B. DAVENPORT, OPIE son of William and Elizabeth Davenport, 29 April 1752.

B. DAVENPORT, JOSEPH son of Fortunatus and Elizabeth Davenport, 7 September 1759.

B. DAVENPORT, GEORGE son of Fortunatus and Elizabeth Davenport, 7 December 1760.

B. DAVENPORT, BETTY HEALE, daughter of Fortunatus and Elizabeth Davenport, 19 May 1765.

B. DAVENPORT, RACHEL daughter of Fortunatus and Elizabeth Davenport, 27 Feb.1767.

B. DAVENPORT, JOHN son of Fortunatus and Elizabeth Davenport, 23 April 1769.

D. DAVENPORT, WILLIAM 7 August 1771

B. DAVENPORT, WILLIAM HEALE FORESTER son of Opie and Nancy Davenport, 4 March 1783.

B. DAVENPORT, DANIEL DOBYNS son of Joseph and Frances Davenport, 6 April 1783.

B. DAVENPORT, SUCKEY NORRIS daughter of Opiy (sic) and Nancy Davenport, 11 November 1787.

B. DAVENPORT, ELIZABETH POPE daughter of George Davenport, 7 February 1790.

M. DAVIS, WILLIAM and Elizabeth Thrift, 23 April 1677.

B. DAVIS, WILLIAM son of William and Elizabeth Davis, 15 March 1677 [1677/8].

M. DAVIS, EDWARD and Mary Paxen, 15 November 1677.

B. DAVIS, JANE daughter of William and Elizabeth Davis, 20 November 1680.

B. DAVIS, ROBERT son of William and Elizabeth Davis, 25 March 1682.

B. DAVIS, RICHARD son of William and Elizabeth Davis, 5 September 1687.

B. DAVIS, JOSEPH son of Joseph and Catharine Davis, 9 January 1693.

B. DAVIS, MARY daughter of Joseph and Susanna Davis, 9 September 1715.

B. DAVIS, WILLIAM son of John and Frances Davis, 10 October 1719.

B. DAVIS, MARY daughter of Joseph and Susanna Davis, 19 October 1721.

D. DAVIS, MARY 25 August 1722.

B. DAVIS, JOHN son of John and Frances Davis, 7 September 1722.

B. DAVIS, WINNIFRED daughter of John and Frances Davis, 11 January 1723/4.

B. DAVIS, SAMUEL son of Joseph and Susanna Davis, 3 March 1723/4.

B. DAVIS, WINNEFRED daughter of Robert and Susanna Davis, 12 January 1724/5.

D. DAVIS, ARTHER 18 January 1725.

D. DAVIS, JOSEPH 5 February 1725.

D. DAVIS, THOMAS 16 March 1725.

B. DAVIS, DESSEMIAH son of John and Frances Davis, 16 August 1725.

B. DAVIS, JOHN son of John and Frances Davis, 16 July 1726.

D. DAVIS, WILLIAM 1 December 1726.

D. DAVIS, JOHN 12 December 1726.

M. DAVIS, ANN and Charles Nichols, 17 August 1727.

M. DAVIS, JOHN and Susanna Hammond, 25 December 1727.

M. DAVIS, JANE and Thomas Randall, 4 October 1728.

B. DAVIS, MARY daughter of John and Frances Davis, 4 May 1729.

B. DAVIS, BETTY daughter of John and Susanna Davis, 7 June 1729.

D. DAVIS, RICHARD 10 October 1729.

D. DAVIS, JOHN 25 December 1730.

M. DAVIS, GRACE and Henry Allard, 15 February 1730/1.

B. DAVIS, JOHN son of John and Susanna Davis, 3 March 1732.

B. DAVIS, BAYLIS daughter of John and Susanna Davis, 21 December 1735.

B. DAVIS, WILLIAM son of Joseph Davis, 16 October 1738.

B. DAVIS, ANN daughter of George and Kathrine Davis, 5 May 1739.

B. DAVIS, JOB son of John and Elizabeth Davis, 17 August 1739.

B. DAVIS, MARY ANN daughter of George and Catherine Davis, 11 December 1741.

B. DAVIS, MARY daughter of Thomas and Mary Davis, 10 February 1742.

B. DAVIS, JOHN son of George and Kathrine Davis, 15 October 1744.

B. DAVIS, CATY daughter of George and Kathrine Davis, 19 April 1747.

D. DAVIS, ROBERT 11 May 1748.

B. DAVIS, SAMUEL son of Thomas and Mary Davis, 19 May 1748.

D. DAVIS, JOHN 27 October 1750.

B. DAVIS, NANNY daughter of Joseph and Mary Davis, 29 April 1751.

B. DAVIS, THOMAS son of Thomas and Mary Davis, 13 February 1754.

B. DAVIS, SALLEY daughter of George and Betty Davis, 5 November 1759.

B. DAVIS, BETTY daughter of George and Betty Davis, 31 October 1761.

B. DAVIS, GEORGE son of George and Betty Davis, 24 May 1766.

B. DAVIS, KATHARINE daughter of John and Ann Davis, 10 December 1770.

B. DAVIS, ANN daughter of John and Ann Davis, 30 December 1772.

B. DAVIS, WILLIAM son of Joseph and Martha Davis, 8 June 1774.

B. DAVIS, LEROY son of Joseph Davis, 8 November 1776.

B. DAVIS, BETTEY daughter of Thomas and Bettey Davis, 1 February 1777.

B. DAVIS, JOHN son of John and Ann Davis, 13 June 1779.

B. DAVIS, JEAN daughter of John and Ann Davis, 19 December 1782.

B. DAVIS, AILCEY daughter of John and Ann Davis, 10 March 1791.

B. DAVIS, REBECCA daughter of William and Hainey Davis, 28 Sept. 1793 [L:7].

B. DAWSEY, WILLIAM son of William and Mary Dawsey, 13 December 1728.

B. DAWSEY, JOHN son of William and Mary Dawsey, 21 May 1731.

B. DAWSEY, THOMAS son of William and Mary Dawsey, 6 March 1733.

D. DAWSON, ELIZABETH 9 October 1725.

B. DAWSON, DAVID son of Sarah Dawson, 13 August 1726.

M. DAWSON, SARAH and Andrew Morgan, 13 November 1730.

D. DAYLEY, TIMOTHY 10 August 1725.

B. DEANE, ISAAC son of Thomas and Elizabeth Deane, 11 February 1794 [L:7].

B. DEATING, NANNY daughter of Christopher and Elizabeth Deating, 25 April 1758.

B. DEATLEY, WILLIAM son of Chris and Eleanor Deatley, 2 June 1763.

D. DEBORD, MARY 29 February 1717.

B. DEBORD, GEORGE son of John and Elizabeth Debord, 20 May 1728.

B. DEBORD, TAMER daughter of Elizabeth Debord, 18 February 1728/9.

B. DEBORD, JOHN son of John and Elizabeth Debord, 30 August 1730.

B. DEEK, ELIZABETH daughter of Joseph and Catharine Deek, 13 July 1704.

B. DEEK, CATHARINE daughter of Joseph and Catharine Deek, 10 June 1707.

B. DEEK, MARY daughter of Joseph and Catharine Deek, 17 July 1710.

B. DEEK, JOSEPH son of Joseph and Catharine Deek, 3 February 1713.

B. DEEK, JOHN son of Joseph and Catharine Deek, 26 December 1715.

D. DEEK, JOHN 1 February 1720.

D. DEEK, JOSEPH 20 February 1720.

D. DEEK, MARY 8 January 1726.

B. DEGGES, WILLIAM son of William and Dorothy Degges, 10 January 1726/7.

    DELLEWAR   SEE; DALE PAGES 37 ---39

B. DELLEWAR, ANN daughter of Abraham and Winnefred Dellewar, 2 April 1717.

B. DEMAR, BETTY "a child of a free Negro woman," 5 May 1779.

M. DEMERITT, LUKE and Judith Win, 13 February 1728/9.

B. DEMERITT, ELIZABETH daughter of Luke and Judith Demeritt, 4 November 1729.

B. DEMERITT, MARY daughter of Luke and Judith Demeritt, 12 September 1731.

D. DERTON, JANE 6 February 1728.

B. DEW, ISHMAEL son of Andrew and Flora Dew, 4 January 1700.

B. DEW, ANDREW son of Andrew and Flora Dew, 1 March 1702.

B. DEW, SAMUEL son of Andrew and Flora Dew, 9 February 1705.

B. DEW, THOMAS and WILLIAM sons of Andrew and Flora Dew, 8 August 1711.

D. DEW, ANDREW 15 November 1726.

D. DEW, THOMAS 12 January 1733.

B. DEW, ANDREW son of Thomas and Ann Dew, 1 April 1733.

B. DEW, SAMUEL son of William and Elizabeth Dew, 14 November 1733.

B. DEW, ISHMAEL son of Thomas and Ann Dew, 15 November 1734.

B. DEW, BETTY daughter of William and Elizabeth Dew, 7 September 1735.

B. DEW, THOMAS son of William and Elizabeth Dew, [day and month not entered] 173

B. DEW, BETTY daughter of Thomas and Ann Dew, 13 December 1737.

B. DEW, JUDITH daughter of Thomas and Ann Dew, 13 May 1743.

B. DEW, ALICE daughter of Thomas and Ann Dew, 14 March 1744.

B. DEW, WILLIAM and ALEXANDER sons of William and Elizabeth Dew, 15 June 1744.

D. DEW, THOMAS 12 August 1750.

D. DEW, WILLIAM 23 May 1769.

B. DICKEN, MARY NORMAN daughter of Richard and Mary Dicken, 25 June 1756.

B. DICKENSON, THOMAS son of Metcalfe and Winifred Dickenson, 2 June 1748.

D. DILLIAN or DALLIAN, MATTHEW 2 October 1737.

D. DIXON, ESTHER 17 January 1749.

D. DOBYNS, EDMOND [day not entered] February 1720.

B. DOBYNS, WILLIAM son of Charles and Sarah Dobyns, 5 March 1724/5.

B. DOBYNS, CHARLES son of Charles and Sarah Dobyns, 11 December 1727.

B. DOBYNS, ANN daughter of Charles and Sarah Dobyns, 12 January 1729.

B. DOBYNS, BETTY daughter of Griffin and Mary Ann Dobyns, 2 March 1731/2.

B. DOBYNS, DANIEL son of Charles and Sarah Dobyns, 21 May 1732.

B. DOBYNS, MARY ANN daughter of Griffin and Mary Ann Dobyns, 24 October 1733.

B. DOBYNS, THOMAS son of Charles and Sarah Dobyns, 19 February 1734.

B. DOBYNS, DRURY son of Griffin and Mary Ann Dobyns, 2 February 1735.

B. DOBYNS, SAMUEL son of Charles and Sarah Dobyns, 15 June 1738.

B. DOBYNS, CATY daughter of Charles and Sarah Dobyns, 11 March 1740.

B. DOBYNS, SAMUEL son of Griffin and Mary Ann Dobyns, 8 September 1740.

B. DOBYNS, GRIFFIN son of Griffin and Mary Ann Dobyns, 23 April 1743.

B. DOBYNS, EDWARD son of Charles and Sarah Dobyns, 30 December 1743.

B. DOBYNS, ABNER son of Charles and Sarah Dobyns, 22 September 1746.

B. DOBYNS, CHARLES son of William and Rebeccah Dobyns, 29 January 1747.

D. DOBYNS, GRIFFIN 10 February 1749.

D. DOBYNS, MARY ANN 12 February 1749.

D. DOBYNS, DRURY son of Griffin and Mary Ann Dobyns, 15 February 1749.

B. DOBYNS, HENRY son of William and Rebeccah Dobyns, 9 March 1749.

B. DOBYNS, WILLIAM son of Griffin and Mary Ann Dobyns, 15 August 1749.

B. DOBYNS, BETTY daughter of Charles and Sarah Dobyns, 23 September 1749.

B. DOBYNS, WILLIAM son of William and Rebecca Dobyns, 1 June 1752.

B. DOBYNS, BETTY daughter of William and Rebecca Dobyns, 23 October 1754.

B. DOBYNS, LEROY son of William and Rebecca Dobyns, 25 December 1756.

B. DOBYNS, THOMAS son of William and Rebecca Dobyns, 21 March 1759.

B. DOBYNS, NEWMAN son of Thomas and Rachel Dobyns, 15 November 1759.

B. DOBYNS, FRANCES daughter of Daniel and Winifred Dobyns, 5 March 1760.

B. DOBYNS, WILLIAM FORRESTER son of Samuel and Winny Dobyns, 17 May 1760.

D. DOBYNS, CHARLES SEN:^R 16 November 1760.

B. DOBYNS, SARAH daughter of William and Rebecca Dobyns, 10 January 1761.

B. DOBYNS, THOMAS son of Thomas and Rachel Dobyns, 20 March 1761.

B. DOBYNS, CHARLES son of Daniel and Winifred Dobyns, 27 December 1761.

B. DOBYNS, MARY ANN daughter of Samuel and Winny Dobyns, 10 February 1763.

B. DOBYNS, FREDERICK son of Charles and Lucy Dobyns, 5 June 1763.

B. DOBYNS, WINIFRED daughter of Daniel and Winifred Dobyns, 20 March 1764.

B. DOBYNS, DANIEL son of Charles and Lucy Dobyns, 18 February 1765.

B. DOBYNS, DANGERFIELD son of Samuel and Winny Dobyns, 30 November 1765.

B. DOBYNS, ANNA daughter of Daniel and Betty Dobyns, 19 January 1767.

B. DOBYNS, CATHARINE daughter of Charles and Lucy Dobyns, 23 May 1767.

B. DOBYNS, BARBARA daughter of Thomas and Rachel Dobyns, 6 October 1767.

B. DOBYNS, REBECCA daughter of William and Rebecca Dobyns, 24 October 1767.

B. DOBYNS, MOLLY daughter of Abner and Winny Dobyns, 14 September 1768.

D. DOBYNS, SARAH 26 September 1768.

B. DOBYNS, BETTY daughter of Daniel and Betty Dobyns, 1 February 1769.

B. DOBYNS, SARAH daughter of Charles and Lucy Dobyns, 7 March 1769.

B. DOBYNS, EPAPHRODITUS son of Abner and Winny Dobyns, 28 February 1770 .

B. DOBYNS, WINIFRED daughter of Edward and Amany Dobyns, 15 August 1770 .

B. DOBYNS, ANN daughter of Charles and Lucy Dobyns, 18 September 1770.

B. DOBYNS, PEGGY daughter of Samuel and Winny Dobyns, 7 November 1770.

B. DOBYNS, DANIEL son of Daniel and Betty Dobyns, 8 June 1771.

B. DOBYNS, ABNER son of Henry and Sarah Dobyns, 19 September 1771.

B. DOBYNS, ABNER son of Abner and Winny Dobyns, 8 January 1772.

B. DOBYNS, LUCY daughter of Charles and Lucy Dobyns, 22 January 1772.

B. DOBYNS, FREDERICK son of Edward and Amony Dobyns, 26 March 1772.

B. DOBYNS, HENRY MISKELL son of Henry and Sarah Dobyns, 19 December 1773.

B. DOBYNS, JOHN son of Abner and Winny Dobyns, 16 January 1774.

B. DOBYNS, EDWARD son of Edward and Amony Dobyns, 19 December 1774.

B. DOBYNS, WILLIAM HENRY son of Thomas and Rachel Dobyns, 23 September 1776.

B. DOBYNS, WASHINGTON son of Samuel Dobyns, 16 September 1777.

B. DOBYNS, BETTY daughter of Henry and Sally Dobyns, 28 December 1777.

B. DOBYNS, THOMAS son of Henry and Sally Dobyns, 10 February 1780.

B. DOBYNS, LAWSON son of Thomas and Rebeckah Dobyns, 26 December 1782.

B. DOBYNS, NANCY HALE daughter of William and Betty Dobyns, 23 September 1783.

B. DOBYNS, DANIEL son of Daniel Dobyns, 1 April 1788.

B. DOBYNS, THOMAS THORNTON and REBECCAH SISSON, twins, son and daughter to Daniel and Frances S. Dobyns, 21 March 1796.

DODSON : DOTSON

B. DODSON, THOMAS son of Charles and Anne Dodson, 15 May 1681.

B. DODSON, ANNE daughter of Charles and Anne Dodson, 16 July 1715.

D. DODSON, CHARLES 1 August 1715.

B. DODSON, MARY daughter of Thomas and Mary Dodson, 5 October 1715.

B. DODSON, JAMES son of Bartholomew and Elizabeth Dodson, 23 December 1716.

B. DODSON, JOSEPH son of Charles and Ruth Dodson, 15 November 1719.

B. DODSON, ABRAHAM son of Thomas and Mary Dodson, 4 April 1723.

B. DODSON, CHARLES son of Charles and Ruth Dodson, 11 July 1723.

B. DODSON, MARY daughter of Lambert and Sarah Dodson, 3 April 1724.

B. DODSON, JOSEPH son of Thomas and Elizabeth Dodson, 21 February 1725.

B. DODSON, JOSHUA son of Thomas and Mary Dodson, 25 May 1725.

B. DODSON, SAMUEL son of Charles and Ruth Dodson, 4 September 1725.

B. DODSON, MARTHA ANN daughter of John and Elizabeth Dodson, 7 November 1725.

D. DODSON, SAMUEL [day and month not entered] 1726.

M. DODSON, GEORGE and Margaret Dagod, 30 April 1726.

B. DODSON, CHARLES son of John and Elizabeth Dodson, 28 August 1726.

M. DODSON, FORTUNATUS and Ellis Goad, 9 September 1726.

B. DODSON, MARY daughter of George and Margaret Dodson, 21 December 1726.

B. DODSON, ELISHA son of Thomas and Mary Dodson, 22 February 1727.

B. DODSON, SOLOMON son of Charles and Ruth Dodson, 4 December 1727.

B. DODSON, LUCY daughter of Fortunatus and Alce Dodson, 12 September 1728.

B. DODSON, THOMAS son of Thomas and Elizabeth Dodson, 3 October 1728.

B. DODSON, LAZARUS son of George and Margaret Dodson, 7 October 1728.

B. DODSON, MOSES son of John and Elizabeth Dodson, 12 January 1729.

B. DODSON, MARGARET daughter of Charles and Ruth Dodson, 23 February 1729.

M. DODSON, ALES [ALICE] and William Creel, 25 November 1729.

B. DODSON, RAWLEIGH son of George and Margaret Dodson, 18 January 1730.

[!sic!]

B. DODSON, RAWLEIGH son of George and Margaret Dodson, 18 February 1730.

D. DODSON, LUCY 9 April 1730.

B. DODSON, MARY daughter of Thomas and Elizabeth Dodson, 16 June 1730.

B. DODSON, ISAAC son of Lambert and Sarah Dodson, 11 September 1730.

B. DODSON, JAMES son of Fortunatus and Alce Dodson, 18 December 1730.

B. DODSON, JOHN son of John and Elizabeth Dodson, 12 August 1731.

B. DODSON, SARAH and BETTY, twins, daughters of Thomas and Elizabeth Dodson, 27 May 1732.

B. DODSON, ANN daughter of Fortunatus and Alice Dodson, 10 November 1732.

B. DODSON, ALICE daughter of Fortunatus and Alice Dodson, 15 March 1734.

D. DODSON, JOHN JUN.^R 27 May 1734.

B. DODSON, NANNY daughter of Lambert and Sarah Dodson, 20 July 1734.

B. DODSON, RUTH [no parents entered], 21 September 1734.

D. DODSON, DANIEL 4 November 1734.

D. DODSON, RUTH 12 April 1735.

B. DODSON, PETER son of John and Elizabeth Dodson, 22 May 1735.

B. DODSON, THOMAS son of George and Margaret Dodson, 25 May 1735.

D. DODSON, SARAH 21 February 1736.

B. DODSON, GEORGE son of James and Elizabeth Dodson, 26 February 1736.

D. DODSON, JOSEPH 2 April 1736.

D. DODSON, FORTUNATUS 9 September 1737.

B. DODSON, HANNAH daughter of Fortunatus and Alice Dodson, 7 October 1737.

B. DODSON, GEORGE son of George and Margaret Dodson, 30 or 31 October 1737.

B. DODSON, FORTUNATUS son of George and Margaret Dodson, 31 March 1740.

D. DODSON, THOMAS 21 November 1740.

B. DODSON, DANIEL son of James and Elizabeth Dodson, 9 December 1740.

B. DODSON, JUDITH daughter of Greenham and Eleanor Dodson, 6 January 1741.

B. DODSON, JESSE son of James and Elizabeth Dodson, 28 August 1743.

M. DODSON, MARY and Robert Galbrath, 29 September 1743.

B. DODSON, MILLION daughter of Abraham and Barbary Dodson, 7 September 1744.

B. DODSON, CHARLES son of James and Elizabeth Dodson, 23 December 1746.

B. DODSON, HANNAH daughter of George and Margaret Dodson, 2 May 1747.

B. DODSON, JUDITH daughter of Charles and Elizabeth Dodson, 3 June 1748.

D. DODSON, MARGERY 27 February 1749.

B. DODSON, WILLIAM son of James and Elizabeth Dodson, 14 December 1749.

B. DODSON, JAMES BOOTH son of Charles and Elizabeth Dodson, 20 July 1750.

B. DODSON, CHARLES son of Charles and Elizabeth Dodson, 20 August 1752.

B. DODSON, FRANCES daughter of Charles and Elizabeth Dodson, 25 February 1755,

B. DODSON, JOHN son of Charles and Elizabeth Dodson, 28 April 1757.

B. DODSON, ALEXANDER son of Charles and Elizabeth Dodson, 14 December 1761

B. DODSON, WILLIAM son of James Dodson, 8 February 1773.

B. DODSON, JAMMEY son of James Dodson, 10 December 1780.

B. DOTSON, SARAH ALPHORD daughter of James Dotson, 28 February 1783.

B. DODSON, ELIZABETH BOOTH daughter of Alexander and Winifred Dodson, 21 May 1783.

B. DODSON, WINNYFRIT daughter of Elxander [Alexander] Dodson, 15 November 1788.

B. DODSON, ABRAHAM son of Rawleigh and Betty Dodson, 17 J ___[?]___ 1789.

B. DODSON, SUCKCAY daughter of Alexander and Winny Dodson, 28 February 1791.

B. DODSON, BETSY BOOTH daughter of Rawleigh and Betty Dodson, 28 October 1791.

B. DODSON, JAMES BOOTH daughter of Alexander and Winneyfret Dodson, 7 March 1795.

D. DOFFIN, ROBERT 6 August 1726.

DOGGETT : DOGGITT : DOGED &c: SEE: DAGOD PAGE 37

M. DOGGETT, ISAAC and Elizabeth Churchwell, 11 December 1729.

B. DOGGITT, ANN daughter of John and Mary Doggitt, 4 October 1725.

B. DOGED, JOHN son of Isaac Doged, 4 December 1730.

B. DOGED, THOMAS son of Richard and Ann Doged, 2 September 1731.

B. DOGED, SAMUEL son of Isaac and Elizabeth Doged, 9 June 1733.

M. DOLPHIN, KATHERINE and John McNamara, 30 April 1730.

M. DOON, ELIZABETH and Thomas Petty, 24 August 1727.

B. DOREN, CHARLES a mulatto belonging to Patrick Doren, 8 December 1715.

D. DORGAN, JUGG 8 January 1724/5.

B. DOSIER, JOHN son of William and Aerrilla Dosier, 10 September 1754.

B. DOSIER, JAMES son of William and Averrilla Dosier, 25 February 1764.

B. DOSSON, FANNY MIDDLETON daughter of Elizabeth Dosson, 28 February 1788.

DOTSON   SEE: DODSON PAGES 47 - 50

B. DOUGHLASS, JUDITH daughter of Edward and Lucy Doughlass, 8 February 1778.

B. DOUGLASS, WINIFRED daughter of James and Sarah Douglass, 1 May 1705.

B. DOUGHLES, JOHN son of William and Mary Doughles, 28 August 1788.

D. DOW, ISHMAELL 15 April 1728.

B. DOWDEN, WINNY daughter of Anthony and Sarah Dowden, 19 June 1725.

D. DOWDEN, ANTHONY 9 March 1726.

B. DOWDIN, ANTHONY son of Anthony and Sarah Dowdin, 28 June 1727.

M. DOWDEN, WINNY and Keene Samford, 28 July 1742.

B. DOWNING, RUTH daughter of Ralph and Honor Downing, 5 September 1686.

B. DOWNING, RALPH son of Ralph and Honor Downing, 15 April 1688.

B. DOWNING, JAMES son of Ralph and Honour Downing, 25 January 1690.

B. DOWNMAN, RAWLEIGH son of William and Million Downman, 24 April 1680.

B. DOWNMAN, WILMOTH daughter of William and Million Downman, 14 December 1681.

B. DOWNMAN, MILLION daughter of William and Million Downman, 21 November 1683.

B. DOWNMAN, WILLIAM son of William and Million Downman, 19 October 1685.

B. DOWNMAN, ROBERT son of William and Million Downman, 2 January 1686.

B. DOWNMAN, ELIZABETH daughter of William and Million Downman, 26 January 1688.

B. DOWNMAN, TRAVERSE son of William and Million Downman, 15 November 1696.

B. DOWNMAN, TRAVERSE son of William and Million Downman, 19 March 1700.

B. DOWNMAN, ROBERT son of William and Anne Downman, 21 May 1720.

B. DOWNMAN, JAMES son of William and Anne Downman, 29 July 1722.

B. DOWNMAN, WILLIAM son of William and Anne Downman, 14 February 1724/5.

B. DOWNMAN, TRAVERSE son of William and Anne Downman, 16 March 1726.

M. DOWNMAN, ELIZABETH and Thomas Pinc[k]ard, 22 April 1727.

B. DOWNMAN, ELIZABETH daughter of William and Ann Downman, 20 August 1728.

D. DOWNMAN, TRAVERSE 25 April 1730.

B. DOWNMAN, JOBEZ son of William and Ann Downman, 12 September 1730.

D. DOWNMAN, JABEZ 26 September 1730.

B. DOWNMAN, ROBERT PORTEUS son of Robert and Elizabeth Downman, 6 May 1744.

B. DOWNMAN, WILLIAM son of Robert and Elizabeth Downman, 15 April 1746.

B. DOWNMAN, ANN daughter of Traverse and Grace Downman, 21 September 1748.

B. DOWNMAN, MILDRED daughter of Robert and Elizabeth Downman, 4 March 1749.

B. DOWNMAN, BETTY daughter of James and Lucy Downman, 10 January 1750.

B. DOWNMAN, GRACE daughter of Traverse and Grace Downman, 4 October 1750.

D. DOWNMAN, GRACE daughter of Traverse and Grace Downman, 11 October 1750.

B. DOWNMAN, ELIZABETH daughter of Robert and Elizabeth Downman, 21 Feby 1752.

D. DOWNMAN, RAWLEIGH son of Robert and Elizabeth Downman, 26 March 1752.

B. DOWNMAN, LUCY daughter of James and Lucy Downman, 30 August 1752.

B. DOWNMAN, WINNY daughter of James and Lucy Downman, 26 December 1753.

B. DOWNMAN, RAWLEIGH son of Robert and Elizabeth Downman, 5 September 1754.

B. DOWNMAN, ANNE daughter of James and Lucy Downman, 9 December 1755.

D. DOWNMAN, ELIZABETH wife of Robert Downman, [not entered] 1756.

B. DOWNMAN, FANNY daughter of James and Lucy Downman, 18 April 1757.

D. DOWNMAN, MARGARET 20 September 1758.

B. DOWNMAN, RAWLEIGH son of James and Lucy Downman, 26 September 1758.

B. DOWNMAN, TRAVERSE son of James and Lucy Downman, 20 January 1760.

B. DOWNMAN, PRISCILLA daughter of James and Lucy Downman, 5 March 1762.

B. DOWNMAN, WINIFRED daughter of Rawleigh and Elizabeth Downman, 11 August 1767.

B. DOWNMAN, WILLIAM son of Rawleigh and Elizabeth Downman, 26 April 1769.

B. DOWNMAN, FRANCES PORTEUS daughter of Robert and Elizabeth Downman, 10 January 1772.

B. DOWNMAN, RICHARD son of Rawleigh and Elizabeth Downman, 28 May 1776.

B. DOWTIN, WINNY daughter of Anthony and Anne Dowtin, 2 August 1752.

B. DOWTIN, ISAAC son of Anthony and Ann Dowtin, 29 April 1755.

B. DOWTIN, ANTHONY son of Anthony and Ann Dowtin, 2 May 1756.

B. DOWTIN, SAMUEL son of Anthony and Ann Dowtin, 11 May 1758.

B. DOWTIN, JOHN son of Anthony and Ann Dowtin, 4 January 1761.

B. DOWTIN, BETTY JONES daughter of Anthony and Mary Dowtin, 19 July 1770.

B. DOZER, WILLIAM son of John and Sarah Dozer, 27 January 1723/4.

B. DOZER, JOHN son of John Dozer, 8 April 1732.

M. DOZIER, ELIZABETH and John King, 29 August 1727.

B. DRAKE, HENRY TAYLOE son of James and Jane Drake, 15 January 1793 [L:7].

B. DRAKE, RICHARD FENDALL son of James and Jane Drake, 6 January 1797 [L:7].

M. DRAPER, RICHARD and Elizabeth Man, 12 September 1680.

B. DRAPER, ELIZABETH daughter of Thomas and Sarah Draper, 7 October 1711.

B. DRAPER, JUDITH daughter of Thomas and Sarah Draper, 5 December 1713.

B. DRAPER, WILLIAM son of Thomas and Sarah Draper, 1 November 1715.

B. DRAPER, MARY daughter of Thomas and Sarah Draper, 25 March 1718.

B. DRAPER, JOSEPH son of Thomas and Sarah Draper, 23 March 1719.

B. DRAPER, JOSHUA son of Thomas and Sarah Draper, 25 March 1721.

B. DRAPER, JAMES son of Thomas and Sarah Draper, 15 February 1723/4.

B. DRAPER, KATHRINE daughter of Thomas and Sarah Draper, 21 September 1728.

M. DRAPER, ELIZABETH and Robert Gibson, 26 January 1730/1.

B. DRAPER, SOLOMAN son of Thomas and Sarah Draper, 20 May 1731.

B. DRAPER, THOMAS son of Thomas and Sarah Draper, 2 September 1733.

D. DRAPER, THOMAS 10 May 1735.

M. DRAPER, MARY ANN and Parmenus Palmer, 30 March 1741.

B. DRAPER, JUDY daughter of William and Catherine Draper, 20 February 1742.

B. DRAPER, JOHN son of William and Kathrine Draper, 14 March 1745.

B. DRAPER, VIRTUE daughter of James and Sarah Draper, 18 October 1746.

B. DRAPER, WINNY daughter of William and Kathrine Draper, 14 February 1746/7.

D. DRAPER, KATHARINE 9 June 1763.

D. DRAPER, WILLIAM 16 October 1765.

B. DRAPER, CATY daughter of John and Leanna Draper, 7 April 1767.

B. DRAPER, JOHN son of John and Leanor Draper, 21 July 1775.

B. DRAPER, POLLY daughter of Leanor Draper, 11 September 1783.

B. DRYASS, WILLIAM son of William and Elizabeth Dryass, 24 February 1729.

B. DUDLEY, BETTY daughter of William and Mary Dudley, 7 September 1719.

B. DUDLEY, THOMAS son of William and Mary Dudley, 3 October 1724.

B. DUDLEY, MARY daughter of William and Mary Dudley, 1 January 1726.

D. DUDLEY, MARY 15 January 1726.

B. DUDLEY, ALEXANDER son of William and Mary Dudley, 4 January 1727.

B. DUDLEY, MARY daughter of William and Mary Dudley, 20 October 1730.

B. DUDLEY, WINNIFRED daughter of William and Mary Dudley, 17 March 1732.

D. DUDLEY, MARY 13 September 1735.

B. DUDLEY, WILLIAM son of William and Mary Dudley, 10 October 1735.

B. DUDLEY, ANN daughter of William and Ann (sic) Dudley, 2 June 1738.

B. DUDLEY, RICHARD son of William and Mary Dudley, 4 March 1742.

B. DUDLEY, KATHRINE daughter of William and Mary Dudley, 5 September 1745.

D. DUDLEY, WILLIAM 8 January 1752.

B. DUDLEY, WILLIAM a bastard child of Ann Taylor, 23 July 1755.

B. DUDLEY, SARAH daughter of Thomas and Elizabeth Dudley, 29 January 1757.

B. DUDLEY, JOHN son of Thomas and Elizabeth Pitman Dudley, 26 August 1759.

B. DUDLEY, WILLIAM son of Alexander and Winny Dudley, 5 December 1762.

B. DUDLEY, FRANCES daughter of Alexander and Winny Dudley, 5 February 1767.

B. DUDLEY, THOMAS and CHARLOTTE son and daughter of Alexander and Winifred Dudley, 12 December 1768.

B. DUGLISS, ALICE RANDAL daughter of Rodham and Magdaline Dugliss, 10 April 1774.

B. DUGLESS, RODHAM and FRANCES son and daughter of Rodham Dugless, 9 April 1777.

B. DUKESHELL, ELIZABETH daughter of Joseph and Elizabeth Dukeshell, 10 Dec. 1686.

DUM   SEE: OLDHAM [!] PAGE 140 - 141

B. DUM, KATHRINE daughter of Peter and Rebeccah Dum, 11 September 1730. [This recording is entered under the letter "O".]

B. DUN, ELIZABETH daughter of William and Anne Dun, 2 April 1711.

B. DUN, NEWMAN son of William and Anne Dun, 18 November 1714.

B. DUN, ANN daughter of William and Anne Dun, 15 November 1716.

D. DUN, PATRICK 13 April 1719.

D. DUN, JOHN 3 July 1719.

D. DUN, ROBERT 12 July 1726.

D. DUNAWAY, MARY 8 July 1722.

M. DUNAWAY, MALACHI and Elizabeth Nell, 23 January 1726/7.

B. DUNAWAY, SAMUEL son of Malachi and Elizabeth Dunaway, 25 December 1728.

B. DUNAWAY, ANNE daughter of Maliciah and Elizabeth Dunaway, 20 December 1731.

B. DUNAWAY, ANN daughter of Malachi and Elizabeth Dunaway, 20 December 1732.

B. DUNAWAY, SARAH ANN daughter of Joseph and Elizabeth Dunaway, 25 July 1733.

B. DUNAWAY, CHARLES son of Malachi and Elizabeth Dunaway, 20 November 1735.

B. DUNAWAY, THOMAS son of John and Peggy Dunaway, 15 March 1769.

B. DUNAWAY, SAMUEL son of Samuel and Peggey Dunaway, 30 May 1776.

B. DURHAM, MARY daughter of Thomas and Dorothy Durham, 5 June 1686.

B. DURHAM, THOMAS son of Thomas and Dorothy Durham, 27 June 1690.

B. DURHAM, JOHN son of Thomas and Dorothy Durham, 23 November 1698.

D. DURHAM, JOHN 23 September 1722.

B. DURHAM, JOHN son of Thomas and Mary Durham, 14 December 1724/5 (sic).

B. DURHAM, MARY daughter of Thomas and Mary Durham, 24 August 1726.

B. DURHAM, SUSANNA daughter of Thomas and Mary Durham, 14 May 1728.

M. DURHAM, MARGARET and Dominick Newgent, 2 December 1729.

B. DURHAM, WILMOTH daughter of Thomas and Mary Durham, 21 May 1730.

B. DURHAM, KATHRINE daughter of Thomas and Mary Durham, 18 March 1731.

B. DURHAM, MILLICENT daughter of Thomas and Mary Durham, 4 August 1734.

D. DURHAM, WILLMOTH 2 October 1734.

D. DURHAM, THOMAS 3 December 1734.

M. DURHAM, SARAH and William Hanks, 26 January 1738.

B. DURHAM, JOSHUA son of John and Sarah Durham, 11 December 1748.

B. DURHAM, NELLY daughter of John and Sarah Durham, 13 March 1750.

D. DURHAM, MARY 8 May 1750.

B. DURHAM, CHARNELL son of John and Sarah Durham, 29 June 1753.

B. DYE, ARTHUR son of Martin and Margaret Dye, 18 May 1673.

B. DYE, THOMAS son of Sarah Dye, 10 April 1721.

E

D. EARTH, THOMAS 23 March 1720.

B. EDMONDS, JOHN son of Robert and Mary Edmonds, 18 May 1773.

B. EDMONDS, SARAH daughter of Robert and Mary Edmonds, 2 September 1776.

M. EDWARDS, WILLIAM and Mary Peace, 16 December 1725.

D. EDWARDS, JOHN 20 November 1726.

M. EDWARDS, MARY and John Spragg, 2 February 1726/7.

B. EFFORD, WILLIAM son of John and Hannah Efford, 1 October 1713.

B. EFFORD, ELIZABETH daughter of John and Hannah Efford, 24 August 1717.

D. EFFORD, HANNAH 19 June 1741.

B. EFFORD, JOHN son of William Efford, 17 August 1741.

B. EFFORD, ZACCARIAH son of John and Frances Efford, 7 August 1747.

D. EFFORD, ZACCARIAH son of John and Frances Efford, 7 November 1747.

B. EFFORD, GEORGE son of John and Frances Efford, 16 November 1748.

B. EFFORD, WILLIAMSON son of William and Sarah Efford, 4 October 1750.

B. EFFORD, ZACHARIAH and MARY twins of John and Frances Efford, 21 Oct. 1750.

B. EFFORD, ZACHARIAS son of John and Frances Efford, 30 January 1752.

D. EFFORD, JOHN 10 December 1753.

B. EFFORD, LEANNA daughter of John and Winifred Efford, 2 June 1762.

B. EFFORD, [name not entered] a child of Elizabeth Efford, 30 January 1776.

B. EFFORD, [name not entered] a child of Elizabeth Efford, 26 February 1778.

B. EFFORD, GEORGE son of Zachariah and Elizabeth Efford, 26 October 1778.

B. EFFORD, ZACHERIAH son of Zacheriah and Elizabeth Efford, 10 February 1782.

B. EIDSON, WILLIAM WHITE son of John and Mary Ann Eidson, 24 June 1791 [L:9].

B. EIDSON, LUCY daughter of Edward and Winifred Eidson, 3 June 1792 [L:9].

B. EIDSON, MATTHEW son of John and Elizabeth Eidson, 17 October 1793 [L:9].

B. EIDSON, JOHN son of John and Elizabeth Eidson, 14 February 1796 [L:9].

B. ELDER, ELIZABETH daughter of William and Anne Elder, 4 September 1712.

B. ELDER, PETER son of William and Anne Elder, 21 May 1715.

B. ELDER, WILLIAM son of William and Ann Elder, 8 October 1717.

B. ELDER, SARAH daughter of William and Ann Elder, 18 July 1718.

B. ELDER, THOMAS son of William and Ann Elder, 11 November 1721.

B. ELDER, JOHN son of William and Anne Elder, 25 November 1723.

B. ELDER, EDMOND son of William and Anne Elder, 21 August 1727.

B. ELDER, CHARLES son of William and Anne Elder, 30 May 1729.

B. ELDER, RUTH daughter of John and Anne Elder, 19 May 1730.

M. ELDER, ELIZABETH and Gregory Glascock, 29 January 1730/1.

B. ELDER, JOSEPH son of William and Ann Elder, 6 September 1731.

B. ELDER, MARY ANN and WINNEFRED daughters of William and Ann Elder, 7 September 1733.

B. ELDER, SAMUEL son of Peter and Amadine Elder, 6 August 1738.

B. ELDER, PETER son of Peter and Amadine Elder, 1 December 1741.

B. ELDER, SILVESTER a bastard child of Mary Elder's, 16 August 1756.

B. ELDER, WINNY a bastard child of Lucy Elder's, 27 September 1756.

ELLIOTT : ELLIT

B. ELLIT, RICHARD son of Richard and Anne Ellit, 22 September 1686.

B. ELLIOTT, THOMAS son of Richard and Jane Elliott, 29 September 1692.

B. ELLIOTT, JEDUTHAN son of William and Margaret Elliott, 2 June 1750.

B. ELLIOTT, NANSY daughter of William and Margaret Elliott, 24 February 1753.

B. ELLIS, PETER son of Peter and Ellenor Ellis, 21 April 1670.

B. ELLIS, ANNE daughter of Peter and Jane Ellis, 2 January 1696.

B. ELLOT, ANN daughter of Richard and Jemima Ellot, 17 July 1716.

B. ELLOT, ISAAC son of Richard and Jemima Ellot, 17 July 1716.

B. ELLOT, ELIZABETH daughter of Richard and Jemima Ellot, 1 December 1718.

B. ELLOT, LUCY daughter of Richard and Jemima Ellot, 21 March 1721/2.

B. ELMORE, ANNE daughter of Peter and Frances Elmore, 29 August 1674.

M. ELMORE, FRANCIS and Anne Allen, 2 December 1677.

B. ELLMORE, JOHN son of Francis and Anne Ellmore, 25 November 1685.

B. ELMORE, DANIEL son of Francis and Ann Elmore, 10 December 1689.

B. ELMORE, ELIZABETH daughter of Francis and Catharine Elmore, 6 July 1693.

B. ELMORE, FRANCIS son of John and Ann Elmore, 12 December 1716.

D. ELMORE, THOMAS 27 February 1717.

D. ELMORE, PETER 2 April 1718.

B. ELMORE, ELIZABETH daughter of John and Anne Elmore, 22 October 1720.

B. ELMORE, MARY daughter of John and Anne Elmore, 11 March 1722/3.

B. ELMORE, JOHN son of John and Anne Elmore, 28 May 1725.

D. ELMORE, JOHN 28 August 1725.

D. ELMORE, ANNE 6 October 1725.

D. ELMORE, PETER 1 December 1725.

D. ELMORE, WILLIAM 16 December 1725.

B. ELMORE, ANNE daughter of John and Anne Elmore, 24 December 1726.

B. ELMORE, JOHN son of John and Anne Elmore, 18 March 1728.

M. ELMORE, CHARLES and Sarah Barton, 11 October 1728.

M. ELMORE, JOHN and Ann Raynolds, 29 November 1728.

D. ELMORE, JOHN 20 November 1729.

B. ELMORE, DANIEL son of John and Anne Elmore, 20 November 1731.

D. ELMORE, ANNE 15 April 1732.

D. ELMORE, CHARLES 18 January 1733.

B. ELMORE, PETER son of Charles and Sarah Elmore, 10 December 1733.

B. ELMORE, JOHN son of John and Alice Elmore, 14 September 1736.

M. ELMORE, FRANCIS and Mary Hammock, 23 February 1738.

B. ELMORE, ALICE daughter of John and Alice Elmore, 23 June 1740.

B. ELMORE, MARY ANN daughter of Francis and Mary Elmore, 4 September 1742.

B. ELMORE, KEZIAH daughter of John and Alice Elmore, 30 November 1744.

B. ELMORE, BETTY ANN daughter of John and Ann Elmore, 29 April 1747.

B. ELMORE, AMMENY daughter of William and Mary Elmore, 7 December 1753.

B. ELMORE, MILLY daughter of William and Mary Elmore, 3 February 1756.

B. ELMORE, OPIE a bastard child of Rachel Elmore's, 15 February 1757.

B. ELMORE, WILLIAM son of George and Elizabeth Elmore, 7 November 1787.

B. ELMORE, JUDITH DODSON daughter of George and Elizabeth Elmore, 8 Jany 1790.

B. ELMORE, GEORGE WASHINGTON son of George and Elizabeth Elmore, 8 March 1792.

B. ELMORE, HARDING NELMS son of William and Frances Elmore, 15 October 1794.

M. ENGLISH, KATHERINE and Thomas Webster, 11 September 1739.

B. ENGLISH, NANCY daughter of William and Caty English, 9 December 1777.

B. ENGLISH, JAMES son of William and Katy English, 21 June 1781.

B. ENGLISH, SUCKEY daughter of William and Katy English, 23 June 1783.

ERSKINE : ERSKING SEE: ARESKIN PAGE 6

M. ERSKING, WILLIAM and Penilopy Barns, 27 May 1726.

M. EUSTACE, JOHN and Alice Corbin Peachey, 6 October 1743.

B. EVANS, RICHARD son of Peter and Diana Evans, 5 August 1688.

B. EVANS, SARAH daughter of Richard and Mary Evans, 24 December 1726.

D. EVENS, CLARK 3 March 1735. [SEE: EVINS, PAGE 61]

EVERET : EVERETT : EVERITT

B. EVERET, WILLIAM son of Daniel and Anne Everet, 15 March 1692.

B. EVERETT, ANNE daughter of William and Margaret Everett, 2 August 1716.

B. EVERETT, ELIZABETH daughter of William and Mary Everett, 14 November 1720.
(sic)

B. EVERETT, LUCRECY daughter of William and Margaret Everett, 2 June 1725.

B. EVERETT, SARAH daughter of William and Margaret Everett, 13 April 1729.

B. EVERETT, DANIEL son of William and Margaret Everett, 8 March 1731/2.

B. EVERETT, GEORGE son of William and Margaret Everett, 7 November 1734.

B. EVERETT, WILLIAM son of William and Margaret Everett, 24 January 1736.

B. EVERETT, RUTH daughter of William and Margaret Everett, 21 June 1742.

B. EVERET, MILLION daughter of Daniel and Frances, Everet, 3 May 1756.

B. EVERET, ANNE daughter of Daniel and Frances Everet, 27 August 1758.

B. EVERET, SARAH daughter of Daniel and Frances Everet, 3 January 1761.

B. EVERET, WILLIAM son of Daniel and Frances Everet, 4 May 1763.

B. EVERIT, JOHN son of William and Winny Everit, 10 February 1783.

B. EVERITT, THOMAS son of William and Winney Everitt, 4 November 1788.

B. EVERITT, RAWLEIGH son of William and Winnefret Everitt, 29 August 1795.

B. EVERIT, CHARLES SIMMONS son of William and Winney Everit, 17 October 1798.

B. EVERIT, BETTEY NUT daughter of William and Winney Everit, 25 February 1802.

B. EVINS, WILLIAM son of Elizabeth Evens, 3 March 1735. [SEE: EVENS, PAGE 60]

D. EWERS, THOMAS 20 February 1749.

F

FANN SEE: FENN PAGE 62

M. FANN, ANNE and Thomas Collee, 13 July 1673.

M. FANN, WILLIAM and Alicia Samford, 23 January 1675. [The bridegroom's surname is in error; it was LUNN. This is proven by the will of William Lunn (16 -1679) of record in Rappahannock County, the marriage of his widow 27 August 1679 to Edward Jones (c.1652-1715) and the will of Alicia (Samford) Lunn Jones' father, James Samford (c.1624-1704) of record in Richamond County]

B. FANN, HENRY son of John and Mary Fann, 23 April 1702.

B. FANN, WINNEFRED daughter of John and Mary Fann , 20 November 1714.

D. FANN, JOHN 20 November 1719.

B. FANN, ANNE daughter of Henry and Winnefred Fann, 1 October 1722.

B. FANN, JOHN son of Henry and Winnefred Fann, 29 November 1724.

B. FANN, LUCRITIA daughter of Judith Fann, 2 February 1726.

B. FANN, ELIJAH son of Henry and Winnefred Fann, 17 September 1727.

M. FANN, WINIFRED and William Hames, 26 November 1730.

B. FANN, WILLOUGHBY son of Judith Fann, 9 December 1730.

B. FANN, ZACHARRAS son of Henry and Winnefred Fann, 20 December 1730.

D. FANN, MARY 20 November 1732.

B. FAUNTLEROY, MARY daughter of More and Margaret Fauntleroy, 28 February 1725.

B. FAUNTLEROY, MORE son of More and Margaret Fauntleroy, 1 October 1728.

B. FAUNTLEROY, JUDITH B. daughter of Robert and Sarah Fauntleroy, 3 March 1799.

D. FAUSTER, ELIZABETH 18 January 1725.

B. FAVER, ELIZABETH daughter of John and Mary Faver, 25 November 1699.

FENN SEE: FANN PAGE 61

D. FENN, HENRY 20 March 1732.

B. FERGUSON, POLLEY daughter of Robert and Sarah Ferguson, 9 January 1792 [L:11].

B. FERGUSON, KETURAH, daughter of William and Mary Ferguson, 11 Aug. 1792 [L:11].

B. FIELD, JAMES son of Thomas and Catharine Field, 4 May 1714.

B. FILYOUNG, GEROGE son of Charles and Catharine Filyoung, 26 May 1729.

D. FILYOUNG, JOHN 31 March 1730/1.

B. FILYOUNG, JOHN son of Charles and Catharine Filyoung, 31 March 1731.

B. FILYOUNG, WILLIAM son of Charles and Catharine Filyoung, 4 April 1732.

D. FILYOUNG, WILLIAM 4 April 1732.

B. FISHER, PHELISHA CARTER daughter of John and Elizabeth Fisher, 28 Sept. 1794 [L:11].

D. FITCHGARRELL, EDWARD 19 January 1722/3.

D. FITCHGARRELL, MARY 10 March 1725.

D. FITCHGARRELL, ALCE 10 November 1732.

B. FLEMING, JOHN son of Alexander and Sarah Fleming, 23 March 1690.

B. FLEMING, MARGARET daughter of Alexander and Sarah Fleming, 25 March 1692.

B. FLEMING, ALEXANDER son of Alexander and Sarah Fleming, 17 April 1696.

B. FLEMING, SARAH daughter of Alexander and Sarah Fleming, 31 April 1698.

B. FLEMING, WILLIAM son of Alexander and Sarah Fleming, 2 December 1706.

B. FLEMING, CHARLES son of Alexander and Sarah Fleming, 20 August 1708.

B. FLEMING, ELIZABETH daughter of Alexander and Sarah Fleming, 18 February 1710.

D. FLEMING, ALEXANDER 5 May 1720.

B. FLEMMING, JOHN son of William and Winney Flemming, 22 April 1782.

B. FLOYD, ELIZABETH daughter of Magnis and Anne Floyd, 16 February 1724/5.

B. FLOYD, MARGARET daughter of Magnis and Anne Floyd, 17 November 1726.

B. FLOYD, MARY daughter of Magnes and Anne Floyd, 14 February 1729.

B. FLOYD, JAMES son of Magnis and Anne Floyd, 5 December 1731.

M. FLOWERS, ELEANOR and Joseph Burn, 3 April 1728.

B. FONES, LETTY daughter of Charles and Bathsheba Fones, 28 December 1792 [L:11].

B. FONES, FANNEY daughter of John and Jenney Fones, 10 September 1795 [L:11].

B. FONES, JOHN JARVICE son of John and Jane Fones, 2 June 1797 [L:11].

D. FORREST, RICHARD 18 July 1722.

B. FORRESTER, ROBERT son of William and Frances Forrester, 24 August 1716.

B. FORRESTER, WILLIAM son of William and Frances Forrester, 9 September 1718.

B. FORRESTER, JAMES son of William and Frances Forrester, 17 September 1720.

B. FORRESTER, MARGARET daughter of William and Frances Forrester, 30 Jan.ᵞ 1722/3.

D. FORRESTER, FRANCES 13 April 1723.

B. FORRESTER, GRIFFIN son of Robert and Bridgett Forrester, 30 April 1766.

B. FORRESTER, WILMUTH ROUT daughter of James and Winney Forrester, 6 May 1781.

B. FORRESTER, ROBERT son of James Forrester, 6 September 1783.

B. FORRESTER, JAMES son of James and Winifred Forrester, 3 May 1786.

M. FOSTER, ANN and Samuel Barber, 30 November 1727.

M. FOSTER, KATHERINE and John Seamons, 17 July 1728.

B. FOSTER, EVE daughter of Edward and Sarah Foster, 24 December 1728.

B. FOUSHEE, CHARLOTTE daughter of James and Mary Foushee, 5 June 1692.

B. FOUSHEE, SUSANNA daughter of James and Mary Foushee, 12 December 1695.

B. FOUSHEE, JOHN son of John and Mary Foushee, 6 September 1697.

B. FOUSHEE, ELIZABETH daughter of John and Elizabeth Foushee, 1 October 1723.

D. FOUSHEE, MARY 3 October 1724.

B. FOWLER, MARTHA daughter of David and Mary Fowler, 19 September 1673.

B. FOWLER, FRANCES daughter of David and Mary Fowler, 4 June 1677.

B. FOWLER, JOHN son of David and Mary Fowler, 30 September 1679.

M. FOWLER, ELIZABETH and Thomas Bryant, 27 June 1729.

D. FOX, RICHARD 22 December 1716.

B. FRANCE, JOSEPH son of John and Katharine France, 6 May 1791 [L:11].

B. FRANCE, FANNEY daughter of John and Katey France, 2 October 1795 [L:11].

B. FRANKLIN, WILLIAM MYNN a base born child, son of Hanner Sisson, 20 April 1798 [L:35].

B. FRANKLIN, ELIZABETH WALKER daughter of Steward and Mary Franklin, 22 May 1798 [L:11].

B. FRANKS, JAMES TEMPLEMAN son of William Franks, 15 December 1795 [L:11].

B. FRESHWATER, MICHAL son of Thomas and Joanna Freshwater, 2 January 1672.

B. FRESHWATER, JOANNA daughter of Thomas and Joanna Freshwater, 30 October 1677.

B. FRESHWATER, ANNE daughter of Thomas and Mary Freshwater, 11 December 1707.

B. FRESHWATER, JOHN son of Thomas and Mary Freshwater, 23 February 1712.

B. FRESHWATER, MARY daughter of Thomas and Mary Freshwater, 31 January 1717.

B. FRESHWATER, GEORGE son of Thomas and Anne Freshwater, 13 February 1725.

B. FRESHWATER, ANNE daughter of Thomas and Anne Freshwater, 19 March 1728.

M. FRESHWATER, MARY and William Linton, 31 March 1730.

B. FRESHWATER, ANNE daughter of Thomas and Anne Freshwater, 24 February 1730/1.

D. FRESHWATER, ANNE 15 March 1731.

FRISTOE : FRISTOW : FRESTOW

M. FRISTOW, ROBERT and Jane Sherman, 1 August 1675.

B. FRISTOW, ROBERT son of Robert and Jane Fristow, 2 May 1676.

B. FRISTOW, JANE daughter of Robert and Jane Fristow, 23 March 1678.

B. FRESTOW, MARY daughter of John and Mary Frestow, 25 June 1682.

B. FRISTOW, CATHARINE daughter of George and Mary Firstow, 14 June 1683.

B. FRISTOW, WILLIAM son of George and Mary Fristow, [not entered] October 1687.

B. FRISTOW, ELIZABETH, daughter of Robert and Anne Fristow, 8 October 1704.

B. FRISTOW, ROBERT son of Robert and Anne Fristow, 25 February 1706.

B. FRISTOW, MARY daughter of Robert and Anne Fristow, 2 December 1711.

B. FRISTOW, ANNE daughter of Robert and Anne Fristow, 17 June 1714.

B. FRISTOW, JANE daughter of Robert and Anne Fristow, 27 April 1719.

D. FRISTOW, ROBERT 6 March 1720.

B. FRYAR, MARY daughter of Edward and Mary Fryar, 11 September 1676.

B. FRYER, ANNE daughter of Edward and Mary Frayer, 21 May 1680.

B. FRAZIER, WILLIAM son of Andrew and Catharine Frazier, 10 April 1721.

B. FULLER, MARY daughter of Thomas and Margaret Fuller, 28 June 1687.

B. FULLER, WILLIAM LEROY son of Betty Fuller, 21 May 1781.

G

D. GADEN, SUSANNAH 4 February 1730/1.

D. GALBRATH, MARGARET wife of Robert Galbrath, 14 January 1741.

M. GALBRATH, ROBERT and Mary Dodson, 29 September 1743.

B. GALLOWAY, MARTHA daughter of John and Elizabeth Galloway, 26 June 1772.

B. GALLOWAY, BETSEY daughter of John and Elizabeth Galloway, 17 February 1776.

B. GARLAND, DOROTHY SMITH daughter of Jesse and Ann Garland, 3 April 1778.

B. GARLAND, WILLIAM GRIFFIN son of Vincent and Elizabeth Garland, 3 February 1793 [L:13].

B. GARNER, WILLIAM son of John and Mary Garner, 22 June 1753.

B. GARNER, PEGGY BARTHEN daughter of James Garner, 21 January 1778.

B. GARNER, BILLY son of James and Susannah Garner, 13 May 1782.

B. GARZIA, KATHRINE daughter of John and Mary Garzia, 4 May 1720.

B. GARZIA, JANE daughter of John and Mary Garzia, 17 December 1721.

D. GARZIA, MARY 13 October 1725.

B. GARZIA, ANNE daughter of John and Mary Garzia, 1 November 1725.

D. GARZIA, ANNE 5 March 1728/9.

B. GARZIA, JOHN son of John and Mary Garzia, 28 September 1731.

B. GASKINS, WILLIAM son of John and Anne Gaskins, 18 June 1758.

B. GASTENS, SALLY daughter of Jessy and Susy Ann Gastens, __ September 1781.

GATHINS : GATHINGS : GAYTHINGS &c:

B. GATHINS, BEHATHELEM daughter of Philip and Jane Gaythings, 4 January 1724/5.

M. GATHINGS, COBHAM and Judith Millner, 26 February 1726/7.

B. GATHINGS, ALICE daughter of Cobham and Judith Gathings, 29 May 1730.

D. GATHINGS, JANE 28 April 1732.

B. GATHINGS, CLARYMAN daughter of Cobham and Judith Gathings, 29 April 1732.

B. GAYTHINGS, JOHN son of Cobham and Judith Gaythings, 25 May 1734.

B. GATHINGS, ANN daughter of Cobham and Judith Gathings, 12 January 1736.

B. GATHINGS, PHILIP son of Cobham and Judith Gathings, 9 June 1740.

B. GATHINGS, LUCY daughter of Cobham and Judith Gathings, 10 November 1742.

GAYTON ⦂ GAYTON ⦂ GAYDON

B. GAYTON, RALPH son of Ralph and Joanna Gayton, 2 October 1680.

B. GAYTON, GEORGE son of Ralph and Joanna Gayton, 22 December 1682.

B. GAYTON, JOHN son of Ralph and Joanna Gayton, 14 September 1684.

B. GAYTON, GEORGE son of George and Elizabeth Gayton, 4 January 1739.

B. GAYDEN, ELIZABETH daughter of George and Elizabeth Gayden, 19 June 1742.

D. GAYDEN, GEORGE son of George Gayden 8 July 1744.

B. GAYTON, WINNY daughter of George and Hannah Gayton, 7 March 1750.

B. GAYDON, JOHN son of George and Hannah Gaydon, 19 April 1753.

B. GEARE, JANE daughter of William and Jane Geare, 25 December 1687.

GEFFREYS ⦂ GEFFERYS &c   SEE⦂ JEFFRIES ⦂ JEFFRYS PAGE 103

B. GEFFRYS, ELIZABETH daughter of Edward and Eliz.^{a} Geffrys, 4 August 1679.

B. GEFFREYS, BETTY daughter of Thomas and Eliz.^{a} Geffreys, 17 October 1710.

B. GEFFREYS, WINNEFRED daughter of Thomas and Eliz.^{a} Geffreys, 23 April 1712.

B. GEFFREYS, HESTER daughter of Thomas and Eliz.^{a} Geffreys, 9 April 1714.

B. GEFFREYS, WILLIAM son of Thomas and Eliz.^{a} Geffreys, 23 July 1716.

D. GEFFERES, ELIZABETH 25 January 1718.

D. GEFFERES, MARY 20 November 1720.

B. GEFFERYS, MARGARET daughter of Thomas and Mary Gefferys, 26 February 1722.

B. GEFFREYS, ANNE daughter of Thomas and Mary Geffreys, 30 June 1724.

B. GEFFERYS, PRISCILLA daughter of Thomas and Mary Gefferys, 3 August 1732.

B. GEFFERYS, TRAVERSE son of Thomas and Mary Geffrys, 6 April 1735.

B. GEFFERY, BETTY HAMMOND daughter of Winifred Geffery, 16 January 1744.

GENINGS   SEE⦂ JENNINGS PAGE 103

D. GENINGS, THOMAS 4 November 1734.

B. GEORGE, NICHOLAS son of Nicholas and Martha George, 29 May 1720. [Nicholas

George, Sr. died testate in Stafford County, Virginia, 1736/7 (Will Book "M", page 249); there are further recordings in regard to this George family in OPR, pages 40-41 and SPR, page 54.]

B. GEORGE, FRANCIS son of Samuel and Sarah George, 12 November 1726.

D. GEORGE, SARAH 11 December 1726.

B. GEORGE, ELIZABETH daughter of Benjamin and Elizabeth George, 8 April 1735.

B. GEORGE, ELIZABETH daughter of David and Magdaline George, 18 April 1771.

B. GEORGE, FANNY daughter of Fortunatus George, 30 December 1790.

GIBBS ፧ GIBS

B. GIBS, PENELLOPE daughter of Richard and Anne Gibs, 1 May 1722.

D. GIBS, RICHARD 1 December 1722.

M. GIBBS, ELIZABETH and Harry Maccay, 19 March 1729/30.

B. GIBSON, SARAH daughter of Robert and Mary Gibson, 10 March 1716.

M. GIBSON, JOHN and Elizabeth Call, 7 August 1729.

B. GIBSON, WILLIAM son of John and Elizabeth Gibson, 24 November 1729.

B. GIBSON, JOSEPH daughter of Robert and Elizabeth Gibson, 25 February 1730.

M. GIBSON, ROBERT and Elizabeth Draper, 26 January 1730/1.

B. GIBSON, RAWLEIGH son of John and Eliz.^{a} Gibson, 29 May 1731.

B. GIBSON, ANN daughter of John and Elizabeth Gibson, 5 January 1732.

D. GIBSON, ROBERT 17 December 1733.

B. GIBSON, MARY daughter of John and Elizabeth Gibson, 8 March 1734.

B. GIBSON, PRISCILLA daughter of John and Elizabeth Gibson, 6 June 1737.

B. GIBSON, WINNY daughter of John and Elizabeth Gibson, 26 February 1740.

B. GIBSON, DUANNA bastard daughter of Sarah Gibson, 23 October 1745.

B. GIBSON, SAMUEL bastard son of Sarah Gibson, 6 June 1747.

B. GIBSON, JOHN bastard son of Sarah Gibson, 2 January 1753.

M. GIBTON, ELIZABETH and Thomas Rawlin[g]s, 2 March 1730/1.

B. GILL, ELIZ.^A daughter of Edward and Mary Gill, 7 September 1702.

B. GILL, EDWARD son of Edward and Mary Gill, 27 June 1705.

B. GILL, JOHN son of Edward and Mary Gill, 6 November 1707.

B. GIMBER, JAMES THOMPSON son of William and Lucy Gimber, 17 February 1792 [L:13].

B. GIMBER, WALTER EVANS son of William and Lucy Gimber, 19 August 1794 [L:13].

B. GLADING, WILLIAM son of William and Mary Glading, 24 June 1727.

B. GLADING, LETTIS daughter of William and Mary Glading, 19 May 1729.

B. GLADMAN, EDWARD son of Thomas and Catherine Gladman, 24 November 1688.

D. GLADMAN, EDWARD 7 October 1728.

B. GLASCOCK, JEAN daughter of Thomas and Ann Glascock, 10 July 1673.

B. GLASCOCK, MARY and ANNE daughters of Gregory and Mary Glascock, 10 November 1673.

B. GLASCOCK, FRANCES daughter of Thomas and Anne Glascock, 14 July 1680.

B. GLASCOCK, MARY daughter of Thomas and Ann Glascock, 22 January 1690.

B. GLASCOCK, JOHN son of Thomas and Sarah Glascock, 14 January 1699.

B. GLASCOCK, GREGORY son of Thomas and Sarah Glascock, 10 March 1700.

B. GLASCOCK, ELIZABETH daughter of Thomas and Sarah Glascock, 20 April 1703.

B. GLASCOCK, THOMAS son of Thomas and Sarah Glascock, 12 April 1705.

B. GLASCOCK, PETER son of Thomas and Sarah Glascock, 13 March 1714.

D. GLASCOCK, THOMAS 8 January 1726.

B. GLASCOCK, SARAH daughter of Gregory and Alice Glascock, 5 November 1727.

M. GLASCOCK, SARAH and Charnel Hightower, 16 January 1727/8.

B. GLASCOCK, GEORGE son of George and Judith Glascock, 14 January 1728.

B. GLASCOCK, MILLION daughter of William and Esther Glascock, 20 February 1728/9.

B. GLASCOCK, ANN daughter of William and Esther Glascock, 29 February 1730.

B. GLASCOCK, WILLIAM son of Gregory and Alice Glascock, 28 May 1730.

B. GLASCOCK, ALCE   25 June 1730.

M. GLASCOCK, FRANCES and Benjamin Millner, 13 July 1730.

M. GLASCOCK, GREGORY and Elizabeth Elder, 29 January 1730/1.

B. GLASCOCK, GRIGORY son of Grigory and Elizabeth Glascock, 21 January 1731/2.

B. GLASCOCK, JESSE son of Gregory and Elizabeth Glascock, 10 May 1733.

B. GLASCOCK, WILLIAM son of William and Esther Glascock, 4 July 1733.

B. GLASCOCK, WILLIAM son of George and Judith Glascock, 1 September 1734.

B. GLASCOCK, TRAVERSE son of Grigory and Elizabeth Glascock, 1 October 1734.

B. GLASCOCK, GEORGE son of William and Esther Glascock, 20 December 1743.

B. GLASCOCK, MILDRED daughter of George and Judith Glascock, 4 November 1749.

B. GLASCOCK, BETTY daughter of William and Esther Glascock, 9 December 1749.

D. GLASCOCK, MILLION   25 October 1750.

B. GLASCOCK, SUSANNA daughter of George and Judith Glascock, 28 November 1751.

B. GLASCOCK, JOHN son of William and Esther Glascock, 24 December 1751.

D. GLASCOCK, MAJOR GEORGE   27 February 1752.

B. GLASCOCK, MILLY daughter of William and Esther Glascock, 24 November 1753.

B. GLASCOCK, WILLIAM CHICHESTER son of William and Elizabeth Glascock, 4 July 1754.

B. GLASCOCK, GEORGE son of George and Judith Glascock, 10 January 1756.

B. GLASCOCK, JDUTIH daughter of George and Judith Glascock, [not entered] 1756.

D. GLASCOCK, JOHN   7 May 1756.

D. GLASCOCK, WILLIAM CHICHESTER son of William and Elizabeth Glascock, 8 August 1756.

B. GLASCOCK, THOMAS son of William and Ann Glascock, 21 September 1756.

D. GLASCOCK, JESSE   1 April 1757.

B. GLASCOCK, SARAH daughter of George and Judith Glascock, 4 October 1761.

B. GLASCOCK, ELIZABETH CHICHESTER daughter of Richard and Hannah Glascock, 27 April 1762.

B. GLASCOCK, RICHARD son of George and Judith Glascock, 23 August 1764.

B. GLASCOCK, GEORGE son of Peter and Elizabeth Glascock, 26 January 1771.

B. GLASCOCK, NANCY daughter of John and Susanna Glascock, 15 June 1771.

B. GLASCOCK, WASHINGTON son of John and Susannah Glascock, 6 August 1775.

B. GLASCOCK, JOHN son of Peter Glascock, 3 September 1776.

B. GLASCOCK, JOHN son of John and Susanna Glascock, 18 April 1777.

B. GLASCOCK, JAMES son of Peter and Elizabeth Glascock, 12 May 1777.

B. GLASCOCK, THOMAS MITCHELL and WINNY BALL son and daughter of John Glascock, 24 December 1782.

B. GLEW, WILLIAM son of William and Constant Glew, 5 January 1682/3.

B. GLEW, SIMON son of William and Constance Glew, 15 August 1686.

B. GLEW, JOHN son of William and Constance Glew, 11 January 1688.

D. GLEW, JOHN 10 May 1721.

B. GOAD, WILLIAM son of Abraham and Catharine Goad, [not entered] August 1693.

B. GOAD, HANNAH daughter of Abraham and Cathrine Goad, [not entered] Nov. 1695.

B. GOAD, JOHN son of Abraham and Catharine Goad, 27 November 1700.

B. GOAD, ABRAHAM son of Abraham and Cathrine Goad, 15 March 1710.

B. GOAD, ANN daughter of William and Mary Goad, 13 February 1713.

B. GOAD, PETER son of Abraham and Kathrine Goad, 27 May 1715.

B. GOAD, WILLIAM son of William and Mary Goad, 29 January 1717.

B. GOAD, JOANNA daughter of John and Kathrine Goad, 1 November 1723.

B. GOAD, ELIZ.^A daughter of John and Kathrine Goad, 12 July 1726.

M. GOAD, ELLIS and Fortunatus Dodson, 9 September 1726.

B. GOAD, JOHN son of John and Kathrine Goad, 1 July 1729.

D. GOAD, WILLIAM 18 January 1732.

B. GOAD, HANNAH daughter of John and Kathrine Goad, 7 April 1732.

B. GOAD, WILLIAM son of John and Kathrine Goad, 3 March 1734.

D. GOAD, ABRAHAM 11 April 1734.

D. GOAD, MARY 20 January 1735.

B. GOAD, SARAH daughter of Abraham and Joanna Goad, 7 April 1736.

D. GOAD, KATHRINE 23 May 1741.

M. GOULDING, MARY and Edward Kelley, 18 April 1726.

B. GOWER, STANDLY son of Francis and Anne Gower, 17 November 1679.

B. GOWER, FRANCIS son of Francis and Anne Gower, 15 April 1682.

B. GOWER, FRANCIS son of John and Ester Gower, 2 February 1706.

B. GOWER, KATHRINE daughter of Standley and Sarah Gower, 24 September 1720.

D. GOWER, FRANCES 7 January 1726. [The Christian name should be FRANCIS; the will of Francis Gower was proved in Richmond County, Virginia, 1726.]

D. GOWER, JOHN 26 September 1726.

D. GOWER, SUSANNAH 11 December 1726.

B. GOWER, FRANCIS son of Francis and Rachel Gower, 15 December 1726.

M. GOWER, SUSANNAH and Henry Williams, 22 December 1726.

M. GOWER, RACHEL and John Branham, 16 March 1726/7.

D. GOWER, WINIFRED 20 May 1727.

M. GOWER, FRANCES and William Sisson, 31 August 1727.

M. GOWER, ELIZABETH and Edward Jones, 26 September 1728.

D. GOWER, FRANCES 10 September 1729.

B. GRAHAM, EDWARD son of Edward and Patience Graham, 10 December 1715.

M. GRAY, THOMAS and Marthew [Martha] Peck, 10 July 1726.

M. GREEN, JOHN and Dorothy Benjamin 24 August 1673.

B. GREEN, ISAAC son of George Green and Anne Bodkin, 12 August 1688.

B. GREEN, WINNEFRED daughter of Richard and Anne Green, 19 December 1693.

B. GREEN, ANNE daughter of Richard and Anne Green, 17 June 1696.

B. GREEN, ELEANOR daughter of Richard and Anne Green, 19 February 1702.

M. GREEN, MARY and Charles Hinds, 9 November 1727.

D. GREENHAM, JEREMIAH 5 December 1752.

B. GREENWOOD, JOHN son of Gerard and Ellinor Greenwood, 20 September 1676.

B. GREENWOOD, GERRARD son of Gerrard and Elenor Greenwood, 19 February 1681. [Gerard Grienwood, "the German Doctor," is mentioned in the records of Old Rappahannock County 1675-1687; the surname is also rendered Greenwood and Greine in these records. Sweeny, p. 52, 97, 137.]

B. GRIFFIN, CORBIN son of LeRoy and Winnefred Griffin, 12 April 1679.

B. GRIFFIN, WINNEFRED daughter of LeRoy and Winnefred Griffin, __ October 1682.

B. GRIFFIN, THOMAS son of LeRoy and Winnefred Griffin, 20 September 1684.

B. GRIFFIN, LEROY son of Thomas and Elizabeth Griffin, 19 January 1711.

B. GRIFFIN, ELIZABETH daughter of Thomas and Eliz.^{a} Griffin, 13 October 1714.

B. GRIFFIN, SARAH daughter of Thomas and Eliz.^{a} Griffin, 7 November 1716.

B. GRIFFIN, ANNE daughter of Thomas and Elizabeth Griffin, 16 January 1718.

M. GRIFFIN, JANE and William Moody, 23 November 1725.

D. GRIFFIN, THOMAS 9 September 1732.

B. GRIFFIN, THOMAS B. son of LeRoy and Mary Ann Griffin, 17 October 1735.

B. GRIFFIN, BETTY daughter of LeRoy and Mary Ann Griffin, 17 March 1736.

B. GRIFFIN, LEROY son of LeRoy and Mary Ann Griffin, 30 December 1738.

B. GRIFFIN, CORBIN son of LeRoy and Mary Ann Griffin, 2 March 1741.

B. GRIFFIN, WILLIAM son of LeRoy and Mary Ann Griffin, 29 January 1742.

B. GRIFFIN, SAMUEL son of LeRoy and Mary Ann Griffin, 20 April 1746.

B. GRIFFIN, CYRUS son of LeRoy and Mary Ann Griffin, 16 July 1748. [This is the birth of the Honorable Judge Cyrus Griffin (16 July 1748 - 14 December 1810), president of Congress, &c. He was educated in England where he met and subsequently married Lady Christina Stuart, daughter of John Stuart, Sixth Earl of Traquair in Scotland, a lady of most distinguished ancestry. Judge Griffin's mother, Mary Ann (Marianne), was the daughter of William and Susanna (Foushee) Bertrand. MRC, p. 17, 81-82.]

D. GRIFFIN, COL. LEROY 9 July 1750.

B.   GRIFFIN, JOHN TAYLOE son of LeRoy and Maryann Griffin, 24 August 1750.

B.   GRIFFIN, ANN CORBIN daughter of LeRoy and Alice Griffin, 19 September 1765.

B.   GRIFFIN, ELIZABETH daughter of LeRoy and Judith Griffin, 18 August 1773.

B.   GRIFFIN, JUDITH daughter of LeRoy and Judith Griffin, 10 March 1775.

M.   GRIGRYE, ANN and Thomas Hinds, 19 April 1731.

   GRIGGS :   GRIGS :   GREGS :   GRIEGS &c.

B.   GREGS, ELIZABETH daughter of Robert and Anne Gregs, 11 May 1701.

B.   GREGS, JOHN son of Robert and Anne Gregs, 6 September 1707.

B.   GREGS, JAMES son of Robert and Anne Gregs, 19 November 1714.

B.   GRIEGS, JANE daughter of Robert and Ann Griegs, 30 March 1719.

B.   GRIEGS, ROBERT son of Robert and Ann Griegs, 16 September 1726.

D.   GRIGGS, JANE   13 December 1726.

D.   GRIGGS, ANNE   14 December 1726.

D.   GRIEGS, ROBERT   16 April   1729.

B.   GREGS, ANNE daughter of James and Alice Gregs, 5 February 1755.

B.   GRIGS, WILLIAM L. son of Lue [? Lee ?] Grigs, 28 April 1788.

M.   GRIMES, SARAH and John Reynolds, 5 August 1674.

B.   GRIMES, FRANCES daughter of Charles and Frances Grimes, 19 November 1717.

B.   GRIMES, ALCE daughter of Charles and Frances Grimes, 24 March 1718/9.

B.   GRIMSTON, JOHN son of John and Barbary Grimston, 20 December 1672.

B.   GRINSTEAD, BARBARY daughter of John and Mary Grinstead, 17 February 1728.

   GRYMES   SEE : GRIMES PAGE 74

B.   GUPTON, STEPHEN son of William and Mary Gupton, 30 November 1703.

B.   GUPTON, THOMAS son of William and Mary Gupton, 1 July 1706.

B.   GUPTON, ELIZABETH daughter of William and Mary Gupton, 25 September 1709.

B.   GUPTON, STEPHEN son of Stephen and Eliz.ᵃ Gupton, 27 November 1713.

B. GUPTON, HENRY son of William and Mary Gupton, 30 December 1713.

B. GUPTON, JOYCE daughter of Stephen and Eliz.^a Gupton, 17 February 1715.

B. GUPTON, SARAH daughter of William and Mary Gupton, 9 February 1717.

B. GUPTON, ELIZABETH daughter of William and Mary Gupton Dec.^d, ___ February 1718. [This entry is not clear; B. should probably be D.]

D. GUPTON, THOMAS ___ February 1718.

D. GUPTON, HENRY ___ April 1719.

B. GUPTON, PETER son of William and Mary Gupton, 1 July 1721.

B. GUPTON, WILLIAM son of William and Eleanor Gupton, 31 January 1722.

D. GUPTOÑ, WILLIAM 21 May 1722.

D. GUPTON, MARY 7 May 1723.

M. GUPTON, STEPHEN and Margaret Coward, 23 January 1728/9.

B. GUPTON, MARY daughter of Stephen and Margaret Gupton, 27 January 1731/2.

B. GUPTON, ELIZABETH daughter of Stephen and Magdalin Gupton, 26 March 1737.

B. GUPTON, WILLIAM son of Stephen and Magdolin Gupton, 12 January 1738.

B. GUPTON, DANIEL "a Mullatto belonging to George Saunders," 1 June 1738.

B. GUPTON, ANNE daughter of Stephen and Magdalen Gupton, 24 November 1740.

B. GUPTON, STEPHEN son of Stephen and Magdalin Gupton, 31 January 1742.

B. GUPTON, WILLIAM GARLAND son of Stephen and Magdalin Gupton, 31 May 1745.

B. GUPTON, VINCENT son of Stephen and Magdalin Gupton, 9 May 1747.

B. GUPTON, HENRIETHA daughter of Stephen and Magdaline Gupton, 8 September 1750.

B. GUPTON, ELIZABETH daughter of William and Caty Gupton, 1 January 1778.

B. GUTRIGE, SUCKEY WILLIAMS daughter of Reubin and Elizabeth Gutrige, 23 November 1797 [L:13].

M. GWIEN, ALICE and Christopher Burn, 2 August 1728.

B. GWILLIAMS, EDGCOMB son of Richard and Mary Gwilliams, 28 February 1742.

B. GWILLIAMS, SARAH HILL daughter of Richard and Mary Gwilliams, 17 April 1746.

B. GWIN, ELIZABETH daughter of David and Catharine Gwin, 31 December 1692.
    [The handsome portrait of Elizabeth Gwynn (31 December 1692—28 January 1745)
    hangs at Mount Airy, the ancestral home of the Tayloe family in Richmond
    County. She married first Stephen Lyde and secondly the Honorable Colonel
    John Tayloe (1687/8-1747). She was the daughter of Major David Gwynn (16 -
    1704) and his wife nee Katherine Griffin (1664-1728), next below. MRC,p.267.]

D. GWIN, KATHRINE 24 September 1728.
    [The handsome portrait of Madam Katherine (Griffin) Fauntleroy Gwynn (16 March
    1664 - 24 September 1728) also hangs at Mount Airy. She was the daughter
    of Colonel Samuel Griffin (1633-1703) of Northumberland County and married
    first in 1678, Colonel William Fauntleroy (c.1655-1685) and secondly Major
    David Gwynn (16 -1704). By her first husband she had three sons and by her
    second husband three daughters; she was the ancestress of many distinguished
    persons. Genealogy of the Virginia Family of Lomax (Chicago, 1913) p. 48-49;
    AP&P, p. 266; W. Randolph Tayloe, The Tayloes of Virginia and Allied Families
    (Berryville, Virginia, 1963) p.2 et seq; 38 V 383-384.]

                                    H

    HABRON   SEE : HEABRON PAGE 91 AND HEBRON PAGE 92

B. HABRON, MOLLEY daughter of George Habron, 14 June 1790.

B. HADDAWAY, KATHARINE daughter of Charles and Elizabeth Haddaway, 26 December
    1760.

M. HADING, ELIZABETH and Daniel O'Neal, 10 May 1674.

    HADLEY   SEE: HEADLEY PAGE 91   AND HEDLEY PAGE 92

B. HAIL, BENJAMIN RUSSEL son of Benjamin and Frances Hail, 28 December 1781.

    HAIMS   SEE : HAMES PAGE 77

M. HAIS, ANNE and John Buxton, 18 February 1730/1.

B. HALL, JOYCE daughter of Elizabeth Hall, 16 September 1719.

M. HALL, JOSEPH and Elizabeth Morgan, 21 April 1729.

B. HALL, SARAH mulatto daughter of Joice Hall, 25 January 1750.

B. HALL, JOHN son of John Hall and Judah, his wife, 2 September 1768; and on
    the next line is written "wife 2^{d} of July."

B. HALL, JOHN OLDHAM son of Sally Hall, 7 November 1781.

B. HALL, NEWMAN son of Williamson and Susannah Hall, 21 March 1792 [L:15].

B. HALL, WILLIAM son of William and Rebecca Hall, 13 August 1792 [L:15].

B. HALL, ANNE daughter of Isaac and Jane Hall, 12 January 1793 [L:15].

B. HALL, WILLIAM son of Richard and Peggy Hall, 24 March 1794 [L:15].

B. HALL, REUBIN son of Williamson and Susanna Hall, 17 April 1794 [L:15].

B. HALL, JAMES son of Isaac and Jane Hall, 15 September 1795 [L:15].

B. HALL, JOHN son of Williamson and Susanna Hall, 7 October 1795 [L:15].

B. HALL, ROBERT son of William and Rebecca Hall, 13 December 1795 [L:15].

B. HALL, REUBIN son of Newman and Nancey Hall, 13 April 1796 [L:15].

B. HALL, POLLEY ANN daughter of Williamson and Susanna Hall, 12 September 1797
    [L:15].

B. HALL, REUBIN son of Isaac and Jane Hall, 25 March 1798 [L:15].

B. HALL, WILLIAM BRAGG son of William and Rebecca Hall, 6 July 1798 [L:15].

B. HALLAT, HENRY son of Mary Hallat, 11 March 1746.

D. HALLOND, HENRY   31 May 1737.

    HAMES   :   HAIMS

B. HAMES, WILLIAM son of William and Elizabeth Hames, 16 July 1711.

B. HAMES, JOHN son of William and Elizabeth Hames, 12 April 1713.

B. HAMES, CHARLES son of William and Elizabeth Hames, 10 September 1715.

B. HAMES, MARGARET daughter of Robert and Hannah Hames, 13 April 1717.

B. HAMES, CHARITY daughter of William and Elizabeth Hames, 1 October 1719.

B. HAMES, MARY ANN daughter of William and Elizabeth Hames, 21 March 1722/3.

M. HAMES, WILLIAM and Winifred Fann, 26 November 1730.

B. HAIMS, CHARLES son of William and Winifred Haims, 22 November 1732.

B. HAIMS, WILLIAM son of John and Ruth Haims, 20 February 1734.

B. HAIMS, EDWARD son of William and Winifrett Haims, 18 July 1735.

B. HAMES, BETTY ANN daughter of John and Ruth Hames, 8 March 1736.

B. HAMES, MARY ANN daughter of William and Winifred Hames, 16 September 1737.

B. HAMES, WILLIAM HARRIS son of Elizabeth Hames, 26 February 1739.

B. HAMES, RACHEL daughter of William and Winifred Hames, 13 December 1739.

B. HAMES, ANN [no parents entered], 26 January 1741.

B. HAMES, JOHN son of William and Winifred Hames, 30 October 1741.

B. HAMES, RANDAL son of William and Winifred Hames, 22 January 1743.

B. HAMES, ANN daughter of Charles and Lucresy Hames, 17 February 1743.

M. HAMILTON, GILBERT and Ann Beale, 4 November 1732.

D. HAMLETT, THOMAS 17 March 1726/7.

HAMMOCK : HAMMACK

B. HAMMOCK, RICHARD son of William and Grace Hammock, 4 May 1674.

B. HAMMOCK, WILLIAM son of William and Alice Hammock, 15 March 1688.

B. HAMMOCK, JANE daughter of William and Christian Hammock, 23 January 1711.

B. HAMMOCK, ELIZABETH daughter of William and Christian Hammock, 15 Sept. 1714.

B. HAMMOCK, ALCE daughter of William and Eleanor Hammock, 4 March 1715.

B. HAMMOCK, JOHN son of William and Eleanor Hammock, 14 December 1718.

B. HAMMOCK, WILLIAM son of William and Eleanor Hammock, 10 May 1720.

B. HAMMOCK, JOHN son of Richard and Frances Hammock, 20 September 1722.

B. HAMMOCK, CHRISTIAN daughter of Benjamin and Elizabeth Hammock, 28 May 1723.

B. HAMMOCK, ALICE daughter of William and Eleanor Hammock, 22 March 1723/4.

B. HAMMOCK, WILLIAM son of William and Margaret Hammock, 14 December 1724.

D. HAMMOCK, ALCE 23 February 1725.

B. HAMMOCK, WILLIAM son of Robert and Anne Hammock, 10 September 1726.

M. HAMMOCK, MARY and Charles Jones, 22 August 1727.

M. HAMMOCK, JANE and John Seamons, 2 September 1727.

M. HAMMOCK, ELIZABETH and John Morgan, 21 August 1729.

D. HAMMOCK, WILLIAM 7 July 1730.

B. HAMMOCK, JOHN son of Robert and Ann Hammock, 3 August 1730.

B. HAMMOCK, BENEDICT son of Benedict and Elizabeth Hammock, 28 August 1732.

B. HAMMOCK, HUGH son of Robert and Ann Hammock, 30 October 1732.

B. HAMMOCK, ELIZABETH daughter of William and Eleanor Hammock, 14 April 1734.

B. HAMMOCK, CATY daughter of William and Elizabeth Hammock, 8 November 1735.

B. HAMMOCK, JOHN son of Benedict and Elizabeth Hammock, 17 August 1736.

B. HAMMOCK, ROBERT son of Robert and Ann Hammock, 17 October 1737.

M. HAMMOCK, MARY and Francis Elmore, 23 February 1738.

B. HAMMOCK, ABIGAL daughter of Benedict and Elizabeth Hammock, 29 June 1739.

B. HAMMOCK, ELEANOR daughter of William and Eleanor Hammock, 7 October 1739.

B. HAMMOCK, BENEDICT son of Robert and Ann Hammock, 4 April 1740.

M. HAMMOCK, JOHN and Mildred Lambert, 26 August 1741.

B. HAMMOCK, WILLIAM son of John and Mildred Hammock, 27 September 1742.

B. HAMMOCK, CHARLES son of John and Susanna Hammock, 29 January 1744.

B. HAMMOCK, LAMBEART son of Robert and Ann Hammock, 16 September 1744.

B. HAMMOCK, ANN daughter of John and Mildred Hammock, 13 March 1745.

B. HAMMOCK, MARY daughter of Robert and Ann Hammock, 10 November 1746.

B. HAMMOCK, WILLIAM son of John and Susanna Hammock, 6 July 1747.

B. HAMMOCK, LEWIS son of Robert and Ann Hammock, 17 June 1749.

B. HAMMOCK, JOHN son of John and Mary Ann Hammock, 19 April 1756.

B. HAMMOCK, CATY daughter of John and Susanna Hammock, 19 April 1756.

B. HAMMOCK, MILLY daughter of Robert and Anne Hammock, 11 January 1757.

B. HAMMOCK, ANN daughter of John and Mary Hammock, 1 April 1758.

B. HAMMOCK, WILLIAM bastard son of Christian Hammock, 9 February 1761.

B. HAMMOCK, SARAH daughter of Benedick and Sarah Hammock, 6 November 1771.

B. HAMMACK, MOLLEY daughter of Benjamin and Sarah Hammack, 22 January 1777.

B. HAMMACK, SARAH daughter of Bendick Hammock, 25 May 17__ [not entered, probably 178?].

B. HAMMOCK, SALLEY daughter of William and Salley Hammock, 12 July 1790.

B. HAMMOCK, POLLEY daughter of William and Sally Hammock, 15 December 1794 [L:15].

B. HAMMOND, JOB son of Job and Elizabeth Hammond, 10 July 1677.

B. HAMMOND, ELIZABETH daughter of Job and Mary Hammond, 10 March 1680.

B. HAMMOND, WILLIAM son of Job and Elizabeth Hammond, 3 September 1682.

B. HAMMOND, MARTIN son of Martin and Mary Hammond, 3 July 1683.

B. HAMMOND, MARY daughter of Martin and Mary Hammond, 24 April 1687.

B. HAMMOND, EDWARD son of Martin and Mary Hammond, 22 November 1689.

B. HAMMOND, THOMAS son of Martin and Mary Hammond, 17 July 1692.

B. HAMMOND, WINNIFRED daughter of Job and Elizabeth Hammond, 22 July 1698.

B. HAMMOND, THOMAS son of Job and Amadine Hammond, 20 April 1702.

B. HAMMOND, SUSANNA daughter of Job and Amadine Hammond, 7 January 1705.

B. HAMMOND, GEORGE son of Martin and Elizabeth Hammond, 2 November 1712.

B. HAMMOND, BETTY daughter of John and Catharine Hammond, 17 October 1713.

B. HAMMOND, MARGARET daughter of Martin and Elizabeth Hammond, 25 July 1714.

B. HAMMOND, MERSY daughter of Job and Amandine Hammond, 17 March 1715.

B. HAMMOND, MARY daughter of Martin and Elizabeth Hammond, 7 April 1715.

D. HAMMOND, MARGARET 25 March 1716.

B. HAMMOND, JOHN son of John and Frances Hammond, 4 August 1716.

B. HAMMOND, CHARLES son of John and Catharine Hammond, 19 November 1716.

B. HAMMOND, ANNE daughter of Edward and Hannah Hammond, 18 March 1717.

D. HAMMOND, ELIZABETH 17 June 1717.

D. HAMMOND, MARY 20 August 1717.

B. HAMMOND, JEMIMA daughter of Martin and Elizabeth Hammond, 27 December 1717.

D. HAMMOND, JEMIMA 5 January 1718.

B. HAMMOND, JEMIMA daughter of Martin Hammond, 14 January 1718.

D. HAMMOND, WILLIAM 25 March 1718.

B. HAMMOND, WILLIAM son of William and Mary Hammond, 16 July 1718.

B. HAMMOND, CATEY daughter of John and Kathrine Hammond, 11 January 1719.

B. HAMMOND, WILLIAM son of Edward and Hannah Hammond, 10 November 1720.

B. HAMMOND, MARTIN son of Martin and Elizabeth Hammond, 4 October 1721.

B. HAMMOND, SAMUEL son of Job and Amadine Hammond, 19 March 1721/2.

B. HAMMOND, JOHN son of John and Kathrine Hammond, 5 February 1722.

B. HAMMOND, MARY ANN daughter of Edward and Hannah Hammond, 20 April 1723.

B. HAMMOND, ELIZABETH daughter of Martin and Elizabeth Hammond, 12 Jany 1725.

B. HAMMOND, DAVID son of John and Kathrine Hammond, 27 April 1725.

B. HAMMOND, JARVIS son of Job and Amadine Hammond, 27 September 1725.

D. HAMMOND, JOB 2 January 1726.

B. HAMMOND, DAVID son of William and Alice Hammond, 13 February 1726.

M. HAMMOND, JOHN and Judith Yeates, 21 February 1725/6.

M. HAMMOND, THOMAS and Ann Morris, 9 June 1726.

D. HAMMOND, ANNE 14 December 1726.

B. HAMMOND, WILLIAM son of John and Judith Hammond, 6 May 1727.

M. HAMMOND, ELIZABETH and Edward Morris, 25 May 1727.

M. HAMMOND, SUSANNA and John Davis, 25 December 1727.

M. HAMMOND, THOMAS and Mary Bryant, 23 September 1728.

M. HAMMOND, JANE and George Hill, 20 December 1728.

B. HAMMOND, LEROY son of John and Kathrine Hammond, 18 February 1728/9.

B. HAMMOND, LUIS (sic) son of Martin and Elizabeth Hammond, 8 January 1729.

B. HAMMOND, JOB son of Job and Amadine Hammond, 25 June 1729.

B. HAMMOND, RICHARD son of Thomas and Mary Hammond, 5 July 1729.

B. HAMMOND, ABSALOM son of John and Judith Hammond, 11 August 1729.

M. HAMMOND, ELIZABETH and Thomas Jesper, 12 November 1730.

B. HAMMOND, STORY son of Martin and Elizabeth Hammond, 19 January 1732.

D. HAMMOND, DANIEL 20 March 1732.

B. HAMMOND, JOHN son of John and Judith Hammond, 29 March 1732.

B. HAMMOND, WINIFRITT daughter of John and Kathrine Hammond, 6 June 1732.

D. HAMMOND, JUDITH 11 September 1733.

D. HAMMOND, ELIZABETH 27 April 1734.

D. HAMMOND, THOMAS 13 May 1734.

D. HAMMOND, STORY 2 June 1734.

D. HAMMOND, MARTIN 6 June 1734.

D. HAMMOND, RICHARD 16 July 1734.

B. HAMMOND, LUCY daughter of John and Elizabeth Hammond, 25 December 1734.

D. HAMMOND, MARTIN 10 December 1735.

B. HAMMOND, JANE daughter of John and Elizabeth Hammond, 5 January 1736.

B. HAMMOND, JEMIMA daughter of George and Elizabeth Hammond, 20 March 1736.

B. HAMMOND, KATHRINE daughter of Thomas and Elizabeth Hammond, 29 April 1738.

B. HAMMOND, MARTIN son of Lewis and Margaret Hammond, 8 May 1738.

D. HAMMOND, JANE 26 September 1738.

B. HAMMOND, HEIRS son of Thomas and Elizabeth Hammond, 15 March 1739.

M. HAMMOND, BETTY and John Hill, 13 August 1739.

B. HAMMOND, NATHAN son of George and Elizabeth Hammond, 29 September 1739.

B. HAMMOND, SARAH daughter of George and Elizabeth Hammond, 18 February 1741.

B. HAMMOND, JANE daughter of John and Elizabeth Hammond, 19 November 1741.

B. HAMMOND, JOB son of William and Elizabeth Hammond, 2 June 1742.

B. HAMMOND, THOMAS son of Thomas and Elizabeth Hammond, 23 December 1742.

B. HAMMOND, MERRYMAN son of Thomas and Elizabeth Hammond, 19 March 1744.

B. HAMMOND, WINNY daughter of John and Elizabeth Hammond, 27 March 1744.

B. HAMMOND, MARTIN son of William and Elizabeth Hammond, 29 September 1744.

B. HAMMOND, CATY daughter of William and Elizabeth Hammond, 2 March 1746.

B. HAMMOND, CATY daughter of John and Ann Hammond, 6 March 1746.

B. HAMMOND, THOMAS and ANN, twins of John and Elizabeth Hammond, 21 April 1746.

D. HAMMOND, KATHRINE wife of John Hammond, 10 October 1746.

B. HAMMOND, CHARLES son of Charles and Elizabeth Hammond, 18 November 1747.

B. HAMMOND, WILLIAM son of John and Betty Hammond, 1 January 1748.

D. HAMMOND, MARTIN son of John and Elizabeth Hammond, 15 January 1748.

B. HAMMOND, KATHARINE daughter of William and Elizabeth Hammond, 1 March 1748.

B. HAMMOND, MARTIN son of John and Elizabeth Hammond, 26 December 1748.

B. HAMMOND, DORCAS daughter of Thomas and Elizabeth Hammond, 8 October 1749.

B. HAMMOND, CHRIS.^R son of William and Elizabeth Hammond, 29 October 1749.

B. HAMMOND, WILLIAM son of Thomas and Elizabeth Hammond, 22 April 1750.

B. HAMMOND, HANNAH daughter of Absolum and Elizabeth Hammond, 18 May 1750.

B. HAMMOND, MARY ANN and LUCY twins of John and Elizabeth Hammond, 2 June 1750.

B. HAMMOND, MARY ANN bastard child of Sukey Hammond, 3 October 1750.

B. HAMMOND, JOHN son of John and Ann Hammond, 17 December 1750.

B. HAMMOND, ABNER son of Charles and Elizabeth Hammond, 31 March 1751.

B. HAMMOND, MARY daughter of William and Elizabeth Hammond, 21 May 1752.

B. HAMMOND, ANN daughter of John and Ann Hammond, 22 May 1752.

B. HAMMOND, JOHN son of William and Katharine Hammond, 24 August 1752.

B. HAMMOND, BETTY daughter of John and Elizabeth Hammond, 11 January 1753.

B. HAMMOND, JUDITH daughter of Absolom and Elizabeth Hammond, 11 April 1753.

B. HAMMOND, ANN daughter of John and Ann Hammond, 22 May 1753.

B. HAMMOND, EPAPHRODITUS son of Charles and Elizabeth Hammond, 17 June 1753.

B. HAMMOND, CHARLES bastard child of Sukey Hammond, 26 August 1753.

B. HAMMOND, WILLIAM son of William and Winifred Hammond, 7 July 1754.

B. HAMMOND, WINNY daughter of John and Ann Hammond, 27 May 1755.

B. HAMMOND, SARAH daughter of Charles and Elizabeth Hammond, 2 June 1755.

B. HAMMOND, CATY daughter of John and Elizabeth Hammond, 11 August 1755.

D. HAMMOND, ABNER son of Charles and Elizabeth Hammond, 24 August 1756.

B. HAMMOND, MARY daughter of Absolom and Elizabeth Hammond, 5 October 1756.

D. HAMMOND, JOB 19 October 1756.

B. HAMMOND, JOSHUA son of John and Ann Hammond, 1 January 1758.

B. HAMMOND, CATY daughter of LeRoy and Mary Ann Hammond, 29 January 1760.

B. HAMMOND, BETTY daughter of Absolom and Elizabeth Hammond, 6 September 1760.

B. HAMMOND, SUSANNA daughter of John and Ann Hammond, 28 September 1760.

B. HAMMOND, DAVID bastard child of Winny Hammond, 13 April 1762.

B. HAMMOND, CATY daughter of William and Katharine Hammond, 11 December 1762.

B. HAMMOND, JANEY daughter of John and Elizabeth Hammond, 11 January 1763.

B. HAMMOND, CATY DOBYNS daughter of Charles and Elizabeth Hammond, 30 Dec. 1763.

B. HAMMOND, JOHN son of John and Elizabeth Hammond, 15 February 1764.

B. HAMMOND, ELIZABETH daughter of John and Elizabeth Hammond, 16 December 1768.

B. HAMMOND, JUDITH daughter of John and Elizabeth Hammond, 24 March 1771.

B. HAMMOND, ELIZABETH daughter of Thomas and Rachel Hammond, [not entered] 1782.

B. HAMMOND, THOMAS son of Thomas and Ann Hammond, 5 January 1783.

B. HAMMONTREE, RUBIN (sic) son of Jonathan and Mary Hammontree, 15 Sept. 1719.

B. HAMMONTREE, ANNE daughter of Jonathan and Mary Hammontree, 19 September 1721.

B. HAMMONTREE, JOHN son of Jonathan and Mary Hammontree, 9 November 1723.

B. HAMMONTREE, DAVID son of Jonathan and Mary Hammontree, 10 October 1726.

M. HAMMONTREE, ANN and James Horgin 17 July 1742.

M. HAND, LAWRENCE and Delline [surname omitted], 14 January 1727/8.

M. HANES, ANN and Truman Palmer, 31 October 1743.

B. HANKS, WILLIAM son of William and Sarah Hanks, 14 February 1679.

B. HANKS, WILLIAM son of William and Hester Hanks, 26 May 1712.

B. HANKS, WILLIAM son of John and Kathrine Hanks, 8 March 1715.

B. HANKS, HANNAH daughter of William and Esther Hanks, 14 February 1717.

B. HANKS, ELEANOR [parents not entered], 18 March 1717.

B. HANKS, ALEXANDER son of Luke and Elizabeth Hanks, 31 October 1719.

B. HANKS, SARAH daughter of William and Esther Hanks, 22 February 1720.

B. HANKS, ELIZABETH [parents not entered], 18 October 1720.

B. HANKS, LUCRETIA daughter of Luke and Elizabeth Hanks, 1 June 1722.

B. HANKS, SARAH daughter of John and Catharine Hanks, 7 April 1723.

B. HANKS, RICHARD son of William and Esther Hanks, 14 August 1723.

B. HANKS, CATHARINE daughter of John and Catharine Hanks, 4 October 1723.

B. HANKS, SUSANNA daughter of William and Hannah Hanks, 18 December 1725.

B. HANKS, JOSEPH son of John and Catharine Hanks, 20 December 1725.

B. HANKS, JOHN son of John and Catharine Hanks, 4 May 1728.

B. HANKS, THOMAS son of William and Esther Hanks, 26 July 1728.

B. HANKS, JAMES son of William and Esther Hanks, 12 February 1732.

D. HANKS, WILLIAM 1 May 1732.

B. HANKS, THOMAS son of John and Catharine Hanks, 1 July 1732.

B. HANKS, ALEXANDER son of John and Catharine Hanks, 2 December 1734.

B. HANKS, TURNER son of Luke and Elizabeth Hanks, 18 June 1737.

M. HANKS, WILLIAM and Sarah Durham, 26 January 1738.

B. HANKS, ELIJAH son of William and Sarah Hanks, 17 December 1740.

B. HANKS, CHARLOTTE daughter of Ann Hanks, 25 December 1740.

B.   HANKS, MOTT son of John and Mary Hanks, 21 April 1742.

B.   HANKS, MILLION daughter of William and Sarah Hanks, 21 August 1742.

M.   HANKS, SUSANNA and William Hightower, 12 October 1743.

B.   HANKS, JUDITH daughter of William and Sarah Hanks, 29 December 1744.

B.   HANKS, ARGILL daughter of William and Sarah Hanks, 2 February 1746.

B.   HANKS, SUSANNA daughter of William and Sarah Hanks, 19 September 1749.

B.   HANKS, HANNAH daughter of William and Sarah Hanks, 11 February 1752.

B.   HANKS, MARTHA daughter of Luke and Sarah Hanks, 26 May 1752.

B.   HANKS, MARY daughter of Turner and Million Hanks, 20 May 1761.

B.   HANKS, JOSEPH son of Thomas and Betty Hanks, 21 February 1764.

B.   HANKS, NANSY (sic) daughter of Thomas and Betty Hanks, 15 September 1766.

B.   HANKS, ELIJAH son of John and Susanna Hanks, 19 October 1766.

B.   HANKS, HANNAH daughter of Turner and Million Hanks, 3 June 1767.

B.   HANKS, GEORGE son of Turner and Sarah Hanks, 22 June 1769.

B.   HANKS, BETTY daughter of Joseph and Ann Hanks, 4 March 1771.

B.   HANKS, LUKE son of Turner and Sarah Hanks, 17 May 1771.

B.   HANKS, RAWLEIGH son of Turner and Sarah Hanks, 1 April 1773.

B.   HANKS, PITMAN son of Turner and Sarah Hanks, 3 December 1776.

B.   HANKS, GEORGE NASH son of Judith Hanks, 30 April 1778.

B.   HANKS, CHITESTER son of Turner and Sarah Hanks, 31 May 1781.

B.   HANKS, WINNY daughter of George and Elizabeth Hanks, 27 October 1781.

D.   HARBER, RICHARD 18 July 1728.

     HARBORN : HARBURN

M.   HARBURN, DAVID and Sarah Peirce, 21 April 1729.

B.   HABBORN, DAVID son of David and Sarah Harborn, 9 August 1730.

B.   HARBORN, MARY daughter of David and Sarah Harborn, 30 June 1732.

HARBURN   SEE: HARBORN   :   HARBURN   PAGE 86

B.   HARDAGE, BETSY REDMAN daughter of Aron and Salley Hardage, 25 December 1796. [L:15]; see Hardige and Hardwick page 87.

B.   HARDIGE, JOHN son of John and Mary Hardige, 17 February 1749.

B.   HARDIGE, JAMES WILLSON "a child baptized for Aaron Hardige," 13 January 1792 [L:15].

M.   HARDING, WILLIAM and Sarah Ball, 14 February 1730/1.
[MRC.,p.87 questioned the surname of the bride - if Bale or Ball; the latter is correct. She was the only daughter of Captain Joseph[3] Ball (c.1680-1721) as Hayden, p.65, states but he errs in stating her mother was Mary Spencer. An Act of the House of Burgesses in May 1732 regarding land in Essex County (British Colonial Office 5/1389, ff.70-71) proves that Captain Joseph[3] Ball married Mary Mottrom, the only child of Spencer Mottrom, Gent. (1670-1700) of Northumberland County, and he was the only son and heir of John Mottrom and his wife née Hannah Fox whose father David[1] Fox of Lancaster County made her a deed poll on 11 November 1662 for 800 acres on Piscataway Creek which fell into Essex County. This land descended to the aforementioned Mary Mott- rom and this Act states she married (1) the aforementioned Captain Joseph[3] Ball and (2) William Loury, Gent. of Essex County and had five children by each spouse all of whom were living in 1732.]

B.   HARDWICK, JOHN son of John and Jane Hardwick, 26 May 1777.

B.   HARDWICK, DANIEL HARRISON son of Aaron and Salley Hardwick, 15 January 1794 [L:15]; see Hardage - Hardige page 87.

B.   HARFORD, DARKY daughter of John and Elizabeth Harford, 15 April 1750.

B.   HARFORD, BETTY BEZLEY daughter of John and Winny Harford, 27 February 1764.

B.   HARFORD, WILLIAM son of John and Winny Harford, 22 March 1767.

B.   HARFORD, HENRY son of John and Winefred Harford, 18 August 1775.

B.   HARFORD, LUCY daughter of John and Winne Harford, 20 January 1778.

B.   HARFORD, HENRY son of William and Sarah Harford, 12 July 1793 [L:15].

B.   HARGROVE, ELIZABETH daughter of Daniel and Mary Hargrove, 6 February 1678.

B.   HARMAN, SARAH daughter of Richard and Sarah Harman, 23 September 1688.

B.   HARPER, ABRAHAM son of Frances Harper, 21 December 1708.

M.   HARPER, ABRAHAM and Katherine Camel, 8 January 1729/30.

B.   HARPER, HENRY son of Henry and Rachel Harper, 17 October 1729.

B. HARRIS, SARAH daughter of Phillip and Mary Harris, 24 October 1702.

B. HARRIS, ANNE daughter of Phillip and Mary Harris, 27 December 1704.

B. HARRIS, PHILLIP son of Phillip Harris, 3 April 1715.

B. HARRIS, ELIZABETH daughter of Phillip and Ann Harris, 8 October 1717.

B. HARRIS, HUGH son of Hugh and Flowro Harris, 18 November 1717.

D. HARRIS, MARY 20 June 1719.

B. HARRIS, WILLIAM son of Philip and Anne Harris, 4 August 1719.

D. HARRIS, PHILLIP 13 JANUARY 1726.

M. HARRIS, ANN and Thomas Tune, 24 July 1727.

M. HARRIS, MARY and Richard Lawson, 22 September 1727.

D. HARRIS, PHILLIP 17 March 1734.

D. HARRIS, ELIZABETH 17 March 1735.

B. HARRIS, PHILIP son of John and Charity Harris, 24 November 1737.

B. HARRIS, MARY daughter of John and Charity Harris, 6 February 1739.

B. HARRIS, HUGH son of John and Charity Harris, 11 April 1743.

B. HARRIS, BETTY daughter of John and Charity Harris, 12 February 1746.

B. HARRIS, JAMES bastard son of Mary Harris, 13 February 1746.

B. HARRIS, NANNY daughter of John and Charity Harris, 20 May 1749.

B. HARRIS, WILLIAM son of John and Charity Harris, 29 June 1751.

B. HARRIS, SALLY daughter of John and Charity Harris, 20 March 1754.

B. HARRIS, GEORGE son of John and Charity Harris, 30 September 1755.

B. HARRIS, SARAH daughter of John and Charity Harris, 11 December 1761.

B. HARRIS, GEORGE HENRY son of Hugh and Sally Harris, 20 November 1789.

B. HARRIS, MOLLEY daughter of William and Molley Harris, 6 October 1795 [L:15]

B. HARRIS, JOSEPH son of William and Molley Harris, 6 January 1797 [L:15].

B. HARRIS, MOURNING son of William and Molley Harris, 8 October 1799 [L:15].

B. HARRISON, ROBERT son of Andrew and Thomasin Harrison, 23 October 1674.

B. HARRISON, WILLIAM son of Andrew and Thomasin Harrison, 14 May 1677.

B. HARRISON, ANNE daughter of Andrew and Thomasin Harrison, 25 June 1679.

B. HARRISON, WILLIAM son of James and Mary Harrison, 31 December 1719.

D. HARRISON, JAMES 29 November 1726.

B. HARRISON, VINCENT son of Benjamin and Eleanor Harrison, 12 July 1747.

B. HARRISON, SUSANNA daughter of Benjamin and Eleanor Harrison, 11 March 1748.

B. HARRISON, ALICE GRIFFIN daughter of George and Betty Harrison, 6 April 1783.

B. HART, LEONARD son of Thomas and Elizabeth Hart, 7 January 1688.

B. HART, THOMAS son of Thomas and Elizabeth Hart, 17 April 1691.

B. HART, BETTY daughter of Leonard and Mary Hart, 5 August 1719.

B. HART, THOMAS son of Leonard and Mary Hart, 25 September 1722.

B. HARTLEY, MARY ANN daughter of William and Winny Hartley, 11 June 1750.

B. HARTLEY, CATY daughter of John and Jane Hartley, 17 December 1763.

B. HARTLEY, SAMUEL son of John and Jane Hartley, 13 July 1768.

B. HARTLEY, KATHARINE daughter of John and Jean Hartley, 22 February 1771.

B. HARTLY, ELIZABETH daughter of Henry and Elizabeth Hartly, 14 November 1672.

B. HARTLY, ANNE daughter of Henry and Elizabeth Hartly, 4 May 1675.

B. HARTLY, ELIZABETH daughter of Henry and Elizabeth Hartly, 22 July 1679.

M. HARUEAR, HARUEAR (sic) and William Beale, 29 April 1729.

M. HARVEY, MARGARET and Lewis Pugh, 2 February 1738.

M. HASTIE, WILLIAM and Ann Roberson, 17 September 1730.

B. HASTIE, WILLIAM son of William and Ann Hastie, 1 June 1731.

B. HASTIE, JOHN son of William and Ann Hastie, 4 October 1735.

B. HATTEN, WILLIAM son of Peter and Molley Hatten, 13 October 1776.

HAW   SEE : HOW PAGE 98

B. HAW, THOMAS son of Henry and Dorcas Haw, 27 November 1726 [see Hawford, p.90].

B. HAWFORD, JOHN son of John Hawford, 25 February 1676.

B. HAWFORD, ELIZABETH daughter of John and Catharine Hawford, 20 October 1680.

B. HAWFORD, JOYCE daughter of Zachariah and Mary Hawford, 14 January 1686.

B. HAWFORD, THOMAS son of John and Catharine Hawford, 5 June 1687.

B. HAWFORD, KATHRINE daughter of Henry and Dorcas Hawford, 8 September 1715.

B. HAWFORD, DORCAS daughter of Henry and Dorcas Hawford, 6 March 1717.

D. HAWFORD, DORCAS 9 March 1717.

B. HAWFORD, ANNE daughter of Henry and Dorcas Hawford, 20 November 1720.

B. HAWFORD, WINNEFRED daughter of Henry and Dorcas Hawford, 20 November 1720.

D. HAWFORD, HENRY 18 January 1721.

B. HAWFORD, HENRY son of Henry and Dorcas Hawford, 19 December 1721.

D. HAWFORD, MARY 16 September 1722.

B. HAW [? ford ?], THOMAS, son of Henry and Dorcas Haw (sic) , 27 November 1726 [See, page 90, line one above].

B. HAWFORD, EDE daughter of Henry and Dorcas Hawford, 12 October 1729.

B. HAWFORD, WILLIAM son of Henry and Dorcas Hawford, 26 May 1732.

B. HAWKINS, ELLIOT son of James and Mary Hawkins, 5 June 1795 [L:15].

B. HAZARD, HENRY son of John and Frances Hazard, 27 October 1713.

B. HAZARD, ELIZABETH daughter of Joseph and Margaret Hazard, 30 March 1736.

B. HAZARD, JOSEPH son of Henry and Elizabeth Hazard, 23 July 1737.

B. HAZARD, JOHN son of Henry and Elizabeth Hazard, 10 January 1739.

B. HAZARD, SUSANNA daughter of Henry and Elizabeth Hazard, 10 May 1744.

B. HAZARD, WILLIAM son of Henry and Elizabeth Hazard, 26 January 1746.

B. HAZARD, HENRY son of Henry and Elizabeth Hazard, 1 March 1749.

B. HAZARD, BETTY daughter of Henry and Elizabeth Hazard, 28 October 1752.

B. HAZARD, NANNY daughter of Henry and Elizabeth Hazard, 11 March 1758.

B. HAZARD, MARTIN son of John and Judith Hazard, 29 November 1764.

B. HAZARD, CHARLES son of William and Agnes Hazard, 18 April 1769.

B. HAZARD, WILLIAM son of John and Judith Hazard, 7 May 1770.

B. HAZARD, JAMES son of Henry and Ann Hazard, 27 November 1773.

B. HAZARD, HENRY HARPER son of John and Judith Hazard, 18 December 1775.

B. HAZZELL, MARY daughter of William and Anne Hazell, 3 April 1692.

B. HAZELL , ANNE daughter of William and Anne Hazell, 2 February 1693.

HEABRON   SEE: HABRON PAGE 76 AND HEBRON PAGE 92

HEADLEY   SEE: HADLEY PAGE 76 AND HEDLEY PAGE 91

B. HEADLEY, ANDREW son of William and Susanna Headley, 13 July 1720.

D. HEADLEY, JOHN 18 April 1724.

B. HEADLEY, MARY daughter of William and Susannah Headley, 26 May 1725.

B. HEADLEY, ANN daughter of William and Susanna Headley, 2 January 1728.

B. HEADLEY, SUSANNA daughter of William and Susanna Headley, 22 August 1731.

B. HADLY, Mary daughter of Henry and Ann Hadley, 28 December 1738.

B. HEADLEY, ANN daughter of Henry and Ann Headley, 19 September 1741.

B. HEADLEY, ROBERT son of Henry and Ann Headley, 24 May 1745.

B. HEADLEY, JAMES son of Henry and Anne Headley, 25 December 1751.

B. HEADLEY, LUKE son of Henry and Ann Headley, 24 May 1754.

B. HEADLEY, WILLIAM son of William and Jane Headley, 13 July 1776.

B. HEADLEY, RICHARD son of Luke and Mary Headley, 18 November 1777.

B. HEADLEY, FANNEY STUARD daughter of Elizabeth Headley, 19 November 1777.

B. HEADLEY, GRIFFIN son of James and Winne Headley, 29 December 1777.

B. HEADLEY, THOMAS son of John and Ann Headley, 19 March 1779.

B. HEADLEY, WILLIAM OLDHAM son of Paul and Salley Headley, 15 August 1797 [L:15].

B. HEAL, ELEANOR daughter of George and Catharine Heal, 9 November 1705.

B. HEAL, GEORGE son of George and Catharine Heal, 4 January 1707.

B. HEAL, ELIZABETH daughter of George and Catharine Heal, 8 March 1710.

M. HEALE, ELIZABETH and William Davenport, 26 November 1728.

M. HEALL, ELIZABETH and John Sydnor, 27 May 1728.

    HEABRON : HEBRON   SEE: HABRON PAGE 76

B. HEBRON, WILLIAM son of George and Jane Hebron, 2 May 1711.

B. HEBRON, JOHN son of George and Jane Hebron, [not entered] July 1712.

B. HEBRON, ELIZABETH daughter of George and Jane Hebron, 3 January 1716.

D. HEBRON, WILLIAM 27 January 1725.

B. HEABRON, GEORGE son of George Heabron, 25 May 1782.

    HEDLEY SEE : HADLEY PAGE 76 and HEADLEY PAGE 91

B. HEDLEY, HENRY son of Henry and Jane Hedley, 10 March 1711.

B. HEDLEY, JOHN son of Henry and Jane Hedley, 29 December 1714.

    HEFFORD   SEE : JEFFORD   PAGE 103

    HEFFORD : HELFORD

M. HELFORD, ZACHARIAS and Elizabeth Lewis, 21 February 1727/8.

B. HEFFORD, SARAH daughter of Zacharias and Elizabeth Hefford, 6 April 1729.

B. HEMES, ANNE daughter of Randolph and Charity Hemes, 22 August 1686.

M. HENDORSON, ELIZABETH and William Taylor, 8 October 1730.

B. HENDREN, SALLY daughter of William and Honora Hendren, 10 May 1737.

B. HENDREN, WINEFRED daughter of William and Honori Hendren, 14 January 1739.

D. HENDREN, WINIFRED 8 September 1740.

B. HENDREN, SALLEY daughter of William and Honori Hendren, 10 May 1741.
                [sic]
B. HENDREN, MARY daughter of William and Honori Hendren, 21 May 1741.

B. HENDREN, ROSEANNA daughter of William and Honor Hendren, 6 March 1743.

B. HENDREN, WILLIAM son of William and Honor Hendren, 30 May 1744.

B. HENDREN, LIDIA daughter of William and Honor Hendren, 29 January 1746.

D. HENDREN, ANN daughter of William and Honor Hendren, 9 September 1749.

B. HENDREN, ANN daughter of William and Honor Hendren, 1 December 1749.

B. HENDREN, DOWNING HOWELL son of William and Honor Hendren, 7 April 1754.

B. HENDREN, ROBERT son of William and Honor Hendren, 20 May 1756.

B. HENDREN, THOMAS son of John and Mildred Hendren, 1 October 1760.

B. HENDREN, WILLIAM son of John and Mary Hendren, 14 September 1761.

D. HENDREN, WILLIAM 2 February 1768.

B. HENDREN, MOLLY daughter of William and Priscilla Hendren, 10 April 1770.

B. HENDREN, CYRUS son of William and Priscilla Hendren, 8 November 1790.

B. HERENTON, JOHN son of Samuel Herenton, 7 June 1777.

B. HERRINGTON, SAMUEL son of John and Betty Herrington, 5 August 1748.

B. HERRINGTON, JOHN son of John and Elizabeth Herrington, 5 October 1751.

B. HICHENS, WILLIAM son of Sarah Hichens, 25 July 1710.

B. HIDE, ELIZABETH daughter of John and Martha Hide, 10 March 1756.

B. HIGGS, MARY daughter of William and Dorcas Higgs, 29 May 1726.

B. HIGGS, JOHN son of William and Dorcas Higgs, 15 October 1729.

[sic]

B. Higgs, ELIZABETH daughter of William and Dorcas Higgs, 24 October 1729.

B. HIGGS, MARY daughter of William and Dorcas Higgs, 3 August 1731.

B. HIGHTOWER, THOMAS son of Joshua and Eleanor Hightower, 20 March 1712.

B. HIGHTOWER, WILLIAM son of John and Mary Hightower, 20 July 1720.

B. HIGHTOWER, CHARNAL son of Joshua and Susanna Hightower, 30 October 1721.

B. HIGHTOWER, ELEANOR daughter of John and Mary Hightower, 10 January 1722.

B. HIGHTOWER, KATHARINE daughter of Joshua and Susanna Hightower, 5 October 1723.

B. HIGHTOWER, JOHN son of John and Mary Hightower, 13 November 1725.

M. HIGHTOWER, CHARNEL and Sarah Glascock, 16 January 1727/8.

B.   HIGHTOWER, JOSHUA son of John and Mary Hightower, 14 September 1728.

B.   HIGHTOWER, ELIZABETH daughter of Charnel and Sarah Hightower, 23 March 1728/9

B.   HIGHTOWER, LETTICE daughter of Joshua and Susanna Hightower, 17 March 1729.

B.   HIGHTOWER, THOMAS son of John and Mary Hightower, 24 May 1731.

B.   HIGHTOWER, SARAH daughter of Charnel and Sarah Hightower, 22 June 1731.

B.   HIGHTOWER, JOSEPH son of Joshua and Susannah Hightower, 13 October 1731.

D.   HIGHTOWER, FRANCES   7 March 1733.

B.   HIGHTOWER, CHARNEL son of Charnel and Sarah Hightower, 22 June 1733.

B.   HIGHTOWER, GEORGE son of John and Mary Hightower, 28 September 1733.

B.   HIGHTOWER, SUSANNAH daughter of Joshua and Susannah Hightower, 13 April 1734.

B.   HIGHTOWER, RAWLEIGH son of Charloner and Sarah Hightower, 7 May 1734.

B.   HIGHTOWER, THOMAS son of Thomas and Kindniss Hightower, 5 February 1736.

B.   HIGHTOWER, ROBERT son of Joshua and Susannah Hightower, 24 September 1737.

B.   HIGHTOWER, RICHARD son of John and Mary Hightower, 27 December 1737.

B.   HIGHTOWER, TAVENER son of Joshua and Susanna Hightower, 22 April 1740.

B.   HIGHTOWER, JOSHUA son of Charnell and Sarah Hightower, 11 June 1741.

M.   HIGHTOWER, WILLIAM and Susanna Hanks, 12 October 1743.

B.   HIGHTOWER, GREGORY son of Charnell and Sarah Hightower, 29 October 1745.

B.   HIGHTOWER, CHARNEL son of Charnel Hightower, 24 January 1747 (sic).

B.   HIGHTOWER, JOHN son of Charnell and Sarah Hightower, 7 July 1747 (sic).

B.   HIGHTOWER, THOMAS son of Charnell and Sarah Hightower, 1 February 1750.

M.   HILL, GEORGE and Mary Clark, 20 October 1726.

M.   HILL, WILLIAM and Sarah Suggitt, 3 March 1726/7.

D.   HILL, JOHN 28 March 1728.

M.   HILL, JOHN and Elizabeth Suggett, 19 July 1728.

M.   HILL, ELEANOR and Gilbert Croswell, 9 December 1728.

M. HILL, GEORGE and Jane Hammond, 20 December 1728.

B. HILL, SARAH daughter of John and Elizabeth Hill, 17 August 1729.

B. HILL, JOHN son of John and Elizabeth Hill, 10 December 1732.

D. HILL, ELIZABETH 17 February 1735.

B. HILL, WILLIAM son of John and Elizabeth Hill, 3 April 1735.

D. HILL, FRANCES 16 August 1736.

M. HILL, JOHN and Betty Hammond, 13 August 1739.

B. HILL, CATY daughter of John and Betty Hill, 26 February 1740.

B. HILL, CHARLES son of John and Elizabeth Hill, 31 December 1742.

B. HILL, ANN daughter of John and Elizabeth Hill, 4 April 1745.

B. HILL, LEROY son of John and Elizabeth Hill, 29 March 1749.

B. HILL, JOSEPH son of John and Betty Hill, 29 April 1751.

B. HILL, JOHN son of John and Sarah Hill, 13 February 1761.

B. HILLIARD, PHILLIP son of Phillip and Eleanor Hilliard, 10 August 1753.

M. HILLMAN, RICHARD and Ann Thomas, 10 July 1729.

B. HINDS, ELIZABETH daughter of Richard and Judith Hinds, 30 March 1678.

M. HINDS, JUDITH and Alexander Swan, 15 November 1678.

B. HINDS, THOMAS son of Richard and Mary Hinds, 11 March 1697.

B. HINDS, RICHARD son of Richard and Mary Hinds, 27 November 1700.

B. HINDS, JOHN son of Richard and Mary Hinds, 3 November 1703.

B. HINDS, JUDITH daughter of Richard and Mary Hinds, 19 April 1708.

B. HINDS, CHARLES son of Richard and Mary Hinds, 27 December 1711.

B. HINDS, JAMES son of Richard and Mary Hinds, 4 April 1715.

D. HINDS, MARY 25 September 1717.

M. HINDS, MARY and John Bryant, 3 August 1726.

M. HINDS, CHARLES and Mary Green, 9 November 1727.

M. HINDS, THOMAS and Ann Grigrye, 19 April 1731.

D. HINDS, SUSANNAH 6 June 1732.

B. HINDS, MARY daughter of James and Patience Hinds, 2 May 1734.

B. HINDS, THOMAS son of Charles and Ann Hinds, 11 December 1738.

B. HINDS, DANIEL son of James and Ann Hinds, 29 January 1739.

M. HINDS, JAMES and Ann Singleton, 23 September 1739.

B. HINDS, RICHARD son of Charles and Ann Hinds, 14 February 1740.

B. HINDS, SARAH daughter of James and Ann Hinds, 25 January 1742.

B. HINDS, JUDITH daughter of Charles and Ann Hinds, 30 March 1743.

D. HINDS, RICHARD 9 November 1745.

B. HINDS, RICHARD son of Charles and Ann Hinds, 20 February 1746.

B. HINDS, ELIZABETH daughter of James and Wilmoth Hinds, 22 December 1748.

B. HINDS, CHARLES son of Charles and Ann Hinds, 4 November 1749.

B. HINDS, JOHN son of James and Wilmoth Hinds, 29 July 1750.

B. HINDS, JOSIAH son of Charles and Anne Hinds, 8 March 1752.

B. HINDS, MARY daughter of James and Wilmoth Hinds, 8 April 1752.

D. HINDS, WILMOTH 5 May 1752.

B. HINDS, CHARLES son of Thomas and Ann Hinds, 20 November 1764.

B. HINDS, JAMES son of Daniel and Martha Hinds, 2 May 1765.

B. HINDS, ELIZABETH daughter of Thomas and Ann Hinds, 16 September 1766.

B. HINDS, ABNER son of Daniel and Martha Hinds, 17 November 1767.

M. HINKLEY, EDWARD and Elizabeth Pridham, 10 July 1726.

M. HINKLEY, ELIZABETH and Moses Hopwood, 10 April 1727.

B. HINSON, ELIZABETH daughter of John and Molly Hinson, 2 January 1795 [L:15].

B. HINSON, SALLEY daughter of John and Molley Hinson, 13 January 1797 [L:15].

B. HIPKINS, LUCINDA COVINGTON daughter of Samuel W. and Catharine Hipkins, 16 June 1798 [L:15].

M. HIX, MARY and Richard Lewis, 3 March 1738.

M. HOBS, WINIFRED and John Welldon, 7 July 1729.

HODSON   SEE :   HUDSON   PAGE 100 AND   HUTSON   PAGE 101

B. HODSON, MARY daughter of Brian and Mary Hodson, 24 October 1682.

HOGAN   :   HOGANS   :   HOGINS

B. HOGINS, MARY daughter of Thomas Hogins, 10 August 1763.

B. HOGAN, FANNY daughter of Thomas and Nanny Hogan, 15 September 1775.

B. HOGANS, GEDETHEN son of Thomas and Ann Hogans, 20 October 1782.

B. HOGAN, NANCY daughter of Travis Hogan, 2 October 1788.

B. HOGAN, CHRISTOPHER son of Travis and Sailey Hogan, 4 January 1791.

B. HOGAN, PATTY PLUMMER daughter of James and Hainie Hogan, 30 April 1799.

M. HOLLAND, THOMAS and Joyce Johnson, 2 August 1675.

M. HOLLAND, MARGARET and William Shaw, 22 November 1680.

B. HOLLIS, THOMAS bastard son of Mary Hollis, 10 April 1746.

D. HOLMES, HANNAH 21 April 1725.

B. HOLT, JAMES HINDS son of Simon and Sarah Holt, 27 April 1764.

M. HOPPER, KATHERINE and William Beages, 5 May 1728.

M. HOPWOOD, MOSES and Elizabeth Hinkley, 10 April 1727.

B. HOPWOOD, MARY ANN daughter of Moses and Elizabeth Hopwood, 9 October 1728.

B. HOPWOOD, RICHARD son of Moses and Elizabeth Hopwood, 8 October 1730.

HORGAN   :   HORGIN

M. HORGIN, JAMES and Ann Hammontree, 17 July 1742.

B. HORGAN, MARY daughter of James and Ann Horgan, 2 November 1744.

M. HORNBY, DANIEL and Winifred Traverse, 28 November 1741.

D. HORNBY, WINIFRED wife of Daniel Hornby, 10 August 1749.

D. HORNBY, DANIEL 14 February 1749 [i.e., 1749/50; see MRC., p. 98].

B. HOULT, JANE RIDGWAY daughter of John and Jane Hoult, 20 January 1797 [L:15].

B. HOULT, THRIZA daughter of John and Jane Hoult, 11 September 1799 [L:15].

HOW   SEE : HAW PAGE 90

M. HOW, ELIZABETH and Richard Brasser, 7 July 1678.

B. HOW, KATHRINE daughter of John and Mary How, 30 October 1719.

B. HOW, JOHN son of John and Mary How, 22 October 1720.

B. HOW, BETTY daughter of John and Mary How, 25 March 1726.

B. HOW, SARAH daughter of John and Mary How, 10 March 1728.

B. HOW, MARY daughter of John and Mary How, 9 March 1729.

B. HOW, DANIEL son of John and Mary How, 2 May 1732.

B. HOW, SOPHIA daughter of Abner and Nancey How, 17 September 1791 [L:15].

B. HOW, HENRY son of James and Rebecca How, 14 January 1792 [L:15].

B. HOW, BETSY daughter of John and Elizabeth How, 20 January 1793 [L:15].

B. HOW, THOMAS son of Abner and Nancey How, 16 January 1794 [L:15].

M. HOWARD, ALICE and Stephen Wells, 3 December 1677.

B. HOWARD, CHARLES son of Thomas and Frances Howard, 15 March 1716.

D. HOWARD, THOMAS 10 May 1716.

M. HOWEND, JAMES and Mary Scurlock, 7 November 1729.

B. HOWARD, WILLIAM son of James and Mary Howard, 20 August 1730.

B. HOWARD, THOMAS son of James and Mary Howard, 19 December 1731.

B. HOWARD, WINNY daughter of Thomas and Mary Howard, 5 February 1731/2.

B. HOWARD, TRAVERSE son of James and Mary Howard, 8 October 1733.

D. HOWARD, TRAVERSE 10 September 1734.

B. HOWARD, NANNY daughter of James and Mary Howard, 16 July 1735.

B. HOWARD, SARAH daughter of James and Mary Howard, 23 March 1736.

B. HOWARD, SPENCER son of James and Mary Howard, 13 May 1739.

B. HOWARD, PATTY daughter of James and Mary Howard, 31 January 1741.

B. HOWARD, JAMES son of James and Mary Howard, 16 November 1743.

D. HOWARD, JAMES 9 March 1749.

B. HOWARD, JAMES son of Thomas and Ann Howard, 26 March 1752.

B. HOWARD, BETTY daughter of Thomas and Ann Howard, 6 February 1754.

B. HOWARD, LEROY son of Thomas and Ann Howard, 28 July 1756.

D. HOWARD, BETTY daughter of Thomas and Ann Howard, 18 September 1756.

B. HOWARD, KATHRINE daughter of William and Alice Howard, 22 April 1757.

B. HOWARD, ISAAC son of Thomas and Ann Howard, 4 April 1761.

B. HOWARD, MARY daughter of William and Alice Howard, 25 March 1762.

B. HOWARD, SARAH daughter of Thomas and Ann Howard, 20 June 1763.

B. HOWARD, WILLIAM son of Spencer and Sarah Howard, 21 July 1763.

B. HOWARD, ELIZABETH daughter of Spencer and Sarah Howard, 25 December 1766.

B. HOWARD, PRESLEY son of Spencer and Sarah Howard, 8 May 1769.

B. HOWARD, ISAAC son of Thomas and Ann Howard, 24 January 1772.

B. HOWARD, KATHARINE daughter of Spencer and Sarah Howard, 17 July 1772.

B. HOWARD, ELLEN daughter of James and Hannah Howard, [not entered] 1773.

B. HOWARD, BETSEY daughter of Thomas and Ann Howard, 21 April 1774.

B. HOWARD, THOMAS son of James and Hannah Howard, 20 June 1775.

B. HOWARD, GEORGE son of James and Hannah Howard, 28 December 1776.

B. HOWARD, JOHN son of James and Hannah Howard, 10 August 1778.

B. HOWARD, VINCENT son of Jerry and Ellen Howard, 24 August 1783.

B. HOWARD, SARAH OLIVER daughter of Jeroboam and Ellen Howard, 22 January 1785.

B. HOWARD, ANN daughter of Jereboam and Ellen Howard, 18 March 1787.

B. HOWARD, EPPY son of Jeroboam and Ellen Howard, 21 September 1788.

D. HOWARD, JOHN son of James and Hannah Howard, 18 November 1788.

B. HOWARD, JOHN son of Jeroboam and Ellener Howard, 24 May 1790.

B. HOWELL, JOHN son of George and Dianna Howell, 18 November 1686.

B. HOWELL, JOHN son of Downing and Alice Howell, 9 December 1752.

B. HOWELL, WILLIAM son of John and Mary Howell, 28 December 1752.

M. HOWEND, JAMES and Mary Scurlock, 7 November 1729 [see, HOWARD, pgs. 98-99].

B. HUDNELL, HANNAH daughter of Richard and Elizabeth Hudnell, 3 September 1682.

  HUDSON   SEE : HODSON PAGE 97 AND HUTSON PAGE 101

B. HUDSON, JUDITH daughter of Rebeccah Hudson, 23 March 1720/1.

D. HUDSON, REBECCA 27 February 1745.

B. HUES, WILLIAM son of William and Hannah Hues, 5 February 1717.

M. HUGELL, ELIZABETH and Hezekiah Turner, 8 June 1674.

D. HUGHES, MARTHA "in the year 1719."

D. HUGHS, WILLIAM 16 February 1717.

B. HUGHS, JAMES HOPKINS son of Reubin and Mary Hughs, 20 April 1791 [L:15].

B. HUGHS, POLLY daughter of Reubin and Mary Hughs, 12 January 1793 [L:15].

  HUGHLET : HUGHLETT

D. HUGHLETT, ANNE 23 April 1716.

D. HUGHLETT, JOHN 15 August 1717.

D. HUGHLETT, ROSE 15 October 1722.

B. HUGHLETT, ANN NASH daughter of Winifritt Hughlett, 10 March 1730.

B. HUGHLETT, LEROY GEORGE son of John and Mary Hughlett, 25 September 1730.

B. HUGHLETT, JOHN son of Winifred Hughlett, 8 April 1733.

B. HUGHLET , BE DE (sic) son of Ephrain and Molly Hughlet, 3 March 1789.

D. HULL, JOSEPH 13 January 1750.

B. HUMPHREYS, HELEN daughter of James and Elizabeth Humphreys, 5 January 1752.

B. HUMPHRIS, ELIZABETH daughter of Elias and Fanney Humphris, 18 January 1784.

B. HUMPHRIS, WINNEY daughter of Elias and Fanney Humphris, 18 November 1786.

B. HUNT, JOHN son of Richard and Mary Hunt, 21 January 1723/4.

M. HUNT, GEORGE and Elizabeth Barber, 5 June 1730.

B. HUNT, WILLIAM son of George and Elizabeth Hunt, 11 April 1731.

B. HUNT, CHARLES son of George and Elizabeth Hunt, 9 January 1732.

B. HUNT, ELIZABETH daughter of George and Elizabeth Hunt, 9 July 1735.

B. HUNT, FRANCES daughter of George and Elizabeth Hunt, 9 March 1736.

B. HUNT, MOLLY daughter of Charles and Mildred Hunt, 15 December 1775.

M. HUNTLY, MARY and John Watson, 7 June 1730.

B. HUNTON, ROBERT son of Alexander and Betty Hunton, 12 November 1759.

B. HUNTON, MARY daughter of Alexander and Betty Hunton, 6 February 1764.

B. HUNTON, BETTY daughter of Alexander and Betty Hunton, 21 April 1765.

B. HUNTON, THOMAS son of Alexander and Betty Hunton, 27 January 1767.

B. HUNTON, NANNY daughter of Alexander and Betty Hunton, 25 May 1774.

B. HUNTON, WILLIAM REU [or REN], son of Alexander and Betty Hunton, 25 July 1776.

HUTSON   SEE : HODSON PAGE 97 AND HUDSON PAGE 100

B. HUTSON, WILLIAM son of Rebeccah Hutson, [day not entered] December 1730.

D. HUTSON, WILLIAM 17 September 1732.

I

INGER   SEE : INGOE PAGE 101

B. INGER, JOHN son of John and Mary Inger, 7 February 1675.

B. INGLESBY, WINNY bastard child of Mary Inglesby, 30 January 1753.

INGOE   SEE : INGER PAGE 101

B. INGOE, JAMES son of John and Mary Ingoe, 26 April 1680.
[MRC., p. 101 errs in stating James Ingo(e) was the elder of the two sons of John and Mary Ingo (Ingoe, Inger); the above recordings show James Ingo(e) (1680-1724/5) was the younger son of John and Mary Ingo(e).]

J

M. JACKMAN, MARY and James Tune, 6 September 1680.

D. JACKSON, ANNE 5 April 1717.

B. JACKSON, ELIZABETH daughter of John and Elizabeth Jackson, 15 January 1718.

B. JACKSON, MARY daughter of David and Ann Jackson, 16 May 1719.

B. JACKSON, NATHANIEL son of Nathaniel and Elizabeth Jackson, 3 December 1719.

B. JACKSON, WILLIAM son of Daniel and Sarah Jackson, 23 April 1721.

B. JACKSON, JUDITH daughter of David and Anne Jackson, 17 October 1721.

B. JACKSON, SARAH daughter of John and Elizabeth Jackson, 26 October 1721.

B. JACKSON, HENRY son of John and Elizabeth Jackson, 6 May 1724.

D. JACKSON, DIER [?] 30 February 1726.

B. JACKSON, ROSAMAN daughter of Daniel and Sarah Jackson, 21 July 1726.

B. JACKSON, ANN daughter of John and Elizabeth Jackson, 7 February 1730.

B. JACKSON, BETTY daughter of Nathaniel and Elizabeth Jackson, 4 October 1730.

B. JACKSON, MARY daughter of John and Elizabeth Jackson, 27 March 1736.

B. JACKSON, SAPPHIA daughter of Daniel and Rebeccah Jackson, 24 September 1737.

B. JACKSON, LUKE and MILLY twins of Daniel and Mary Jackson, 5 August 1758.

B. JACKSON, EPHIAH "born of Beckey Jackson," 19 July 1776.

B. JACKSON, HENRY ALLISON son of William Jackson, 11 October 1793 [L:17].

M. JACOBS, JOHN and Mary Cary, 8 November 1680.

D. JACOBS, MARY 11 February 1722/3.

B. JACOBUS, ELIZABETH daughter of Angel and Elizabeth Jacobus, 14 November 1680.
    [It was a typographical error on page 102, MRC, where it was stated Angell
    Jacobus married (1) by 1688 Elizabeth Clark(e); this should have been by 1678
    also the references which prove this date were inadvertently omitted - they
    are the wills of Henry and Joan Clark, the parents of Elizabeth (Clark) Jacob
    which are fully abstracted in Sweeny, pages 75, 90.]

B. JAMERSON, JOHN bastard child of Ann Jamerson, 5 July 1753.

B. JAMESBOLTEZER, MARY daughter of Peter and Mary Jamesboltezer, 30 Sept. 1712.

B. JAMESBOLTEZER, ELIZABETH daughter of Peter and Mary Jamesboltezer, 4 February 1714.

JASPER   SEE :   JESPER   :   JASPER PAGE 104

D. JEFFERY, CHARLES 1 March 1740.

D. JEFFERY, BRIDGETT 20 February 1749.

B. JEFFERYS, JOHN son of William and Mary Jefferys, 29 January 1752.

B. JEFFERYS, WILLIAM LOVELACE son of William and Mary Jefferys, 13 March 1754.

JEFFORD   SEE : HEFFORD PAGE 92

B. JEFFORD, JOHN son of Zacharias and Elizabeth Jefford, 16 November 1730.

JEFFRIES   SEE : JEFFERY : JEFFERYS PAGE 103 AND GEFFREYS PAGE 67

JENKINS   :   JENKINGS

B. JENKINGS, CHARLES son of Edward and Ann Jenkings, 19 July 1735.

B. JENKINS, EDWARD son of Edward and Ann Jenkins, 15 September 1737.

B. JENKINS, JENKINS (sic) son of Edward and Ann Jenkins, 12 March 1738.

B. JENKINS, WINNY daughter of William and Elizabeth Jenkins, 23 April 1774.

B. JENKINS, ELIZABETH OLDHAM daughter of William and Priscilla Jenkins, 20 January 1781.

B. JENKINS, NANCY daughter of William and Priscilla Jenkins, 20 May 1783.

B. JENKINS, MATTHEW son of Jeremiah and Elizabeth Jenkins, 23 March 1791 [L:17].

B. JENKINS, SUCKEY daughter of Daniel and Katey Jenkins, 5 June 1793 [L:17].

B. JENKINS, MARTHA daughter of James and Martha Jenkins, 10 July 1793 [L:17].

B. JENKINS, REUBIN TAYLOR son of William and Sarah Jenkins, 16 Jany 1794 [L:17].

B. JENKINS, NANCEY daughter of Jeremiah and Elizabeth Jenkins, 12 November 1794 [L:17].

B. JENKINS, WILLIAM son of Daniel and Katey Jenkins, 10 March 1797 [L:17].

JENNINGS   SEE : GENINGS PAGE 67

B. JENNINGS, HANNAH daughter of Henry and Eleanor Jennings, 2 February 1701.

B. JENNINGS, ELEANOR daughter of Henry and Eleanor Jennings, 24 April 1704.

M. JENINGS, ANN and John Wilcox, 2 March 1729/30.

B. JENNINGS, WILLIAM son of James and Elizabeth Jennings, 1 April 1792 [L:17].

B. JENNINGS, ELIZABETH daughter of James and Elizabeth Jennings, 18 February 1794 [L:17].

B. JENNINGS, SALLEY daughter of James and Elizabeth Jennings, 23 August 1796 [L:17].

M. JEOFFREY, MARGARET and Charles Bryant, 30 November 1738.

    JESPER : JASPER

B. JESPER, ANNE daughter of Richard and Sarah Jesper, 8 October 1682.

B. JASPER, RICHARD son of Richard and Sarah Jasper, 21 April 1687.

B. JASPER, THOMAS son of Richard and Sarah Jasper, 2 October 1689.

B. JESPER, THOMAS son of Thomas and Anne Jesper, 21 September 1705.

B. JESPER, MARY daughter of Thomas and Anne Jesper, 3 May 1708.

B. JESPER, ELIZABETH daughter of Thomas and Sarah Jesper, 22 May 1712.

B. JESPER, ANN daughter of Thomas and Sarah Jesper, 5 December 1714.

B. JESPER, MARY ANN daughter of Edward and Eleanor Jesper, 23 September 1715.

B. JESPER, RICHARD son of Thomas and Sarah Jesper, 10 June 1717.

B. JESPER, SIMON son of Thomas and Sarah Jesper, 13 January 1720.

D. JESPER, ELIZABETH 2 August 1720.

D. JESPER, EDWARD 15 March 1720/1.

B. JESPER, SARAH daughter of Thomas and Sarah Jesper, 21 February 1723/4.

D. JESPER, ELIZABETH 19 February 1725.

M. JESPER, MARY and Michael Connell, 8 September 1727.

D. JESPER, SARAH 20 August 1728.

D. JESPER, MARY ANN 22 June 1729.

B. JESTER, SARAH daughter of Thomas and Sarah Jesper, 11 November 1729.

M. JESPER, THOMAS and Elizabeth Hammond, 12 November 1730.

B. JESPER, WILLIAM son of Thomas and Elizabeth Jesper, 13 September 1731.

B. JESPER, THOMAS son of Thomas and Elizabeth Jesper, 14 April 1735.

D. JESPER, WILLIAM 19 October 1735.

B. JESPER, WILLIAM son of Thomas and Elizabeth Jesper, 16 September 1737.

B. JESPER, DANIEL son of Thomas and Elizabeth Jesper, 30 October 1739.

B. JESPER, ANN daughter of Thomas and Elizabeth Jesper, 14 December 1742.

B. JESPER, BETTY daughter of Thomas and Elizabeth Jesper, 3 November 1745.

D. JESPER, SARAH 24 January 1749.

B. JESPER, ANN daughter of John and Mary Jesper, 30 September 1755.

B. JESPER, ELIZABETH daughter of Thomas and Ann Jesper, 3 October 1757.

D. JESPER, ELIZABETH 25 October 1757.

B. JESPER, THOMAS son of John and Mary Jesper, 4 November 1757.

B. JESPER, ROBERT son of Thomas and Ann Jesper, 6 February 1760.

B. JESPER, ANN daughter of Thomas and Ann Jesper, 27 September 1762.

B. JESPER, THOMAS son of Daniel and Katharine Jester, 24 March 1764.

B. JESPER, WILLIAM son of Thomas and Ann Jesper, 14 April 1765.

B. JESPER, JOHN son of William and Sarah Jesper, 31 May 1765.

B. JESPER, SARAH daughter of Thomas and Ann Jesper, 29 July 1767.

B. JESPER, MILLY daughter of Thomas and Anne Jesper, 6 April 1769.

B. JESPER, JOHN son of Thomas and Ann Jesper, 7 March 1771.

B. JESPER, MARY ANNE daughter of Thomas and Anne Jesper, 24 August 1776.

B. JESPER, THOMAS son of Thomas and Elizabeth Jesper, 14 April 1777.

B. JESPER, EDWARD son of Daniel and Catharine Jesper, 16 June 1777.

B. JESPER, FANNY daughter of Thomas and Tuanor [?] Jesper, 1 April 1782.

B. JESPER, [Not Entered] a child of Robert and Elizabeth Jesper, 14 Dec. 1782.

B. JESPER, NANCEY DUNNAWAY daughter of George and Elizabeth Jesper, 1 February 1797.

B. JESPER, DANIEL son of George and Elizabeth Jesper, 29 November 1798.

B. JOHNSON, CHRISTOPHER son of Christopher and Joyce Johnson, 24 August 1673.

M. JOHNSON, JOYCE and Thomas Holland, 2 August 1675.

D. JOHNSON, ALEXANDER 28 December 1726.

B. JOHNSTON, WILLIAM son of William and Lucy Johnston, 11 December 1734.

M. JONES, EDWARD and Alicia Lunn, 27 August 1679. [See page 61]
[The bride was the daughter of James Samford (c.1624-1704) and widow of
William Lunn (16 -1679) who died testate in Rappahannock County (Sweeny,
p. 82). She left isse by each spouse. MRC, p. 155.]

B. JONES, JOHN son of Edward and Alicia Jones, 22 August 1680.

B. JONES, AUSTIN son of Edward and Priscilla Jones, 10 May 1682.

B. JONES, MERCY daughter of Edward and Alicia Jones, 13 May 1682.

B. JONES, SAMFORD son of Edward and Alicia Jones, 13 April 1684.

B. JONES, ANNE daughter of Rotherwick and Mary Jones, 16 June 1685.

B. JONES, HANNAH daughter of Edward and Priscilla Jones, 20 March 1686.

B. JONES, JOHN son of Rotherwick and Mary Jones, 16 May 1689.

B. JONES, CHARLES son of Edward and Alicia Jones, 28 August 1697.

B. JONES, SAMFORD son of John and Elizabeth Jones, 13 April 1708.

B. JONES, BETTY daughter of John and Elizabeth Jones, 7 July 1711.

B. JONES, ALICIA daughter of John and Elizabeth Jones, 1 August 1713.

B. JONES, ISAAC son of Edward and Margaret Jones, 5 September 1715.

D. JONES, SAMFORD 27 September 1716.

B. JONES, EDWARD son of Edward and Margaret Jones, 16 March 1717.

B. JONES, WILLIAM son of Edward and Ruth Jones, 8 June 1719.

B. JONES, KATHRINE daughter of Elisha and Christian Jones, 29 December 1719.

B. JONES, JEREMIAH son of William and Mary Jones, 10 February 1720.

B. JONES, ELIZABETH daughter of Edward and Margaret Jones, 5 October 1720.

D. JONES, ELISHA 29 January 1721.

B. JONES, WILMOTH daughter of Edward and Ruth Jones, 23 July 1722.

D. JONES, DANIEL 30 October 1722.

D. JONES, MARGARET 16 December 1722.

B. JONES, JAMES son of Richard Jones, 6 August 1724.

B. JONES, ALICIA daughter of Charles and Mary Jones, 20 February 1724/5.

D. JONES, JANE 29 May 1725.

M. JONES, JOHN and Sarah Mountjoy, 30 November 1725.

B. JONES, SUSANNA daughter of Charles and Mary Jones, 2 January 1726.

D. JONES, MARY 1 February 1726.

M. JONES, WILLIAM and Katherine Smith, 16 February 1725/6.

M. JONES, CHARLES and Mary Hammock, 22 August 1727.

B. JONES, WILLOUGHBY son of Edward and Ruth Jones, 12 March 1727/8.

B. JONES, RACHEL daughter of Richard and Elizabeth Jones, 22 May 1728.

D. JONES, EDWARD 15 August 1728.

D. JONES, ALICIA 20 September 1728.

M. JONES, EDWARD and Elizabeth Gower, 26 September 1728.

B. JONES, SAMFORD son of Charles and Mary Jones, 27 December 1728/9 (sic).

B. JONES, WILLIAM son of Edward and Elizabeth Jones, 7 November 1729.

M. JONES, ELIZABETH and John Seamons, 30 November 1729.

B. JONES, WILLIAM son of Thomas and Hannah Jones, 10 January 1729/30.

M. JONES, OWIN and Jane Wilkerson, 19 January 1730/1.

B. JONES, DAVID son of Owin and Jane Jones, 10 February 1731.

B. JONES, ALICIA daughter of Charles and Mary Jones, 14 June 1731.

B. JONES, GRIFFIN son of Richard and Elizabeth Jones, 11 November 1732.

B. JONES, MARGARET daughter of Edward and Elizabeth Jones, 8 July 1734.

B. JONES, JOHN son of Edward and Elizabeth Jones, 20 February 1737.

D. JONES, JOHN 24 February 1737.

B. JONES, NANNY daughter of Charles and Mary Jones, 29 April 1738.

D. JONES, EDWARD 2 September 1739

M. JONES, MARY and Cornelius Todd, 17 December 1739.

B. JONES, SAMFORD son of Charles and Mary Jones, 30 December 1740.

B. JONES, SARAH daughter of Samford and Mary Jones, 27 August 1742.

D. JONES, JOHN 25 March 1743.

B. JONES, BETTY daughter of Charles and Mary Jones, 26 March 1743.

B. JONES, MARTHA daughter of John and Ann Jones, 21 November 1744.

B. JONES, WILMOTH daughter of Richard and Elizabeth Jones, 29 June 1745.

B. JONES, WINIFRED daughter of Samford Jones, 1 September 1745.

B. JONES, FRANKEY daughter of Humphry and Kathrine Jones, 18 October 1746.

B. JONES, JOHN son of William and Mary Ann Jones, 26 November 1747.

B. JONES, LISHA daughter of Samford and Mary Jones, 1 December 1747.

B. JONES, BETTY daughter of Richard and Elizabeth Jones, 21 February 1748.

B. JONES, BETTY daughter of William and Mary Ann Jones, 16 March 1748.

B. JONES, EDWARD son of Charles and Mary Jones, 16 May 1748.

B. JONES, RICHARD son of John and Ann Jones, 28 October 1748.

B. JONES, WINIFRITT daughter of Edward and Jane Jones, 12 November 1749.

D. JONES, JANE 8 December 1749.

B. JONES, CATY daughter of William and Mary Ann Jones, 5 January 1750.

B. JONES, ELIZABETH daughter of John and Ann Jones, 27 February 1750.

B. JONES, JANE daughter of Samford and Mary Jones, 8 July 1750.

B. JONES, ELIZABETH daughter of Edward and Barbara Jones, 30 July 1751.

B. JONES, JOHN son of John and Anne Jones, 25 February 1753.

B. JONES, WINNY daughter of William and Mary Ann Jones, 29 March 1753.

B.   JONES, JOHN son of Charles and Alice Jones, 1 April 1753.

B.   JONES, LUCY daughter of Edward and Barbara Jones, 17 November 1753.

D.   JONES, WILLIAM 14 March 1754.

B.   JONES, ELIZABETH daughter of John and Ann Jones, 14 January 1755.

B.   JONES, LEANAH daughter of Charles and Alice Jones, 7 February 1755.

B.   JONES, MARGARET daughter of Edward and Barbara Jones, 7 February 1756.

B.   JONES, WILLIAM son of William and Mary Ann Jones, 15 May 1756.

D.   JONES, EDWARD 15 February 1757.

B.   JONES, EDWARD son of William and Mary Ann Jones, 7 April 1759.

B.   JONES, MARY ANN daughter of William and Mary Ann Jones, 22 July 1761.

B.   JONES, ABNER son of David and Mary Jones, 13 March 1765.

B.   JONES, LUCY daughter of David and Mary Ann Jones, 27 January 1768.

B.   JONES, CHARLES son of Samford and Christian Jones, 3 June 1771.

B.   JONES, SPENCER son of David and Mary Ann Jones, 17 March 1772.

B.   JONES, ELIZABETH daughter of John and Susanna Jones, 22 March 1772.

B.   JONES, EDWARD son of Edward and Hannah Jones, 14 August 1776.

B.   JONES, LAMBARD HAMMACK son of Stanford and Cristan Jones, 17 November 1776.

B.   JONES, WILLIAMSON PAYNE son of Edward and Hannah Jones, 24 January 1779.

B.   JONES, FRANCES daughter of Edward and Hannah Jones, 13 June 1783.

D.   JONES, HANNAH wife of Edward Jones, 1 January 1786 "the mother of the three
     children next above mentioned," says the recording meaning Edward (1776),
     Williamson Payne (1779) and Frances (1783).

B.   JONES, RICHARD son of Richard and Elizabeth Jones, 8 November 1791.

Bp. JONES, [not entered] a child of Charles Jones, 16 September [not entered,
     but probably circa 1793]; [L:17]; [no date of birth entered; only baptismal].

B.   JONES, SUSANNA daughter of Vincent and Sally Jones, 9 August 1794. [L:17].

B.   JONES, NANCY daughter of Jeremiah Nash and Elizabeth Jones, 8 December 1795
     [L:17.]

B. JONES, WILLIAM son of Vincent and Salley Jones, 4 December 1796 [L:17].

B. JONES, POLLY daughter of Thomas and Rachel Jones, 21 June 1799 [L:17].

D. JORDEN, LAMBERT 29 March 1719.

B. JORDEN, ANNE daughter of William and Sarah Jorden 20 April 1728.

K

D. KEACEY, JOHN 14 February 1729.

KELLEY : KELLY   SEE : SKELLEY : SKELLY   PAGE 169

B. KELLEY, JOHN son of James and Elizabeth Kelley, 1 April 1711.

M. KELLEY, EDWARD and Mary Goulding, 18 April 1726.

D. KELLEY, SARAH 9 September 1728.

B. KELLEY, THOMAS son of Bridget Kelley, 11 August 1741.

B. KELLY, SUSANNAH WILLSON daughter of John and Jenny Kelly, 21 January 1791 [L:19].

B. KELLY, GEORGE PAYNE son of John and Jenny Kelly, 6 April 1793 [L:19].

B. KELLY, NANCEY daughter of James and Mary Kelly, 16 May 1793 [L:19].

B. KELLY, JOHN son of James and Mary Kelly, 11 November 1794 [L:19].

B. KELLY, RICHARD son of John and Jenny Kelly, 12 November 1794 [L:19].

B. KELLEY, SALLEY daughter of James and Mary Kelley, 26 August 1796 [L:19].

B. KELLEY, POLLY DYE daughter of James and Mary Kelley, 18 February 1798 [L:19].

B. KELLY, CATY daughter of James and Mary Kelly, 12 December 1799 [L:19].

B. KEM, JAMES son of Henry and Betty Kem, 2 June 1738.

M. KEN, JOANNA and Joseph Polley, 4 May 1677.

B. KENDALL, SALLEY daughter of William and Peggy Kendall, 4 Sept. 1797 [L:19].

B. KENNAN, THOMAS son of Robert and Ann Kennan, 14 July 1751.

B. KENNAN, MARY daughter of Robert and Anne Kennan, 17 October 1753.

B. KENNAN, FRANCES daughter of John and Sarah Kennan, 29 July 1774.

B. KILBURN, SARAH daughter of Henry and Elizabeth Kilburn, 5 January 1721.

B. KILBURN, THOMAS son of Henry and Elizabeth Kilburn, 29 November 1724.

D. KILBURN, THOMAS   12 March 1724/5.

M. KILLINGSBY, ELIZABETH and Emanuel Conserve, 22 January 1675.

B. KINCHELOE, CORNELIUS son of John and Elizabeth Kincheloe, 8 October 1721.

B. KINCHELOE, DANIEL son of John and Elizabeth Kincheloe, 8 January 1723/4.

B. KING, MARY daughter of Edward and Elizabeth King, 9 March 1692.

B. KING, MARY daughter of William and Mary King, 19 August 1713.

B. KING, ANNE daughter of Julian and Sarah King, 2 June 1716.

D. KING, SUSANNA 10 September 1716.

M. KING, WILLIAM and Mary Piarse, 14 June 1727.

M. KING, JOHN and Elizabeth Dozier, 29 August 1727.

M. KING, ALICE and Thomas Crolorir, 13 October 1729.

B. KIRCUM, MARY daughter of James and Elizabeth Kircum, 12 February 1771.

B. KIRK, ISAAC son of George and Mary Kirk, 27 November 1745.

B. KIRK, MILLERY daughter of George and Mary Kirk, 28 October 1747.

D. KIRK, GEORGE 24 January 1749

B. KIRK, MARY daughter of James and Lurancy Kirk, 12 June 1752.

B. KIRK, JUDITH daughter of John and Winney Kirk, 23 February 1778.

B. KIRK, WILLIAM son of John Kirk, 28 May 1791 [L:19].

B. KIRK, JAMES LEWIS a child baptized for Frances Kirk, 10 May 1793 [L:19].

KIRTLEY   SEE : KURTLEY PAGE 112

B. KIRTLEY, BEHETHALINE daughter of John and Chloe Kirtley, 21 May 1772.

KNASH   SEE : NASH PAGE 135 - 136

B. KNASH, JAMES WINDER son of Winder and Salley Knash, 6 August 1790.

B. KOOKMAN, GEORGE son of William and Elizabeth Kookman, 14 February 1789.

B. KOOKMAN, MOLLEY daughter of William and Elizabeth Kookman, 11 February 1791.

KURTLEY   SEE : KIRTLEY   PAGE   111

D. KURTLEY, JOHN 9 July 1727.

D. KURTLEY, KATHRINE 14 July 1727.

L

D. LADDEN, WILLIAM 23 March 1733.

B. LAMBERT, ANNE daughter of William and Anne Lambert, 14 February 1699.

B. LAMBERT, JOHN son of William and Anne Lambert, 25 November 1702.

B. LAMBERT, ELIZABETH daughter of William and Anne Lambert, 4 December 1704.

B. LAMBERT, WILLIAM son of William and Anne Lambert, 1 August 1711.

B. LAMBERT, RICHARD son of Hugh and Anne Lambert, 14 February 1715.

D. LAMBERT, WILLIAM 6 March 1715.

B. LAMBERT, HUGH son of Hugh and Anne Lambert, 4 May 1718.

B. LAMBERT, WILLIAM son of Hugh and Anne Lambert, 15 June 1720.

B. LAMBERT, JOHN son of Hugh and Ann Lambert, 19 April 1722.

B. LAMBERT, JOHN son of William and Sarah Lambert, 25 January 1723/4.

B. LAMBERT, LEWIS son of Hugh and Anne Lambert, 19 August 1724.

B. LAMBERT, JANE daughter of John and Frances Lambert, 27 November 1724.

B. LAMBERT, WILLIAM son of William and Sarah Lambert, 25 September 1726.

B. LAMBERT, THOMAS son of Hugh and Anne Lambert, 1 October 1726.

B. LAMBERT, MARY daughter of William and Sarah Lambert, 28 January 1727.

B. LAMBERT, COLSTON son of John and Frances Lambert, 2 April 1727.

B. LAMBERT, HUGH son of William and Sarah Lambert, 27 July 1729.

B. LAMBERT, RANA daughter of Hugh and Ann Lambert, 5 August 1729.

B. LAMBERT, ANNE daughter of William and Sarah Lambert, 14 April 1731.

B. LAMBERT, PERCEIS son of John and Frances Lambert, 15 April 1731.

M. LAMBEART, ELIZABETH and Robert Christie, 23 April 1731.

D. LAMBERT, GARVIS 26 October 1732.

B. LAMBERT, SARAH daughter of John and Frances Lambert, 29 September 1733.

D. LAMBERT, JOHN 24 January 1734.

D. LAMBERT, MARY 22 August 1734.

B. LAMBERT, JOSEPH son of John and Frances Lambert, 18 September 1735.

B. LAMBERT, JAMES son of William and Sarah Lambert, 8 April 1736.

B. LAMBERT, JOHN WADE son of John and Frances Lambert, 30 August 1738.

B. LAMBERT, JARVIS son of John and Frances Lambert, 9 March 1740.

D. LAMBERT, FRANCES 27 June 1741.

M. LAMBERT, MILDRED and John Hammock, 26 August 1741.

B. LAMBERT, JOSEPH son of William and Sarah Lambert, 22 September 1741.

B. LAMBERT, JOHN son of William and Mary Lambert, 16 December 1741.

B. LAMBERT, WILLIAM son of William and Mary Lambert, 18 November 1743.

B. LAMBERT, SARAH daughter of William and Sarah Lambert, 28 March 1744.

B. LAMBERT, MARY ANN daughter of William and Mary Lambert, 17 November 1745.

B. LAMBERT, JAMES son of William and Mary Lambert, 1 September 1750.

B. LAMBERT, JOANNA daughter of William and Mary Lambert, 17 January 1756.

B. LAMBERT, MILLY daughter of William and Mary Lambert, 12 February 1757.

B. LANDMAN, JOHN son of William and Catharine Landman, 25 December 1710.

B. LANDMAN, WILLIAM son of William and Kathrine Landman, 15 July 1712.

B. LANDMAN, GEORGE son of William and Kathrine Landman, 4 April 1715.

B. LANDMAN, JAMES son of William and Kathrine Landman, 22 October 1717.

B. LANDMAN, DANIEL son of William and Kathrine Landman, 13 October 1720.

B. LANDMAN, MARY daughter of William and Kathrine Landman, 14 May 1723.

B. LANDMAN, KATHRINE daughter of William and Kathrine Landman, 8 November 1726.

M. LASE, ANN and Daniel Carill, 26 February 1726/7.

B. LAUGHE, ELEANOR daughter of Thomas and Sarah Laughe, 3 September 1713.

B. LAUGHE, THOMAS son of Thomas and Sarah Laughe, 11 April 1722.

D. LAW, JOHN 12 December 1722.

B. LAWSON, CHRISTOPHER son of John and Mary Lawson, 17 June 1716.

B. LAWSON, ELIZABETH daughter of John and Mary Lawson, 17 February 1719.

B. LAWSON, JOANNA and KATHRINE daughters of John and Mary Lawson, 17 March 1721.

B. LAWSON, ANNE daughter of John and Mary Lawson, 22 September 1725.

B. LAWSON, SARAH daughter of Richard and Mary Lawson, 21 February 1727.

M. LAWSON, RICHARD and Mary Harris, 22 September 1727.

D. LAWSON, THOMAS 29 March 1729.

B. LAWSON, THOMAS son of Richard and Mary Lawson, 24 December 1730.

B. LAWSON, LUCY daughter of John and Mary Lawson, 3 March 1731/2.

D. LAWSON, MARY wife of John Lawson, 16 July 1740.

B. LAWSON, BETTY daughter of Christopher and Sarah Lawson, 9 March 1743/4.

B. LAWSON, JOANNA daughter of Christopher and Sarah Lawson, 17 April 1746.

B. LAWSON, EPAPHRODITUS son of Christopher and Sarah Lawson, 23 February 1747/8.

B. LAWSON, CATY daughter of Christopher and Sarah Lawson, 11 April 1751.

B. LAWSON, LUCY daughter of Christopher and Sarah Lawson, 29 January 1756.

B. LAWSON, SARAH daughter of John and Ann Lawson, 27 February 1769.

D. LAWSON, CHRISTOPHER 19 June 1772.

B. LAWSON, PETER a child baptized for Richard Lawson, 12 June 1791 [L:21].

D. LEACH, EDMOND 1 July 1756.

B. LEACOCK, REBECCA BAILEY daughter of Daniel and Nancey Leacock, 9 March 1792 [L:21].

D. LECOOCK, DENNIS 17 March 1730.

B. LEE, WILLIAM son of William and Dorothy Lee, 14 May 1704.

B. LEE, CHARLES son of William and Dorothy Lee, 18 September 1706.

B. LEE, RICHARD son of William and Dorothy Lee, 9 April 1711.

B. LEE, JOHN son of William and Dorothy Lee, 11 October 1713.

D. LEE, THOMAS 4 October 1719.

B. LEE, KATHRINE daughter of Charles and Jane Lee, 18 May 1737.

B. LEE, PETER son of William and Mary Lee, 30 January 1750.

B. LEE, JOHN son of William and Mary Lee, 22 December 1757.

B. LEE, NANCY daughter of Charles and Jane Lee, 26 September 1766.

B. LEE, WILLIAM son of Charles and Jane Lee, 1 November 1770.

B. LEELESS, BETTY daughter of Dennis and Ann Leeless, 4 April 1752.

B. LEGG, RUTH daughter of Thomas and Sarah Legg, 25 March 1721.

D. LEGG, ELIZABETH 7 October 1722.

B. LEGG, FORTUNATUS son of Thomas and Sarah Legg, 6 April 1723.

B. LEGG, SARAH daughter of Thomas and Sarah Legg, 12 October 1725.

B. LEGG, DAVENPORT son of Thomas and Sarah Legg, 8 September 1728.

B. LEGG, GEORGE son of Thomas and Sarah Legg, 18 March 1733.

B. LELAND, BALDWIN MATTHEWS, son of John and Judith Leland, 11 March 1778.

D. LEU, ELIZABETH 5 December 1726.

D. LEU, RICHARD 10 December 1726.

B. LEWIS, ELIZABETH daughter of Edward and Mary Lewis, 8 March 1674.

B. LEWIS, JOANNA daughter of Edward and Mary Lewis, 8 September 1676.

B. LEWIS, BENJAMIN son of Thomas and Mary Lewis, 10 September 1685.

B. LEWIS, THOMAS son of Thomas and Mary Lewis, 5 December 1692.

B. LEWIS, JANE daughter of Edward and Mary Lewis, 30 July 1693.

B. LEWIS, WILLIAM son of Thomas and Mary Lewis, 9 September 1695.

B. LEWIS, LEWIS (sic) son of Edward and Mary Lewis, 30 September 1695,

B. LEWIS, FRANCES daughter of Robert and Sarah Lewis, 13 February 1708,

B. LEWIS, JOYCE daughter of Charles and Mary Lewis, 26 July 1712.

B. LEWIS, JOHN son of Thomas and Joyce Lewis, 7 November 1713.

B. LEWIS, JAMES son of Robert and Sarah Lewis, 23 August 1714.

B. LEWIS, THOMAS son of Thomas and Joyce Lewis, 29 January 1715.

D. LEWIS, JOHN 26 February 1715.

B. LEWIS, KATHRINE daughter of Charles and Mary Lewis, 1 August 1715.

B. LEWIS, EDWARD son of Charles and Mary Lewis, 12 February 1718.

B. LEWIS, CHARLES son of Charles and Mary Lewis, 4 August 1720.

D. LEWIS, THOMAS 7 August 1720.

B. LEWIS, MARY daughter of Thomas and Joyce Lewis, 30 October 1720.

B. LEWIS, BETTY daughter of Charles and Mary Lewis, 5 September 1722.

B. LEWIS, JOHN son of William and Sarah Lewis, 26 December 1724/5.

B. LEWIS, THOMAS son of Thomas and Joyce Lewis, 8 January 1726.

B. LEWIS, ELIZABETH daughter of William and Sarah Lewis, 29 January 1726.

M. LEWIS, ELIZABETH and Zacharias Helford, 21 February 1727/8.

B. LEWIS, MARY daughter of William and Sarah Lewis, 26 January 1728/9.

B. LEWIS, WINIFRED daughter of Thomas and Joyce Lewis, 17 March 1728/9.

D. LEWIS, FRANCES 4 February 1730/1.

B. LEWIS, JESSE son of Thomas and Ann Lewis, 26 March 1731.

B. LEWIS, ANNE daughter of William and Sarah Lewis, 19 June 1731.

B. LEWIS, MARY ANN daughter of Thomas and Ann Lewis, 23 April 1733.

B. LEWIS, BENJAMIN son of Thomas and Ann Lewis, 13 July 1735.

B. LEWIS, MARGARET daughter of William and Sarah Lewis, 24 February 1736.

B. LEWIS, JOANNA daughter of Thomas and Ann Lewis, 14 December 1737.

M. LEWIS, RICHARD and Mary Hix, 3 March 1738.

B. LEWIS, CATY daughter of Thomas and Ann Lewis, 1 October 1740.

B. LEWIS, JOHN son of Willoughby and Henrietta Lewis, 13 December 1751.

B. LEWIS, REBECCA daughter of George and Magdaline Lewis, 11 March 1757.

B. LEWIS, CHARLES NELMS son of James and Alse Lewis, 26 June 1773.

B. LEWIS, ELIZABETH daughter of James and Alse Lewis, 14 February 1775.

B. LEWIS, SAMUEL son of Mary Magdalene Lewis, 29 January 1777.

B. LEWIS, BRIDGETT daughter of James and Alse Lewis, 5 March 1777.

B. LEWIS, ELIZABETH daughter of Jeremiah Lewis, 4 January 1778.

B. LEWIS, ALSE daughter of James and Alse Lewis, 4 September 1779.

B. LEWIS, JAMES son of William and Agatha Lewis, 7 July 1781.

B. LEWIS, HANNAH daughter of James and Alse Lewis, 22 January 1782.

B. LEWIS, NANCY daughter of William and Agenes Lewis, 24 October 1782.

B. LEWIS, FANNEY daughter of James and Alse Lewis, 12 October 1784.

B. LEWIS, JAMES son of James and Alse Lewis, 31 May 1787.

B. LEWIS, CHARLES son of John and Rebeckey Lewis, 25 December 1787.

B. LEWIS, REBECCA daughter of William Lewis, 20 September 1788.

B. LEWIS, JUDA daughter of William and Agga Lewis, 15 February 1792.

B. LEWIS, JOSEPH BRYANT son of William and Agga Lewis, 6 September 1794.

B. LEWIS, SAMUEL GRIFFIN son of William and Agga Lewis, 9 April 1796.

B. LIGHTFOOT, ANN daughter of Daniel and Lisha Lightfoot, 8 May 1743.

B. LIGHTFOOT, WILLIAM son of Daniel and Lisha Lightfoot, 21 July 1745.

B. LIGHTFOOT, BETTY daughter of Daniel and Licia Lightfoot, 5 May 1750.

B. LIGHTFOOT, SAMUEL son of Daniel and Licia Lightfoot, 1 November 1752.

D. LIGHTFOOT, DANIEL 26 March 1755.

B. LIGHTFOOT, THOMAS son of Daniel and Licia Lightfoot, 31 March 1755.

B. LIGHTFOOT, DANIEL son of William and Sarah Lightfoot, 20 February 1768.

B. LIGHTFOOT, ELIZABETH daughter of William and Sarah Lightfoot, 23 June 1769.

B. LIGHTFOOT, WILLIAM son of William and Sarah Lightfoot, 4 May 1771.

B. LIGHTFOOT, ANN daughter of Daniel and Mary Lightfoot, 21 January 1773.

B. LIGHTFOOT, JOHN son of William and Sarah Lightfoot, 19 February 1773.

B... LIGHTFOOT, SARAH daughter of William and Sarah Lightfoot, 1 May 1775.

B. LIGHTFOOT, SAMUEL son of William and Sally Lightfoot, 25 September 1778.

B. LIGHTFOOT, THADDEUS SMITH son of Thomas and Lucy Lightfoot, 19 July 1781.

M. LIGHTFOOT, THOMAS and Million Miskell, 2 October 1789.

B. LIGHTFOOT, LUCY MISKELL daughter of Thomas and Million Lightfoot, 2 Oct.1790.

B. LIGHTFOOT, JOHN NEWMAN BROCKENBROUGH son of Thomas and Million Lightfoot, 6 May 1792. [His birth was twice recorded; see below].

B. LIGHTFOOT, JOHN NEWMAN BROCKENBROUGH son of Thomas and Milley Lightfoot, 6 May 1792 [L:21].

M. LILLIS, MARY and John Nichols, 5 March 1727/8.

B. LINE, WILLIAM ALEXANDER son of Thomas and Susanna Line, 4 Oct. 1797 [L:21].

B. LINKHORN, ANN daughter of John and Ann Linkhorn, 18 October 1717.

M. LINTON, WILLIAM and Mary Freshwater, 31 March 1730.

LITTARELL : LITTERELL   SEE : LUTTREL   PAGE   120

B. LITTARELL, MOSES son of Richard and Mary Ann Littarell, 24 September 1747.

B. LUTTERELL, JUDITH daughter of Richard and Mary Lutterell, 22 December 1751.

B. LITTERELL, MARY daughter of Richard and Mary Litterell, 27 August 1753.

B. LITTERELL, BETTY daughter of James and Frances Litterell, 18 September 1755.

B. LITTERELL, RICHARD son of Richard and Mary Litterell, 2 December 1755.

B. LITTERELL, JOHN son of Richard and Mary Litterell, 28 October 1757.

B. LITTERELL, JOHN HEARTLEY son of William and Elizabeth Litterell, 27 April 1769.

B. LITTERELL, WINIFRED, daughter of William and Elizabeth Litterell, 14 Feb. 1771.

B. LOE, THOMAS son of Judith Loe, 20 April 1719.

B. LOE, WILLIAM son of Charles and Suffica Loe, 22 December 1777.

B. LONG, THOMAS son of Thomas and Mary Long, 4 January 1700.

D. LONG, JAMES 15 February 1726.

B. LONGWITH, WILLIAM son of John and Elizabeth Longwith, 21 July 1792 [L:19].

D. LONGWORTH, MARY 15 April 1719.

B. LONGWORTH, FRANCES daughter of Burgis and Isabel Longworth, 21 Feby 1722/3.

B. LONGWORTH, JOHN son of Burgis and Isabella Longworth, 3 October 1725.

D. LONGWORTH, WILLIAM 9 November 1726.

D. LONGWORTH, ATITHER 23 November 1726.

M. LONGWORTH, MILLISENT and Luke Thornton 2 January 1727/8.

B. LONGWORTH, MARY daughter of Burgas and Isabela Longworth, 22 July 1728.

B. LONGWORTH, BETTY daughter of Burgis and Isabella Longworth, 22 Dec. 1731.

B. LONGWORTH, FANNEY daughter of George Longworth, 29 July 1797 [L:21].

D. LOOK, JOHN 27 July 1726.

B. LOVELACE, ELIZABETH daughter of Charles and Bridgett Lovelace, 19 March 1720.

B. LOVELACE, WILLIAM son of Charles and Bridgett Lovelace, 27 May 1723.

B. LOVELACE, ELIZABETH daughter of Charles and Bridgett Lovelace, 16 April 1725.

B. LOVELACE, RUTH daughter of James and Mary Lovelace, 3 April 1726.

B. LOVELACE, SARAH daughter of Charles and Bridgett Lovelace, 28 April 1727.

B. LOVELACE, MARY daughter of Charles and Bridgett Lovelace, 27 February 1728.

B. LOVELACE, CHARLES son of Charles and Bridget Lovelace, 13 March 1733.

B. LOVELACE, LIDIA daughter of Charles and Bridget Lovelace, 4 October 1735.

B. LOVELACE, JOHN son of Charles and Bridget Lovelace, 7 September 1737.

B. LOVELACE, THOMAS son of Charles and Bridget Lovelace, 27 February 1739.

D. LOVELACE, CHARLES 5 December 1755 aged 59 years.

B. LOVELACE, ELIZABETH daughter of Charles and Joanna Lovelace, 26 Feby 1759.

B. LOVELACE, LUCY daughter of Charles and Joanna Lovelace, 16 February 1761.

B. LOVELACE, JOANNA daughter of Charles and Joanna Lovelace, 16 November 1763.

B. LOVELACE, CHARLES son of Charles and Joanna Lovelace, 3 September 1766.

D. LOVES, ROBERT 4 February 1726.

B. LOWES, MARTHA daughter of Elizabeth Lowes, 30 January 1735.

B. LUCAS, HENRY son of Henry and Jane Lucas, 23 March 1677.

B. LUCAS, FRANCIS son of Henry and Jane Lucas, 1 September 1680.

B. LUCAS, STEPHEN son of Francis and Anne Lucas, 27 July 1713.

D. LUCAS, ANNE 9 December 1715.

B. LUCAS, JOHN son of Francis and Anne Lucas, 27 September 1717.

B. LUCAS, THOMAS son of Francis and Anne Lucas, 19 June 1719.

B. LUCAS, HENRY son of Francis and Anne Lucas, 14 November 1720.

B. LUCAS, THOMAS son of Thomas and Mary Lucas, 26 August 1725.

D. LUCAS, WILLIAM 12 December 1726.

B. LUCAS, FRANCIS son of Thomas and Eleanor Lucas, 2 November 1743.

B. LUCAS, ANN daughter of Thomas and Eleanor Lucas, 25 April 1745.

B. LUCAS, ELEANOR daughter of Thomas and Eleanor Lucas, 3 April 1748.

B. LUCAS, SARAH daughter of Thomas and Eleanor Lucas, 31 October 1749.

LUN : LUNN [SEE : PAGES 61 and 106]

B. LUN, MARY daughter of William and Alicia Lun, 12 September 1673.

B. LUN, ROGER son of William and Alicia Lun, 28 February 1676.

M. LUNN, ALICIA and Edward Jones, 27 August 1679.

LUTTREL   SEE : LITTARELL : LITTERELL   PAGE 118

B. LUTTREL, JAMES son of James and Susanna Luttrel, 10 August 1728.

B. LUTTREL, RICHARD son of James and Susanna Luttrel [not entered; probably circa 1730].

M. LYELL, JONATHAN and Mary Stanfield, 16 October 1729.

B. LYELL, LIDIA daughter of Jonathan and Mary Lyell, 14 December 1730.

B. LYELL, JOHN son of Jonathan and Mary Lyell, 12 February 1732.

B. LYELL, LEEANNAH daughter of Jonathan and Mary Lyell, 3 March 1736.

B. LYELL, ANN daughter of William and Elizabeth Lyell, 20 March 1737.

B. LYELL, JONATHAN son of Jonathan and Mary Lyell, 12 October 1737.

B. LYELL, WINIFRED daughter of Jonathan and Mary Lyell, 18 February 1738.

B. LYELL, ROBERT son of Jonathan and Mary Lyell, 18 May 1739.

D. LYELL, JOHN 24 May 1741.

B. LYELL, JOSEPH son of Jonathan and Mary Lyell, 22 May 1742.

D. LYELL, ELIZABETH daughter of William and Elizabeth Lyell, 19 October 1747.

B. LYELL, ELIZABETH daughter of William and Elizabeth Lyell, 20 June 1751.

D. LYELL, ELIZABETH 20 June 1751.

LYNE   SEE : LINE PAGE 118

MC

D. MC BANE, ANGUISH 8 October 1717.

B. MC CALL, ELIZABETH daughter of Archibald and Katharine McCall, 10 February
    1765. [See: MRC., p. 122; "The Correspondence of Archibald McCall and George
    McCall, 1777-1784" in 73 V 312-353, 425-454.]

B. MC CALLEY, MARY daughter of Charles and Ann McCalley, 18 May 1737.

B. MC CALLEY, JOHN son of Charles and Ann McCalley, 28 March 1740.

B. MC CALLY, ANN daughter of Charles and Ann McCally, 16 June 1745.

B. MC CALLY, CHARLES son of Charles and Ann McCally, 14 July 1749.

B. MC CALLY, HANNAH daughter of Charles and Ann McCally, 9 September 1757.

B. MC CARTY, CATHARINE daughter of Denis and Elizabeth McCarty, 16 April 1678.

B. MC CARTY, DANIEL son of Daniel (sic) and Elizabeth McCarty, 19 March 1680/1.
    [As there was no Daniel McCarty marriageable by 1680, it is my opinion that

this entry is an error and ought to record the birth of Dennis son of Dennis
and Elizabeth (Billington) McCarty. Several authorities, including Hayden,
p.86-87, assure us that Captain Daniel McCarty (1679-1724), son of Dennis
and Elizabeth (Billington) McCarty, was born in 1679 as his tombstone states
he "departed this life the fourth of May 1724 in the forty-fifth year of his
age," so this birth on 19 March 1680/1 could hardly apply to him. Further-
more, both Meade (vol. II, p.173) and Hayden, p.86, indicate Captain Daniel
McCarty had a brother Dennis McCarty but they fail to give any detail of him.
A Dennis McCarty of St.John's Parish, King William County, left a will dated
28January 1733 "and shortly died" says a Caroline County deed dated 2 January
1745/6 by which his executrix, Elizabeth McCarty, sold 200 acres of which he
died possessed in St. Margaret's Parish to her son, William Madison, and re-
cited the title (Caroline County Misc. Papers, #22656, VSL:AD). MRC., p. 123
and 246 records two marriages of Captain Daniel McCarty (1679-1724), the
first on 19 October 1698 when he was about 19. However, as no other Daniel Mc
Carty of this period is recognized in the Richmond County area, two deeds of
record there prove perplexing and seem to indicate he had two wives when yet
in his 'teens as they record the purchase of 160 acres on 27 March 1697 and
the sale of it 15 June 1698 by Daniel McCarty and Barbary, his wife. These
deeds in Richmond County DB#3, p. 3 and 15 recite the title of the land.]

M. MC CARTY, SARAH and Thomas Beale   27 April 1728.

M. MC CARTY, CHRAIN and Mary Mozingo, 30 December 1729.

M. MC CARTY, BILLINGTON and Ann Barber, 16 June 1732.

B. MC CARTY, DANIEL son of Billington and Ann McCarty, 22 October 1733.

B. MC CARTY, BILLINGTON son of Billington and Ann McCarty, 3 October 1736.

B. MC CARTY, THADDEUS son of Billington and Ann McCarty, 1 April 1739.

D. MC CARTY, DANIEL son of Billington and Ann McCarty, 6 August 1739.

B. MC CARTY, CHARLES BARBER son of Billington and Ann McCarty, 23 August 1741.

B. MC CARTY, ANN a bastard daughter of Mary McCarty, 1 March 1743.

D. MC CARTY, ANN   7 January 1753.

B. MC CARTY, DANIEL son of Billington and Elizabeth McCarty, 24 August 1757.

B. MC CARTY, BILLINGTON son of Billington and Elizabeth McCarty, 18 March 1759.

B. MC CARTY, THADDEUS son of Billington and Elizabeth McCarty, 1 September 1763.

B. MC CARTY, FANNY daughter of Charles and Winny McCarty, 3 August 1765.

B. MC CARTY, ELIZABETH DOWNMAN daughter of Billington and Elizabeth McCarty,
    30 March 1768.

B. MC CARTY, TARPLEY son of Charles and Winny McCarty, 16 February 1711.

123

D. MC CARTY, BILLINGTON 24 March 1771.

B. MC CARTY, WINNEY daughter of Charles and Winney McCarty, 4 September 1775.

B. MC CARTY, JOHN son of Charles and Winney McCarty, 7 June 1777.

B. MC CARTY, MILDRED SMITH daughter of Thad.[s] and Mary McCarty, 21 Nov. 1780.

B. MC CARTY, SARAH daughter of Thaddeus and Mary McCarty, 23 December 1782.

B. MC CARTY, ELOISA TOMLIN first daughter of Bartholomew and Elizabeth McCarty, 9 January 1789.

D. MC CAUEY, DANIEL 10 July 1726.

B. MC DANIEL, BILLINGTON and CATHARINE, son and daughter of Timothy and Catharine McDaniel, 5 January 1711. [These twins and their brother John were the children of Timothy McDaniel and his wife née Katherine McCarty (1678-1713), sister of Captain Daniel McCarty; this is proven by these recordings and Richmond County Court Order Book #7, p. 240, 5 March 1717/18. See also MRC., p. 246.]

B. MC DANIEL, JOHN son of John and Anne McDaniel, 17 August 1719.

B. MC DANIEL, JOHN son of John and Anne McDaniel, 22 October 1721.

B. MC DANIEL, JAMES son of Mary McDaniel, 10 November 1728.

B. MC DANIEL, MILLION daughter of Randal and Susanna McDaniel, 20 April 1752.

B. MC DANIEL, SUSANNA daughter of Randal and Susanna McDaniel, 1 May 1755.

B. MC ELLIGOT, WILLIAM son of Thomas and Ann McElligot, 1 March 1770.

D. MC GWIN, SARAH 20 June 1729.

MC INDREE   SEE : MC KINDREE PAGE 124

B. MC INDREE, DOROTHY daughter of James and Mary McIndree, 3 December 1749.

B. MC KAY, WILLIAM son of the Rev. William and Barbara McKay, 31 May 1741.

B. MC KAY, HANNAH daughter of the Rev. William and Barbara McKay, 30 March 1743.

B. MC KAY, JOHN son of the Rev.[d] William and Barbara McKay, 13 February 1744/5.

B. MC KAY, ANN daughter of the Rev. Wm. and Barbara McKay, 1 October 1747.

B. MC KAY, FITZHUGH son of the Rev. Wm. and Barbara McKay, 24 August 1753.

B. MC KAY, KATHARINE daughter of the Rev. Wm. and Barbara McKay, 13 Dec. 1757.

MC KELDO : MC KELDOE : MC KILDOE

B. MC KELDO, JOHN son of James and Eleanor McKeldo, 20 December 1745.

D. MC KILDOE, JOHN son of James and Eleanor McKildoe, 6 October 1747.

B. MC KILDOE, ELIZABETH daughter of James and Eleanor McKildoe, 28 August 1748.

B. MC KILDO , JAMES son of James and Eleanor McKildo, 15 February 1750.

B. MC KELRAY, JESSE son of Bryant and Catharine McKelray, 25 December 1716.

B. MC KENNY , TRAVERSE son of William and Winifred McKenny, 5 September 1734.

B. MC KENNY, WILLIAMACCUS son of William and Winifred McKenny, 9 May 1737.

D. MC KINNY, WILLIAM 19 November 1746.

B. MC KENNY, JANE daughter of John and Elizabeth McKenny, 26 December 1766.

M. MC KENNY, REBECCA and James Samford 3 April 1772.

MC KINDREE   SEE : MC INDREE PAGE 123

B. MC KINDREE, CATY daughter of James and Mary McKindree, 29 October 1753.

MC MAHON : MC MAHONE : MC MAUHAN : MC MOHHANN : MC MALIAN

B. MC MOHHANN, THOMAS son of Arthur and Frances McMohhann, 18 June 1715.

B. MC MOHHANN, ELEANOR daughter of Arthur and Frances McMohhann, 4 May 1718.

B. MC MOHHANN, JOHN son of Arthur and Frances McMohhann, 18 March 1720/1.

B. MC MAUHAN, FRANCES daughter of Arthur and Frances McMauhan, 6 February 1723/4.

D. MC MAUHAN, JOHN 18 February 1724/5.

B. MC MALIAN, MARY daughter of Arthur and Frances Mc Malian, 23 May 1730.

D. MC MAHON, ARTHUR 31 March 1734.

B. MC MAHONE, WINNY a bastard child of Frances McMahone, 6 June 1750.

MC MILLEN : MC MULLIN

B. MC MULLIN, MARY daughter of Stephen and Lettice McMullin, 25 August 1728.

B. MC MILLEN, JANE daughter of Stephen and Lettice McMullin, 26 July 1730.

125

M.   MC MAMARA, JOHN and Katherine Dolphin, 30 April 1730.

D.   MC NEAL, GEORGE   20 July 1722.

B.   MC VAY, GEORGE son of Hugh and Winnefred McVay, 16 September 1711.

B.   MC VAY, HUGH son of Hugh and Winnefred McVay, 20 April 1713.

B.   MC VAY, THOMAS son of Hugh and Winnefred McVay, 5 July 1719.

B.   MC VAY, JOHN son of Hugh and Winnefred McVay, 20 July 1722.

B.   MC VEY, DAVID son of Hugh and Ruth McVey, 20 January 1744.

B.   MC VEY, HUGH son of Hugh and Ruth McVey, 9 May 1747.

B.   MC VEY, JOHN son of Hugh and Ruth McVey, 25 March 1751.

                                    M

M.   MACCAY, HENRY [HARRY] and Elizabeth Gibbs, 19 March 1729/1730.

M.   MACKGYAR, MARY and Phileman Bird, 25 February 1727/8.

M.   MACKGYER, ELIZABETH and Joab Tillery, 27 August 1730.

M.   MAJOR, CATHERINE and John Allen, 15 November 1678.

M.   MAN, ELIZABETH and Richard Draper, 12 September 1680.

B.   MANAY, BARBARA daughter of Hugh and Winnefred Manay, 25 January 1716.

B.   MANEIR, VSHEIR son of John and Anne Maneir, 31 August 1715.

D.   MANIRE, ANNE 6 September 1731.

B.   MANIRE, JOHN son of William and Ann Manire, 18 October 1737.

B.   MANIRE, ELIZABETH daughter of William and Ann Manire, 30 April 1740.

D.   MANRIN, ANNE 15 November 1726.

D.   MANY, WINIFRED 2 March 1726. [SEE ; MANAY PAGE 125]

B.   MARCH, WILLIAM son of William and Elizabeth March, 15 February 1683.

B.   MARCH, JOHN son of William and Elizabeth March, 19 June 1687.

B.   MARCH, JOHN son of William and Leah March, 9 April 1704.

B. MARCH, SARAH daughter of William and Leah March, 11 February 1705.

B. MARCH, ELIZABETH daughter of William and Leah March, 24 May 1708.

B. MARCH, MARY daughter of William and Leah March, 19 December 1711.

D. MARCH, SARAH 15 January 1719.

D. MARCH, JOHN 3 September 1724.

D. MARCHAND, ELIZABETH 8 October 1730.

D. MARCHANT, ESTHER 28 January 1730.

B. MARKS, WILLIAM son of William and Patience Marks, 25 June 1682.

B. MARKS, JOHN and WILLIAM twin sons of James and Sarah Marks, 4 December 1792 [L:23].

B. MARKS, ELIAS son of John and Lettice Marks, 18 August 1793 [L:23].

B. MARKS, REUBIN son of James and Sarah Marks, 14 September 1794 [L:23].

B. MARKS, SUZANNER daughter of James and Frances Marks, 1 November 1799 [L:23].

B. MARMADUKE, SARAH KELLY daughter of Daniel and Rebecca Marmaduke, 20 September 1793 [L:23].

B. MARMADUKE, CHRISTOPHER son of Daniel and Rebecca Marmaduke, 3 June 1795 [L:23].

B. MARSHALL, MARY daughter of Abraham and Thomasin Marshall, 7 January 1699. [See, MRC., p. 32.]

M. MARSY, JOHN and Anne Canes, 11 July 1680.

B. MARSY, ANNE daughter of John and Anne Marsy, 28 December 1681.

B. MARTIN, THOMAS son of Jane Martin, 28 December 1724.

M. MARTIN, NICHOLAS and Frances Petty, 15 November 1728.

B. MASON, MILLION daughter of Thomas and Elizabeth Mason, 10 October 1699.

B. MASON, TRAVERSE son of Nathaniel and Hannah Mason, 20 March 1733.

B. MASON, ELIZABETH daughter of Nathaniel and Hannah Mason, 22 January 1735.

B. MASON, ROBERT son of Nathaniel and Hannah Mason, 15 December 1737.

B. MASON, NATHAN son of Nathaniel and Hannah Mason, 13 February 1748/9.

B. MASON, THOMAS son of Nathaniel and Hannah Mason, 25 November 1751.

B. MASON, WILLIAM son of Nathaniel and Hannah Mason, [not entered] 1755.

B. MASON, CATY daughter of William and Sarah Mason, 5 September 1755.

B. MASSINGS, MICHAEL son of Edward and Margaret Massings, 6 September 1687.

MATHEWS : MATTHEWS : MATHIS

B. MATTHEWS, ANDREWS son of James and Elizabeth Matthews, 24 February 1683/4.

B. MATHEWS, JOANNAH daughter of Robert and Sarah Mathews, 3 April 1718.

B. MATHEWS, SARAH daughter of Robert and Sarah Mathews, 30 April 1720.

B. MATHIS, JOSHUA son of Robert and Sarah Mathis, 19 July 1724.

D. MATHIS, JOSHUA 12 September 1724.

B. MATHEWS, ROBERT son of Robert and Sarah Mathews, 25 April 1727.

B. MATHEWS, THOMAS son of Robert and Sarah Mathews, 14 May 1729.

D. MATHEWS, ROBERT 26 March 1734.

MATHIS SEE : MATHEWS : MATTHEWS : MATHIS PAGE 127

M. MAXWELL, HERBERT and Ann Alverson, 7 October 1729.

MEALEY : MEALY SEE MELIA PAGE 127

B. MEDDOWS, BETTY daughter of Dorothy Meddows, 15 November 1724.

B. MEEKS, JUDITH daughter of Richard and Mary Meeks, 1 April 1730.

M. MEEKS, MARY and Luke Millner, 19 August 1731.

B. MEEKS, ANN daughter of Richard and Mary Meeks, 21 April 1732.

D. MEEKS, MARTHA daughter of Richard and Mary Meeks, 4 October 1740.

B. MEEKS, BETTY daughter of Richard and Mary Meeks, 15 June 1742.

B. MEEKS, THOMAS son of Thomas and Anne Meeks, 19 September 1744 (sic).

B. MEEKS, WILLIAM son of Thomas and Ann Meeks, 21 December 1744 (sic).

B. MELIA, JOHN son of Samuel and Massee Melia, 27 August 1798.

B. MERCY, WINNEFRED daughter of John and Jane Mercy, 2 July 1677.

M. METCALFE, ELIZABETH and Samuel Bailey, 2 December 1725.

B. MIDDLETON, MATTHEW son of William and Elizabeth Middleton, 19 March 1791 [L:23].

D. MILLER, MARGARET 15 January 1722/3.

D. MILLER, MARY 25 August 1723.

D. MILLER, WILLIAM 18 January 1724/5.

D. MILLER, JOHN 23 January 1724/5.

D. MILLER, JOHN 25 August 1726.

D. MILLER, ELIZABETH 24 December 1726.

D. MILLER, BENJAMIN 15 October 1730.

D. MILLOR, ELIZABETH 10 October 1732.

D. MILLER, JOHN 3 June 1744.

D. MILLER, JOAN __ September 1745.

[N.B. The evidence is prima facia that neither the court clerks of Richmond County or the transcriber of NFPR were meticulous and therefore various similiar names must be carefully scrutinized. The surnames Mil(1)ner and Miller have been carelessly recorded and only by the closest examiniation of both the parochial and court records can they be separated. WB#5, p. 466, 5 Nov. 1744, records the will of John Miller and on the following page the inventory of the estate of John Millner is recorded per order of court 5 Nov. 1744. COB#11, p. 421, 5 Nov. 1744 indicates the will of John Milner was proven in court and his estate ordered to be appraised in the usual manner. It is obvious some of these Millers were actually Mil(1)ners.]

B. MILLER, THOMAS son of Jacob and Aimey Miller, 13 March 1794 [L:23].

B. MILLER, ANNE daughter of Jacob and Aimey Miller, 26 February 1797 [L:23].

MILLNER : MILNER [See: MILLER recordings above and comment.]

B. MILNER, LUKE son of John and Elizabeth Milner, 5 September 1708.

B. MILNER, BENJAMIN son of John and Elizabeth Milner, 27 January 1710.

B. MILNER, JOHN son of John and Elizabeth Milner, 25 March 1718.

B. MILNER, BETTY daughter of William and Mary Milner, 21 August 1723.

B. MILNER, WINIFRED daughter of William and Judith Milner, 28 January 1724/5.

M. MILLNER, JUDITH and Cobham Gathings, 26 February 1726/7.

M. MILLNER, BENJAMIN and Frances Glascock, 13 July 1730.

B. MILNER, BENJAMIN son of Benjamin and Frances Milner, 25 December 1730.

M. MILLNER, LUKE and Mary Meeks, 19 August 1731.

B. MILNER, JOHN son of Luke and Mary Milner, 9 July 1732.

B. MILLNER, LUKE son of Luke and Mary Millner, 31 December 1734.

B. MILLNER, DOROTHY daughter of Luke and Mary Millner, 16 February 1736.

B. MILLNER, MARK son of Luke and Mary Millner, 18 February 1739.

B. MILLNER, ELIZABETH daughter of Luke and Mary Millner, 16 November 1742.

B. MILLNER, ANN daughter of Luke and Mary Millner, 25 February 1744.

B. MILNER, LUKE son of John and Margaret Milner, 17 September 1750.

D. MILLNER, LUKE 28 January 1753.

B. MILNER, JOHN son of John and Margaret Milner, 16 February 1754.

B. MILNER, BEVERLY son of John and Margaret Milner, 2 March 1757.

B. MILNER, ROBERT DUDLEY son of John and Margaret Milner, 14 March 1762.

B. MILNER, BETTY daughter of Mark and Sarah Milner, 3 November 1762.

B. MILLS, ELIZABETH daughter to William Mills, 26 January 1679.

B. MILLS, ELIZABETH daughter of John and Esther Mills, 9 August 1682.

B. MILLS, GEORGE son of John and Mary Mills, 4 March 1719.

D. MILLS, GEORGE [not entered] January 1721.

B. MILLS, MILLS (sic) daughter of John and Mary Mills, 27 September 1722.

B. MILLS, ANNE daughter of Thomas and Mary Mills, 9 June 1726.

M. MILLS, MARY and William Dasey, 8 January 1727/8.

B. MILTON, ANNE daughter of Richard and Anne Milton, 31 August 1720.

B. MILTON, ELIZABETH daughter of Richard and Anne Milton, 26 March 1723.

B. MILTON, SARAH daughter of Richard Milton, 18 May 1728.

B. MINTY, ABIGAL daughter of Edward and Margaret Minty, 29 February 1719.

B. MINTY, MARGARET daughter of Edward and Margaret Minty, 22 June 1723.

B. MINTY, EDWARD son of Edward and Margaret Minty, 24 September 1725.

D. MINTY, EDWARD 27 December 1726.

B. MISKELL, JOHN son of William and Elizabeth Miskell, 6 February 1714.

D. MISKELL, WILLIAM JUN:^R^ 30 August 1715.

B. MISKELL, GEORGE son of William and Elizabeth Miskell, 12 November 1716.

D. MISKELL, THOMAS 20 February 1718.

D. MISKELL, CHARLES 20 May 1719.

D. MISKELL, WILLIAM SEN:^R^ 23 March 1720.

B. MISKELL, REBECCAH daughter of Henry and Winifred Miskell, 20 January 1724/5.

B. MISKELL, DORCAS daughter of Henry and Winifred Miskell, 26 June 1726.

B. MISKELL, JONATHAN son of Henry and Winifred Miskell, 2 March 1728.

B. MISKELL, WILLIAM son of Henry and Winifred Miskell, 5 March 1729.

B. MISKELL, NEWMAN son of Henry and Winifred Miskell, 21 January 1731.

B. MISKELL, DANIEL son of Henry and Winifred Miskell, 3 March 1733.

B. MISKELL, RACHEL daughter of Henry and Winifred Miskell, 12 January 1735.

B. MISKELL, DAVID son of Henry and Winifred Miskell, 24 October 1737.

B. MISKELL, BETTY daughter of Henry and Winifred Miskell, 20 December 1739.

B. MISKELL, WINIFRED daughter of Henry and Winifred Miskell, 20 July 1741.

B. MISKELL, JEREMIAH son of Henry and Winifred Miskell, 5 March 1742.

D. MISKELL, JOHN 18 May 1744.

B. MISKELL, METCALFE and ALICE twins of Henry and Winifred Miskell, 4 February 1745.

D. MISKELL, JONATHAN 8 September 1745.

B. MISKELL, AUSTIN son of Henry and Winifred Miskell, 19 February 1747.

D. MISKELL, AUSTIN son of Henry and Winifred Miskell, 4 March 1747.

D. MISKELL, METCALFE son of Henry and Winifred Miskell, 20 July 1748.

B. MISKELL, WILLIAM son of George and Cathrine Miskell, 1 March 1749.

B. MISKELL, MILLION daughter of Henry and Winifred Miskell, 25 June 1749.

B. MISKELL, SARAH daughter of Henry and Winifred Miskell, 28 May 1753.

B. MISKELL, GEORGE son of George and Magdalene Miskell [not entered] Dec. 1753.

B. MISKELL, HENRY son of George and Magdaline Miskell, 5 July 1756.

B. MISKELL, JOHN son of Daniel and Ann Miskell, 10 February 1757.

B. MISKELL, RACHEL daughter of David and Elizabeth Miskell, 28 December 1758.

B. MISKELL, FRANCES daughter of William and Betty Miskell, 10 September 1759.

B. MISKELL, JONATHAN son of Daniel and Ann Miskell, 24 September 1759.

B. MISKELL, HENRY and JOHN twins of David and Elizabeth Miskell, 12 July 1760.

B. MISKELL, PEGGY daughter of William and Betty Miskell, 4 February 1762.

D. MISKELL, DAVID 4 February 1764.

B. MISKELL, WILLIAM son of William and Betty Miskell, 27 October 1765.

D. MISKELL, WINIFRED [day not entered] January 1766.

B. MISKELL, AUSTIN son of William and Betty Miskell, 1 September 1772.

B. MISKELL, SUSANNAH daughter of Charles and Nancy Miskell, 12 April 1778.

B. MISKELL, SALLY daughter of William and Winny Miskell, 28 May 1780.

B. MISKELL, THOMAS son of Charles and Ann Miskell, 2 November 1781.

B. MISKELL, WINNEFRED daughter of Charles and Ann Miskell, 21 March 1783.

B. MISKELL, WILLIAM son of William and Winney Miskell, 24 October 1786.

B. MISKELL, THOMAS son of Charles and Ann Miskell, 21 March 1787.

B. MISKELL, NEWMAN son of George and Sarah Miskell, 20 November 1787.

M. MISKELL, MILLION and Thomas Lightfoot, 2 October 1789.

B. MISKELL, SARAH daughter of George and Sarah Miskell, 25 February 1790.

B. MISKELL, LUCY daughter of George and Sarah Miskell, 14 November 1791.

B. MISKELL, CATY daughter of George and Sara Miskell, 29 October 1793.

B. MISKELL, CATYAN LAURINDA SMITH daughter of Henry and Hannah Miskell, 27 April 1802.

D. MITCHELL, ELIZABETH 9 December 1722.

D. MITCHELL, KATHRINE 12 December 1722.

D. MITCHELL, MARY 4 April 1750.

B. MITCHEL , WINNY BROKS daughter of Edmon and Vilet Mitchel, 7 January 1785.

B. MITCHEL , WILLIAM son of Edmon and Vilet Mitchel, 4 January 1788.

B. MOCAY, SARAH daughter of Henry and Elizabeth Mocay, 22 July 1731.

D. MOGOMERY, ESTHER 7 June 1727.

D. MONGHON, ROBERT 14 October 1726.

M. MOODY, WILLIAM and Jane Griffin, 23 November 1725.

MOORE : MORE

B. MOORE, KATHRINE daughter of Thomas and Frances Moore, 25 November 1717.

B. MOORE, BETTY daughter of Thomas and Frances Moore, 7 August 1719.

D. MORE , WILLIAM 17 April 1726.

B. MOORE, WILLIAM son of Michael and Alice Moore, 27 March 1744.

B. MOORE, DANIEL son of John and Rebecca Moore, 20 August 1780.

B. MORE , JOHN   son of John More, 25 May 1788.

B. MOORE, SALLY daughter of Reubin and Sally Moore, 11 February 1793 [L:23].

B. MOORE, [not entered], a child of Garland Moore, 31 May 1794 [L:23].

B. MORGAN, CHARLES son of Anthony and Elizabeth Morgan, 28 September 1680.

B. MORGAN, BRIDGETT daughter of Anthony and Elizabeth Morgan, 14 Sept.^{r}- 1682.

B. MORGAN, ANNY daughter of Anthony and Elizabeth Morgan, 14 March 1684.

B. MORGAN, BARBARA daughter of John and Barbara Morgan, 23 July 1686.

B. MORGAN, ANTHONY son of Anthony and Elizabeth Morgan, 20 November 1686.

B. MORGAN, JOHN son of John and Barbara Morgan, 27 December 1687.

B. MORGAN, ELIZABETH daughter of William and Anne Morgan, 20 March 1691.

B. MORGAN, WILLIAM son of William and Anne Morgan, 2 May 1715.

B. MORGAN, THOMAS son of William and Anne Morgan, 1 June 1716.

B.   MORGAN, ANNE daughter of William and Elizabeth Morgan, 20 September 1718.

B.   MORGAN, LAMBERT son of William and Elizabeth Morgan, 11 May 1720.

B.   MORGAN, JOSHUA son of William and Elizabeth Morgan, 10 Nov. 1720 (sic).

B.   MORGAN, BETTY daughter of William and Elizabeth Morgan, 21 May 1722.

B.   MORGAN, LEANNAH daughter of William and Elizabeth Morgan, 14 August 1722.

B.   MORGAN, JOYCE daughter of William and Elizabeth Morgan, 24 January 1724.

B.   MORGAN, JUDITH daughter of William and Elizabeth Morgan, 5 October 1724.

D.   MORGAN, LORANE 4 December 1726.

D.   MORGAÑ, WILLIAM 12 December 1726.

B.   MORGAN, ELIZABETH daughter of William and Elizabeth Morgan, 24 Feby 1727.

D.   MORGAN, WILLIAM 28 April 1727.

B.   MORGAN, PETER son of David and Winifred Morgan, 26 March 1728.

M.   MORGAN, ELIZABETH and Joseph Hall, 21 April 1729.

M.   MORGAN, JOHN and Elizabeth Hammock, 21 August 1729.

M.   MORGAN, ELIZABETH and William Askins, 23 December 1729.

B.   MORGAN, DAVID son of Andrew and Sarah Morgan, 3 February 1730.

M.   MORGAN, ANDREW and Sarah Dawson, 13 November 1730.

B.   MORGAN, WILLIAM son of John and Elizabeth Morgan, 10 December 1730.

B.   MORGAN, ANDREW son of Andrew and Sarah Morgan, 16 March 1732.

B.   MORGAN, JOHN son of John and Elizabeth Morgan, 13 November 1732.

D.   MORGAN, ANDREW 29 June 1734.

B.   MORGAN, DANIEL son of Andrew and Sarah Morgan, 25 June 1735.

B.   MORGAN, NANNY daughter of John and Elizabeth Morgan, 11 September 1735.

B.   MORGAN, DAVID son of David and Winnifred Morgan, 25 August 1736.

B.   MORGAN, MARGARET daughter of Andrew and Sarah Morgan, 5 February 1737.

B.   MORGAN, ELIZABETH SAMFORD daughter of Lamberth and Mafy Morgan, 15 June 1744.

B. MORGAN, WINIFRED a bastard child of Abigal Morgan, 14 March 1750.

B. MORGAN, WINNY daughter of Lambert and Mary Morgan, 11 April 1750.

B. MORGAN, BENJAMIN son of Andrew and Sarah Morgan, 11 February 1753.

B. MORGAN, ANN daughter of Lambert and Mary Morgan, 17 November 1753.

B. MORGAN, SAMUEL son of Lambert and Mary Morgan, 22 March 1755.

B. MORGAN, ELIZABETH daughter of Lambert and Mary Morgan, 19 February 1758.

B. MORGAN, POLLY daughter of Andrew and Winifred Morgan, 12 July 1791 [L:23].

B. MORRIS, ELIZABETH daughter of Edward and Elizabeth Morris, 5 August 1688.

B. MORRIS, TAMAI daughter of John and Anne Morris, 1 June 1725 (sic).

B. MORRIS, ELIZABETH daughter of John and Anne Morris, 25 August 1725 (sic).

M. MORRIS, ANN and Thomas Hammond, 9 June 1726.

M. MORRIS, EDWARD and Elizabeth Hammond, 25 May 1727.

B. MORRIS, DORCAS daughter of Edward and Elizabeth Morris, 20 April 1728.

B. MORRIS, WINIFRED daughter of Edward and Elizabeth Morris, 24 April 1731.

B. MORRIS, HAMMOND son of Edward and Elizabeth Morris, 5 December 1733.

B. MORRIS, ANN daughter of Edward and Elizabeth Morris, 23 April 1739.

B. MORRIS, JESSE son of Edward Morris, 10 October 1742.

B. MORRIS, WILLIAM SON OF Hammond and Mary Morris, 28 February 1754.

E. MORRIS, JESSE son of Hammond and Mary Morris, 7 March 1756.

B. MORRIS, TRAVERSE son of Hammond and Mary Morris, 12 June 1758.

B. MORRIS, THOMAS LYNE son of Simon and Susanna Morris, 19 January 1795 [L:23].

B. MORRIS, POLLEY daughter of Simon and Susanna Morris, 23 February 1798 [L:23].

B. MORRIS, WILLIAM KELLY son of John and Mahala Morris, 16 September 1799 [L:23].

M. MORRISON, JOSEPH and Margaret Scurlock, 9 December 1739.

MORROW : MUROW

M. MORROW, ANDREW and Deborah Sherlock, 1 October 1728.

B.   MUROW, MARY ANN daughter of Andrew and Deborah Murow, 22 April 1730.
[See, MRC., p. 164.]

B.   MORTON, WILLIAM STROTHER son of John and Margaret Morton, 28 November 1794
[L:23].

B.   MOSS, CHARLOTTE daughter of John and Sarah Moss, 18 February [not entered;
circa 1792; L:23.]

B.   MOTHERSHEAD, JAMES son of John and Milley Mothershead, 2 September 1791.

B.   MOTHERSHEAD, HENRY son of Nathaniel and Ann Mothershead, 22 December 1793
[L:23].

M.   MOUNTJOY, SARAH and John Jones, 30 November 1725.

M.   MOUNTJOY, ALVIN and Ellin Thornton, 3 May 1728.

M.   MOZINGO, SARAH and John Chanler, 25 August 1729.

M.   MOZINGO, MARY and Chrain McCarty, 30 December 1729.

M.   MOZINGO, MARGARET and Francis Chandler, 18 July 1731.

B.   MOZINGO, WINNEY daughter of Edward and Betsey Mozingo, 28 February 1793,
[L:23].

B.   MOZINGO, PIERCE son of John and Eleanor Mozingo, 26 August 1793 [L:23].

B.   MOZINGO, PEGGY PIERCE daughter of Edward and Betsey Mozingo, 22 March 1796
[L:23].

B.   MUCHEROY, THOMAS son of Adam and Isabel Mucheroy, 27 July 1732.

B.   MUCKELRY, ADAM son of Adam Muckelry, 8 April 1730.

MUROW   SEE : MORROW   PAGES 134 - 135

B.   MURPHY, WINIFRED daughter of James and Elizabeth Murphy, 7 October 1723.

B.   MURPHY, ANNE daughter of James and Elizabeth Murphy, 2 October 1725.

N

NASH   SEE : KNASH PAGE 111

B.   NASH, ELIZABETH daughter of Thomas and Agathy Nash, 6 August 1725.

B.   NASH, THOMAS son of Thomas and Agathy Nash, 3 January 1726.

B.   NASH, SOLOMAN son of William and Ann Nash, 8 April 1726.

D. NASH, ELIZABETH 3 November 1726.

D. NASH, ANNE 12 November 1726.

D. NASH, JOHN 15 November 1726.

M. NASH, WILLIAM and Margaret Brian, 30 May 1729.

B. NASH, JOHN son of Thomas and Agathy Nash, 2 December 1729.

M. NASH, ANN and Thomas Barber, 28 January 1729/30.

B. NASH, JOHN son of William and Mary Nash, 20 April 1730.

D. NASH, WILLIAM [day not entered] October 1732.

M. NASH, HANNAH and Richard Nash, 30 October 1743.

M. NASH, RICHARD and Hannah Nash, 30 October 1743.

D. NASH, THOMAS 29 November 1748.

B. NASH, ELIZABETH daughter of William and Judith Nash, 20 October 1751.

B. NASH, PITMAN and HANNAH twins of Richard and Hannah Nash, 11 March 1752.

B. NASH, AGATHA daughter of William and Judith Nash, 7 January 1754.

B. NASH, THADDEUS son of George and Sarah Nash, 29 November 1775.

B. NASH, EPPY son of Pittman and Milley Nash, 29 June 1778.

B. NASH, JEREMIAH son of John and Mary Nash, 22 August 1781.

B. NASH, HANNAH daughter of George and Lucy Nash, 2 October 1781.

B. NASH, SALLY daughter of Pitman and Betty Nash, 15 January 1783.

B. NASH, SALLY daughter of George and Lucy Nash, 8 June 1787.

B. NASH, HENRY CARPENTER son of James and Jane Nash, 6 June 1791, [L:25].

B. NASH, WINIFRED THORNTON daughter of George Nash, 18 Februrary 1792 [L:25].

B. NASH, PEGGY daughter of James and Jane Nash, 15 November 1794 [L:25].

B. NASH, SUCKEY daughter of John and Molly Nash, 26 November 1794 [L:25].

B. NASH, VINCENT CARPENTER son of John and Molley Nash, 28 August 1797 [L:25].

B. NASH, JAMES KELLY son of William and Elizabeth Nash, 17 November 1797 [L:25]

B. NASH, SAMUEL son of James and Jane Nash, 5 March 1798 [L:25].

B. NAYLOR, ELIZABETH daughter of John and Mary Naylor, 25 September 1712.

B. NAYLOR, HANNAH daughter of John and Mary Naylor, 4 February 1715.

D. NAYLOR, MARY 16 September 1717.

B. NAYLOR, ANNE daughter of John and Anne Naylor, 20 February 1720.

D. NAYLOR, ANNE 27 August 1722.

B. NAYLOR, JOYCE 2 December 1722.

D. NAYLOR, JOYCE 3 October 1725.

B. NEAL, MARY daughter of Owen and Sarah Neal, 6 July 1716.

B. NEAL, JOHN son of Charles and Ann Neal, 26 December 1716.

M. NEIVES, SARAH and Dennis Rian, 24 October 1729.

M. NELL, ELIZABETH and Malachi Dunaway, 23 January 1726/7.

M. NELMS, JOSHUA and Sarah Northen, 12 February 1728/9.

M. NELSON, ALEXANDER and Prudence Pettey, 8 January 1729/30.

D. NELSON, WILLIAM 15 January 1730.

B. NELSON, WILLIAM son of Alexander and Prudence Nelson, 21 October 1730.

B. NETHERCUTT, ROBERT son of John and Mary Nethercutt, 6 August 1686.

B. NETHERCUTT, JOHN son of John and Mary Nethercutt, 2 September 1687.

M. NEWGENT, DOMINICK and Margaret Durham, 2 December 1729.

B. NEWGENT, ELIZABETH daughter of Dominick and Margaret Newgent, 22 June 1732.

B. NEWGENT, SARAHELLEN, daughter of Dominick and Margaret Newgent, 6 Sept. 1733.

B. NEWGENT, DUDLEY son of Dominick and Margaret Newgent, 9 March 1737.

B. NEWGENT, FRANCES daughter of Dominick and Margaret Newgent, 1 January 1739.

D. NEWGENT, ELIZABETH daughter of Dominick and Margaret Newgent, 20 Sept. 1739.

B. NEWGENT, THOMAS son of Dominick and Margaret Newgent, 18 April 1753.

B. NUGIENT, BETSY daughter of Arthur and Letty Nugient, 6 July 1781.

B. NEWMAN, BETSEY CRASH daughter of George and Alice Newman, 11 December 1792 [L:25].

B. NEWMAN, DELPHA JENKINS daughter of John and Susanna Newman, 5 July 1793 [L:25].

B. NEWMAN, JOSEPH son of George and Ailcey Newman, 1 July 1795 [L:25].

B. NEWMAN, MARTHA PHILISHA daughter of John and Susanna Newman, 10 March 1797 [L:25].

B. NEWMAN, JAMES a base born child of Fanney Newman, 6 March 1799 [L:25].

B. NEWSOM, ANN daughter of John and Elizabeth Newsom, 25 September 1744.

B. NEWSOM, ROBERT son of John and Elizabeth Newsom, 1 April 1748.

B. NEWSOM, HANNAH daughter of John and Elizabeth Newsom, 1 March 1748/9.

B. NEWSOM, ROBERT son of Jeremiah and Rachel Newsom, 2 November 1753.

B. NEASOM, RACHEL DAVENPORT, daughter of Robert and Caty Neasom, 29 April 1781.

B. NEASOME, EPAPHRODITUS LAWSON son of Robert and Caty Neasome, 18 March 1786.

B. NEWSOM, CATY LAWSON son of Robert and Caty Newsom, 5 September 1788.

B. NEWTON, THOMAS son of Willoughby and Sarah Newton, 20 December 1723/4.

B. NEWTON, ELIZABETH daughter of Henry and Elizabeth Newton, 30 Sept. 1726.

B. NEWTON, REBECCAH daughter of Willoughby and Sarah Newton, 6 October 1726.

D. NICHOLS, JOHN 25 March 1714.

B. NICHOLS, WINNEFRED daughter of John and Elizabeth Nichols, 8 February 1721.

B. NICHOLS, SARAH daughter of Charles and Eleanor Nichols, 28 February 1721.

D. NICHOLS, SARAH 28 August 1723.

B. NICHOLS, JOHN son of Charles and Eleanor Nichols, 29 July 1724.

B. NICHOLS, LETTICE daughter of Charles and Eleanor Nichols, 15 October 1726.

D. NICHOLS, ELEANOR 15 November 1726.

B. NICHOLS, CHARLES son of Charles and Ann Nichols, 12 March 1727 [? 1727/8 ?].

M. NICHOLS, CHARLES and Ann Davis, 17 August 1727.

M. NICHOLS, JOHN and Mary Lillis, 5 March 1727/8.

D. NICHOLS, LETTIS 27 October 1731.

D. NICHOLS, CHARLES 8 January 1738.

M. NICHOLS, MARY and William Raven, 30 November 1738.

B. NICHOLS, AGNES daughter of Charles and Jemima Nichols, 28 September 1749.

B. NICHOLS, ELEANOR daughter of John and Eleanor Nichols, 28 September 1750.

B. NICHOLS, GEORGE son of Charles and Jemima Nichols, 18 February 1752.

B. NICHOLS, CHARLES and JEMIMA twins of Charles and Jemima Nichols, 16 February 1755.

B. NICKEN, LUCY daughter of Susannah Nicken, 19 April 1791.

B. NORTHEN, SARAH daughter of Edm. and Elizabeth Northen, 22 July 1713.

B. NORTHEN, EDMUND son of Edm. and Elizabeth Northen, 2 August 1715.

B. NORTHEN, WILLIAM son of Edm. and Elizabeth Northen, 30 March 1719.

D. NORTHEN, SAMUEL 20 November 1726.

M. NORTHEN, SARAH and Joshua Nelms, 12 February 1728/9.

B. NORTHEN, JEMIMA a bastard child of Elizabeth Northen, 14 September 1738.

B. NORTHEN, ABIGAL daughter of William and Abigal Northen, 17 March 1748.

B. NORTHEN, JAMES son of Peter and Jane Northen, 7 January 1774.

B. NORTHEN, EDWARD JONES son of George and Margaret Northen, 3 March 1774.

B. NORTHEN, LUCY BARBER daughter of George and Margaret Northen, 1 February 1776.

B. NORTHEN, GEORGE son of George and Peggy Northen, 22 December 1779.

B. NORTHEN, EDMUND son of George and Margaret Northen, 2 January 1782.

B. NORTHEN, PETER SMITH son of Peter and Jenny Northen, 23 March 1785.

B. NORTHEN, BARBARY BAKER daughter of George and Margaret Northen, 2 Jan.y 1787.

B. NORTHEN, SAMUEL son of George and Margaret Northen, 28 January 1789.

B. NORTHEN, POLLY daughter of George and Margaret Northen, 4 June 1792.

B.   NORTON, ANNE daughter of Nathaniel and Anne Norton, 10 July 1721.

B.   NORTON, WILLIAM son of Nathaniel and Anne Norton, 11 March 1723/4.

B.   NORTON, SARAH daughter of Nathaniel and Anne Norton, 23 November 1726.

B.   NORWOOD, NANCY daughter of John and Ann Norwood, 8 October 1770.

O

B.   OGLEBE, ELIZABETH daughter of John and Margery Oglebe, 26 June 1719.

B.   OGLEBE, WILLIAM son of John and Margery Oglebe, 9 September 1721.

B.   OGLEBE, RUTH daughter of John and Marg Oglebe, 2 July 1725.

D.   OGLEBE, WILLIAM 21 March 1726/7.

B.   OGLEBY, daughter of John and Margery Ogleby, 8 December 1732.

     OLDHAM   SEE : DUM [!] PAGE 55

B.   OLDHAM, MARGARET daughter of John and Sarah Oldham, 6 January 1709.

B.   OLDHAM, ELIZABETH daughter of Hannah Oldham, 1 September 1711.

B.   OLDHAM, MARY daughter of John and Sarah Oldham, 25 June 1712.

B.   OLDHAM, ELIZABETH daughter of John and Sarah Oldham, 12 May 1715.

B.   OLDHAM, JOHN son of James and Junefred Oldham, 30 June 1715.

B.   OLDHAM, SARAH daughter of John Oldham, 24 January 1718.

B.   OLDHAM, BETTY daughter of James and Junefred Oldham, 29 May 1718.

B.   OLDHAM, SARAH daughter of John and Sarah Oldham, 4 December 1718.

B.   OLDHAM, NANNE daughter of James and Junefred Oldham, 1 July 1720.

B.   OLDHAM, JANE daughter of John and Sarah Oldham, 6 October 1721.

B.   OLDHAM, JAMES son of James and Junefred Oldham, 13 November 1722.

M.   OLDHAM, PETER and Rebecca Alverson, 17 February 1728/7 (sic).

D.   OLDHAM, WILLIAM 23 October 1728.

B.   OLDHAM, WILLIAM son of William and Priscilla Oldham, 3 November 1728.

M. OLDHAM, PRISCILLA and Henry Williams, 22 January 1729/30.

M. OLDHAM, MARGARET and John Connelly, 26 February 1729/30.

B. DUM (sic), KATHRINE, daughter of Peter and Rebeccah Dum, 11 September 1730.

D. OLDHAM, REBECCAH 19 September 1730.

D. OLDHAM, JAMES 20 February 1754.

B. OLDHAM, WILLIAM son of William and Mary Oldham, 4 September 1770.

B. OLIFF, PEGGY MUSE daughter of George and Elizabeth Oliff, 22 May 1798 [L:27].

B. OLIFFE, MOLLY daughter of James and Anne Oliffe, 3 April 1793 [L:27].

B. OLIVER, WILLIAM son of William and Elizabeth Oliver, 8 October 1766.

M. O'NEAL, DANIEL and Elizabeth Hading, 10 May 1674.

B. O'NEAL, OWIN son of James and Jane O'Neal, 19 March 1732.

D. OSBORNE, JOHN 3 November 1726.

B. OSBORNE, JOHN son of Thomas and Mary Osborne, 26 November 1726.

D. OSBORNE, MARY 29 November 1726.

B. OSBORNE, MARY daughter of Thomas and Margaret Osborne, 24 November 1727 (sic).

B. OSBORNE, MARY daughter of Thomas and Mary Osborne, 24 November 1727 (sic).

M. OSBORNE, THOMAS and Frances Smith, 11 February 1726/7.

B. OSBORNE, ANNE daughter of Thomas and Mary Osborne, 18 March 1729.

OWENS : OWINS

D. OWINS, EDWARD 9 April 1729.

B. OWINS, BETTY daughter of Benjamin and Bridget Owins, 25 October 1748.

B. OWENS, GEORGE son of Benjamin and Bridget Owens, 24 December 1750.

B. OWENS, WINIFRED daughter of Benjamin and Bridget Owens, 29 October 1752.

B. OWENS, WILLIAM son of Benjamin and Bridget Owens, 7 January 1755.

B. OWENS, LUCY daughter of Benjamin and Bridget Owens, 22 February 1757.

P

PACK   SEE : PECK   PAGE 145

B. PACK, PACK (sic) daughter of John and Mary Pack, 11 October 1703.

PACKET : PACKETT

B. PACKET, JEREMIAH son of John and Elizabeth Packet, 17 August 1720.

B. PACKET, ELIZABETH daughter of John and Elizabeth Packet, 5 September 1722.

B. PACKET, MARY daughter of Gabriel and Kathrine Packet, 21 April 1727.

B. PACKETT, PRESSLEY son of John and Elizabeth Packett, 6 July 1727.

M. PACKET, ELIZABETH and Charles Bragg, 11 June 1728.

D. PACKETT, PRESLEY 20 September 1728.

B. PACKETT, SARAH daughter of John and Elizabeth Packett, 10 December 1729.

B. PACKETT, KATHRINE daughter of Gabriel and Kathrine Packett, 30 August 1730.

D. PACKETT, ELIZABETH 19 January 1730/1.

B. PAG, JENNNER [? JEMIMA ?] 17 August 1718 [no parents entered].

PALLEY   SEE : POLLEY   PAGE 149

D. PALLEY, JOHN 18 January 1743.

B. PALLEY, FRANCES daughter of John and Frances Palley, 25 August 1744.

B. PALMER, ELIZABETH daughter of Robert and Prudence Palmer, 10 November 1699.

B. PALMER, ESTHER daughter of Robert and Prudence Palmer, 20 September 1701.

B. PALMER, JOSEPH son of Robert and Prudence Palmer, 23 June 1704.

B. PALMER, PARMENAS and PRUDENCE son and daughter of Robert and Martha Palmer, 27 May 1719.

B. PALMER, TRUMAN son of Robert and Martha Palmer, 28 April 1721.

B. PALMER, PAUL son of Nathaniel and Sarah Palmer, 28 July 1721.

B. PALMER, KATHARINE daughter of Nathaniel and Sarah Palmer, 15 December 1722.

B. PALMER, WILLIAM son of Robert and Martha Palmer, 20 December 1723.

D. PALMER, WILLIAM 20 December 1723.

B. PALMER, THOMAS son of Robert and Martha Palmer, 12 October 1725.

B. PALMER, WILLIAM son of Robert and Martha Palmer, 18 February 1726.

D. PALMER, JOHN 3 September 1730.

M. PALMER, JANEY and George Blewford, 26 January 1730/1.

D. PALMER, ROBERT 12 March 1732.

B. PALMER, RAWLEIGH son of Joseph and Ann Palmer, 24 November 1733.

B. PALMER, ISAAC son of Joseph and Ann Palmer, 23 February 1738.

M. PALMER, PARMENUS and Mary Ann Draper, 30 March 1741.

B. PALMER, JOHN son of Joseph and Ann Palmer, 20 October 1741.

M. PALMER, TRUMAN and Ann Hanes, 31 October 1743.

D. PALMER, MARY 15 November 1743.

B. PALMER, WILLIAM son of Joseph and Ann Palmer, 27 May 1745.

B. PALMER, THOMAS son of Permenas and Mary Palmer, 9 November 1745.

B. PALMER, ROBERT son of Joseph and Ann Palmer, 27 August 1748.

D. PALMER, JOSEPH 24 March 1749.

B. PALMER, JOSEPH son of Rawleigh and Eleanor Palmer, 27 February 1757.

B. PALMER, JOHN son of William and Elizabeth Palmer, 27 April 1770.

B. PALMER, WILLIAM son of William and Elizabeth Palmer, 23 March 1772.

B. PALMER, ALICE daughter of Isaac and Betty Palmer, 9 September 1772.

B. PALMER, SAMUEL son of William and Betty Palmer, 31 January 1777.

B. PALMER, BETTY daughter of William and Betty Palmer, 30 December 1781.

B. PALMER, CHARLES son of William and Bettey Palmer, 3 August 1789.

B. PARDOE, JOHN son of Elizabeth Pardoe, [day not entered] April 1737.

PARSONS   SEE : PERSON   PAGE 146

B. PARSONS, BETTY daughter of Elizabeth Parsons, 28 November 1731.

M. PARTRIDGE, JOHN and Frances Creswell, 6 April 1678.

M. PAXEN, MARY and Edward Davis, 15 November 1677.

B. PAYNE, ROSE daughter of Hannah Payne, 31 March 1728.

B. PAYNE, WILLIAM son of Hannah Payne, 27 July 1730.

B. PAYNE, SARAH daughter of Hannah Payne, 17 August 1732.

B. PAYNE, THOMAS son of Hannah Payne, 20 March 1735.

M. PEACE, MARY and William Edwards, 16 December 1725.

B. PEACHEY, ROBERT son of Samuel and Elizabeth Peachey, 21 March 1673.

B. PEACHEY, SAMUEL son of William and Pheebe Peachey, 4 September 1699.
    [I should like to correct errors and omissions in regard to Captain Samuel
    Peachey (4 September 1699 - 2 October 1750) and his wives in MRC., pgs. 122,
    155, 246; Hayden, p. 87 and AP&P(2), p. 401. He was thrice married: (1) in
    1720 or 1721 to Katherine McCarty, daughter of Captain Daniel McCarty (1679-
    1724) per recording 9 November 1721 (Westmoreland County D&W#7,pgs.256-261)
    by whom he had Elizabeth Peachey (1721-1792), next below, who married Doctor
    Nicholas Flood (1715-1768); (2) on 13 May 1725 to Winifred Griffin who was
    the mother of all the other children of Captain Peachey; (3) per marriage
    contract dated 16 February 1749/50, to Judith (Steptoe) Lee (170?-1755) widow
    of Richard Lee, Gentleman, (1691-1735) of Northumberland County, both of whom
    died testate there but only the will of Mrs. Peachey remains of record.]

B. PEACHEY, ELIZABETH daughter of Samuel and Kathrine Peachey, 18 November 1721.

B. PEACHEY, ALICE CORBIN daughter of Samuel and Winnefred Peachey, 16 May 1726.

B. PEACHEY, PHEBE daughter of Samuel and Winifred Peachey, 18 December 1727.

B. PEACHEY, WILLIAM son of Samuel and Winifred Peachey, 14 April 1729.

B. PEACHEY, WINNY GRIFFIN daughter of Samuel and Winifred Peachey, 26 Feby 1730.

B. PEACHEY, SAMUEL son of Samuel and Winifred Peachey, 6 February 1732.

B. PEACHEY, THOMAS GRIFFIN son of Samuel and Winifred Peachey, 23 December 1734.

B. PEACHEY, LEROY son of Samuel and Winifred Peachey, 19 June 1736.

B. PEACHEY, ANN daughter of Samuel and Winifred Peachey, 24 August 1738.

M. PEACHEY, ALICE CORBIN and John Eustace, 6 October 1743.

B. PEACHEY, SAMUEL son of William and Million Peachey, 16 December 1749.

D. PEACHEY, WINIFRED daughter of Samuel Peachey, 3 September 1750.

D. PEACHEY, CAPTAIN SAMUEL 2 October 1750.

B. PEACHEY, WINIFRED daughter of William and Million Peachey, 8 January 1752.

B. PEACHEY, ELIZABETH GRIFFIN daughter of LeRoy and Betty Peachey, 20 October 1761.

B. PEACHEY, ALICE daughter of William and Elizabeth Peachey, 2 July 1762.

B. PEACHEY, SUSANNA daughter of William and Elizabeth Peachey, 14 Sept. 1764.

B. PEACHEY, ANN daughter of William and Elizabeth Peachey, 15 October 1766.

B. PEACHEY, SAMUEL son of LeRoy and Betty Peachey, 12 October 1767.

B. PEACHEY, LEROY son of LeRoy and Betty Peachey, 21 August 1770.

B. PEACHEY, THOMAS GRIFFIN son of William and Elizabeth Peachey, 10 Nov. 1770.

B. PEACHEY, WILLIAM TRAVERSE son of William and Elizabeth Peachey, 7 Jan.y 1773.

B. PEACHEY, ELIZABETH daughter of William and Elizabeth Griffin Peachey, 3 December 1775.

B. PEARCE, KATHRINE daughter of John and Anne Pearce, 8 February 1719.

B. PEARCE, ANNE daughter of John and Anne Pearce, 26 March 1720.

B. PEARCE, HANNAH daughter of John and Mary Pearce, 23 November 1722.

PECK   SEE : PACK   PAGE   142

B. PECK, JOHN son of John and Mary Peck, 14 June 1709.

D. PECK, ANN 5 May 1721.

M. PECK, MARTHEW [MARTHA] and Thomas Gray, 10 July 1726.

D. PECK, JOHN 20 December 1726.

M. PECK, JANE and Edward Bates, 16 January 1729/30.

B. PECURE, MOSES son of William and Anne Pecure, 30 March 1729.

M. PEIRCE, SARAH and David Harburn, 21 April 1729.

PENDERGRASS   SEE : SPENDERGRASS   PAGE 173

B. PENDERGRASS, WINNEFRED daughter of James and Rebeccah Pendergrass, 25 August 1721.

M. PENDLE, MARY and Clark Short, 2 March 1730/1.

PENLEY   SEE : PENLY   PAGE   146

M.   PENLEY, THOMAS and Sarah Stone, 30 January 1728/9.

B.   PENLEY, WILLIAM son of Thomas and Sarah Penley, 15 November 1729.

B.   PENLE_, THOMAS son of Thomas and Sarah Penle, 6 June 1732.

B   PENLEY, ALICE daughter of Thomas and Sarah Penley, 7 March 1733.

B.   PENLEY, JOSHUA son of Thomas and Sarah Penley, 25 June 1736.

D.   PENLEY, THOMAS   22 March 1736.

D.   PENLEY, MARY   14 January 1749.

PENLY   SEE : PENLEY   PAGE   146

B.   PENLY, THOMAS son of William and Mary Penly, 8 June 1709.

B.   PENLY, MARY daughter of William and Mary Penly, 3 January 1712.

PERSON   SEE : PARSONS   PAGE   143

D.   PERSON, BETTY   31 December 1731.

B.   PETTY, CHRISTOPHER son of Christopher and Anne Petty, 2 March 1696.

B.   PETTY, JOHN son of Christopher and Mary Petty, 9 February 1698.

B.   PETTY, PETTER (sic) son of Christopher and Mary Petty, 15 February 1700.

B.   PETTY, WILLIAM son of Christopher and Mary Petty, 19 September 1712.

B.   PETTY, JOSEPH son of Christopher and Mary Petty, 26 October 1713.

B.   PETTY, MARY daughter of Christopher and Ann Petty, 6 October 1717.

B.   PETTY, CHRISTOPHER son of John and Frances Petty, 25 December 1723.

B.   PETTEY, WILMOTH daughter of John and Frances Pettey, 28 January 1725.

D.   PETTY, CHRISTOPHER   28 November 1725.

D.   PETTY, JOHN   13 March 1726.

D.   PETTY, PETER   13 December 1726.

M.   PETTY, THOMAS and Elizabeth Doon, 24 August 1727.

B.   PETTEY, FRANCIS MOORE son of Thomas and Elizabeth Pettey, 27 June 1728.

M. PETTY, FRANCES and Nicholas Martin, 15 November 1728.

M. PETTEY, PRUDENCE and Alexander Nelson, 8 January 1729/30.

D. PETTY, WILLIAM 28 March 1734.

B. PETTY, GEORGE son of Joseph and Betty Petty, 19 March 1740.

D. PETTY, CHRISTOPHER 16 December 1740.

B. PETTY, RAWLEIGH son of Joseph and Betty Petty, 1 January 1742.

B. PETTY, JOSEPH son of Joseph and Betty Petty, 18 September 1744.

B. PHILLIPS, ELIZABETH daughter of John and Elizabeth Phillips, 3 December 1674.

B. PHILLIPS, JOHN son of John and Elizabeth Phillips, 23 December 1676.

B. PHILLIPS, BRYANT son of John and Elizabeth Phillips, 13 February 1678.

M. PHILLIPS, JEREMIAH and Anne Brooks, 3 June 1678.

B. PHILLIPS, MARY daughter of John and Elizabeth Phillips, 7 October 1681.

B. PHILLIPS, THOMAS son of John and Elizabeth Phillips, 27 October 1684.

B. PHILLIPS, TOBIAS son of John and Elizabeth Phillips, 12 January 1687.

B. PHILLIPS, SAMUEL son of James and Mary Phillips, 30 November 1689.

B. PHILLIPS, ANNE daughter of John and Elizabeth Phillips, 23 September 1690.

B. PHILLIPS, WILLIAM son of Jeremiah and Anne Phillips, 4 September 1693.

B. PHILLIPS, MARGARET daughter of John and Ann Phillips, 1 August 1712.

D. PHILLIPS, JOHN "in the year 1715."

B. PHILLIPS, ELIZABETH daughter of Tobias and Hannah Phillips, 18 November 1715.

B. PHILLIPS, MARY ANN daughter of William and Anne Phillips, 11 December 1715.

D. PHILLIPS, ELIZABETH [not entered] 1717.

B. PHILLIPS, ELIZABETH daughter of william and Ann Phillips, 9 February 1717.

B. PHILLIPS, FRANCES daughter of Tobias and Hannah Phillips, 10 March 1718.

B. PHILLIPS, JANE daughter of Tobias and Hannah Phillips, 21 June 1720.

B. PHILLIPS, RICHARD son of Tobias and Hannah Phillips, 20 January 1722.

M. PHILLIPS, KATHERINE and George Thompson, 21 February 1725/6.

B. PHILLIPS, WILLIAM son of Robert and Elizabeth Phillips, 10 June 1728.

D. PHILLIPS, TOBIAS 1 November 1739.

B. PHILLIPS, TOBIAS son of George and Hannah Phillips, 25 January 1750.

D. PHILLIPS, ELIZABETH 20 December 1750.

B. PHILLIPS, SARAH daughter of George and Hannah Phillips, 11 July 1753.

B. PHILLIPS, JOSEPH son of John and Mary Phillips, 25 July 1753.

B. PHILLIPS, ANNE daughter of Joshua and Sarah Phillips, 15 May 1754.

B. PHILLIPS, FRANCES daughter of George and Hannah Phillips, 20 December 1755.

B. PHILLIPS, JOHN son of John and Elizabeth Phillips, 4 January 1756.

B. PHILLIPS, WILLIAM son of Joshua and Sarah Phillips, 18 April 1757.

D. PHILLIPS, FRANGES daughter of George and Hannah Phillips, 27 July 1757.

B. PHILLIPS, GEORGE son of George and Hannah Phillips, 20 March 1758.

B. PHILLIPS, BRYANT son of John and Elizabeth Phillips, 14 April 1758.

B. PHILLIPS, WILLIAM son of George and Hannah Phillips, 7 October 1760.

B. PHILLIPS, GEORGE son of John and Betty Phillips, 28 April 1761.

B. PHILLIPS, MILLY daughter of John and Betty Phillips, 4 April 1763.

M. PIARSE, MARY and William King, 14 June 1727.

PICRAFT   SEE : PYCRAFT   PAGE   154

D. PICRAFT, JOHN 3 December 1731.

D. PIERCE, JOHN 8 November 1726.

D. PIERCE, DANIEL 9 December 1726.

M. PINCKARD, THOMAS and Elizabeth Downman, 22 April 1727.

B. PLUMMER, JOHN son of Thomas and Elizabeth Plummer, 19 April 1735.

B. PLUMMER, THOMAS and BETTY twins of Thomas and Elizabeth Plummer, 31 March 1736; they both died 10 April 1736.

D. PLUMMER, ELIZABETH 29 March 1749.

B. PLUMMER, ANNE daughter of Daniel and Winifred Plummer, 22 May 1752.

B. PLUMMER, ELIZABETH daughter of Daniel and Winfred Plummer, 26 January 1756.

M. PLUMMER, JOHN and Sarah Smith, 7 May 1756.

B. PLUMMER, MARY daughter of John and Sarah Plummer, 4 March 1757.

B. PLUMMER, ELIZABETH daughter of John and Sarah Plummer, 25 August 1759.

B. PLUMMER, SARAH daughter of John and Sarah Plummer, 25 November 1761.

B. PLUMMER, THOMAS son of John and Sarah Plummer, 13 March 1764.

B. PLUMMER, REBECCA daughter of John and Sarah Plummer, 15 May 1767.

D. PLUMMER, REBECCA daughter of John and Sarah Plummer, 18 September 1768.

B. PLUMMER, REBECCA WILLOUGHBY daughter of John and Sarah Plummer, 10 March 1769.

D. PLUMMER, JOHN 4 August 1771.

POLLEY   SEE : PALLEY   PAGE 142

M. POLLEY, JOSEPH and Joanna Ken, 4 May 1677.

B. POLLEY, BETTY daughter of John and Frances Polley, 26 November 1740.

M. POLLING, SIMON and Jean Wade, 19 October 1673.

B. POOL, ELIZABETH daughter of Edward and Mary Pool, [not entered] 1671.

B. POPE, FORTUNATUS son of John and Elizabeth Pope, 17 July 1757.

B. POPE, JOSEPH son of John and Elizabeth Pope, 20 February 1767.

B. POPE, GEORGE son of John and Elizabeth Pope, 3 January 1773.

B. POPE, SALLY daughter of LeRoy Pope, 6 January 1776.

B. POPE, NICHOLAS son of LeRoy and Elizabeth Pope, 20 February 1778.

D. POTTER, JOHN 24 January 1735.

D. POTTS, THOMAS 22 September 1742.

B. POUND, ELIZABETH daughter of John and Deborah Pound, 12 October 1709.

B. POUND, LEWIS son of John and Deborah Pound, 4 June 1712.

B. POUND, JOHN son of John and Deborah Pound, 2 August 1713.

B. POUND, JOHN son of John and Sarah Pound, 4 November 1715.

B. POUND, SAMUEL son of Samuel and Sarah Pound, 9 November 1715.

B. POUND, DEBORAH daughter of John and Deborah Pound, 9 February 1716.

B. POUND, THOMAS son of Thomas and Margaret Pound, 7 April 1717.

D. POUND, JOHN 7 November 1718.

B. POUND, ELIZABETH daughter of Thomas and Margaret Pound, 30 June 1719.

B. POUND, PETER son of Samuel and Sarah Pound, 25 March 1722.

D. POUND, PETER 23 October 1722.

B. POUND, WILLIAM son of Samuel and Sarah Pound, 16 October 1724.
    [Samuel Pound moved from Richmond County to Germanna, the county seat of
    Orange County, Va., and on 14 June 1735 received a lease from Governor
    Alexander Spotswood for 100 acres adjoining the courthouse (Orange County
    DB#1, p.125). On 28 June 1750, Samuel Pound, aged about 60 years, made a
    deposition in Orange County court and stated his son, William Pound, was
    born 16 October 1724 and that he hired him to John Smith, undersheriff to
    William Russell, Gent., and was in the said Smith's service at the time the
    plaintiff's writ was served on Theophelas Eddins (Orange County Judgment
    File #13 in suit Anthony Strother vs Theophelas Eddins, Thomas Weatherby
    and William Pound). There are recordings in Orange and Culpeper counties in
    regard to members of the Pound family.]

D. POUND, ELIZABETH 22 November 1726.

D. POUND, SAMUEL 5 January 1730.

B. POUND, SAMUEL son of Samuel and Sarah Pound, 2 September 1730.

B. POWELL, MARY daughter of John and Michall Powell, 4 January 1690.

B. POWELL, JOHN son of John and Michall Powell, 26 January 1692.

B. POWELL, HEZEKIAH son of John and Michall Powell, 1 December 1695.

B. POWELL, WILLIAM son of John and Michall Powell, 18 June 1698.

B. POWELL, ANNE daughter of John and Michall Powell, 20 May 1703.

B. POWELL, JOHN son of John and Michall Powell, 23 May 1705.

D. POWELL, JOHN 15 December 1727.

D. PRATT, JOHN 18 June 1729.

B. PRATT, SAMUEL PUGH son of John and Lydda Pratt, 13 November 1791 [L:29].

M. PRESSION, ELIZABETH and Richard Appleby, 17 November 1728.

M. PRESEON , ANN and Dennis Camron, 1 December 1728.

B. PRICE, JOHN HILL son of Arjalon and Caty Price, 22 February 1762.

PRIDHAM SEE : BRIDHAM PAGE 21

B. PRIDHAM, JOHN son of Christopher and Mary Pridham, 29 December 1703.

B. PRIDHAM, ANNE daughter of Christopher and Mary Pridham, 5 October 1705.

B. PRIDHAM, ELIZABETH daughter of Christopher and Mary Pridham, 12 October 1710.

B. PRIDHAM, CHRISTOPHER son of Christopher and Mary Pridham, 19 December 1712.

B. PRIDHAM, EDWARD son of Christopher and Mary Pridham, 4 March 1714.

B. PRIDHAM, CATHRINE daughter of Christopher and Mary Pridham, 25 January 1717.

B. PRIDHAM, GEORGE BRYER son of Christopher and Mary Pridham, 9 June 1720.

B. PRIDHAM, WILLIAM son of Christopher and Mary Pridham, 6 August 1722.

B. PRIDHAM, THOMAS son of Christopher and Mary Pridham, 20 May 1724.

M. PRIDHAM, ELIZABETH and Edward Hinkley, 10 July 1726.

D. PRIDHAM, WILLIAM 6 October 1729.

D. PRIDHAM, CHRISTOPHER 13 March 1730/31.

Baptized, PRIDHAM, EDWARD son of Christopher Pridham, 6 January 1794 [L:29].

B. PRITCHARD, WILLIAM son of James and Anne Pritchard, 31 March 1680.

B. PRITCHET, ALESEY CONWAY daughter of Rodham Pritchet, 13 September 1781.

B. PRITCHET, NANCY daughter of Thomas Pritchet, 25 February 1788.

B. PRITCHETT, SAMUEL CONWAY son of Rhodom and Judith Pritchett, 15 May 1790.

B. PRITCHETT, WILLIAM SETTLE son of Thomas and Sarah Pritchett, 6 December 1791 [L:29].

B. PROCTOR, ABRAHAM son of Isaac and Ruth Proctor, 19 November 1742.

B. PROCTOR, SARAH daughter of Isaac and Ruth Proctor, 20 December 1744.

B.   PROCTOR, BETTY daughter of Isaac and Ruth Proctor, 4 March 1746.

B.   PROCTOR, NANNY daughter of Isaac and Ruth Proctor, 16 April 1749.

D.   PROCTOR, NANSY daughter of Isaac and Ruth Proctor, 15 October 1750.

B.   PROSSER, SAMUEL son of William and Elizabeth Prosser, 29 December 1777.

B.   PROSSER, ANN daughter of William and Betty Prosser, 16 April 1780.

B.   PROSSER, ELIZABETH EPPERSON daughter of William and Elizabeth Prosser, 13 September 1782.

D.   PUEN, JAMES   25 November 1726.

B.   PUGH, JOHN son of Lewis and Anne Pugh, 29 April 1704.

B.   PUGH, DAVID son of Lewis and Anne Pugh, 25 December 1706.

B.   PUGH, ELIZABETH daughter of Lewis and Anne Pugh, 19 March 1708.

B.   PUGH, HENRY son of Lewis and Anne Pugh, 2 March 1710.

B.   PUGH, WILLOUGHBY son of Lewis and Anne Pugh, 3 May 1711.

B.   PUGH, ANNE daughter of Lewis and Anne Pugh, 14 November 1715.

B.   PUGH, Laurence son of Laurence and Ann Lugh, 2 March 1718.

M.   PUGH, LEWIS and Margaret Harvey, 2 February 1738.

B.   PUGH, ANN daughter of Lewis and Margaret Pugh, 23 October 1744.

B.   PUGH, SARAH RICHARDS daughter of Lewis and Nancey Pugh, 31 Aug. 1792 [L:29].

B.   PUGH, LEWIS son of Lewis and Nancey Pugh, 27 October 1797 [L:29].

D.   PULLEN, HENRY 4 January 1722.

B.   PULLEN, HENRY son of Henry and Mary Pullen, 6 June 1753.

B.   PULLEN, BETTY daughter of Henry and Mary Pullen, 4 February 1755.

B.   PULLEN, JAMES son of Henry and Mary Pullen, 9 April 1756.

B.   PULLEN, GEORGE son of Henry and Mary Pullen, 8 June 1758.

B.   PULLEN, JOHN son of Henry and Mary Pullen, 10 May 1760.

B.   PULLEN, JEDUTHUN son of Jehu and Mary Pullen, 5 August 1762.

B.   PULLEN, MOSES son of Jehu and Mary Pullen, 22 July 1764.

B. PULLEN, JONATHAN son of Jehu and Mary Pullen, 12 February 1766.

B. PULLEN, BETSY CREEL daughter of William Pullen, 11 September 1783.

B. PULLIN, JESSE son of Jesse and Peggy Pullin, 5 January 1792 [L:29].

B. PULLIN, JAMES son of Everard and Catharine Pullin, 11 September 1793 [L:29].

B. PULLIN, REBECCA daughter of Everard and Catharine Pullin, 8 Dec.1796 [L:29].

B. PULLIN, SUSANNA daughter of Everard and Catharine Pullin, 20 March 1798[do].

PURCELL   SEE : PUSSELL : PURSELL : PURCELL &c. PAGE 153

B. PURNEY, THOMAS son of Mary Purney, 10 December 1735.

PURSELL   SEE : PAGE 153

B. PURTLE, MARY daughter of Robert and Kathrine Purtle, 20 August 1719.

PUSSELL   : PURSELL : PURCELL &c.

B. PUSSELL, HENRY son of David and Billender Pussell, 20 April 1682.

B. PUSSELL, JOHN son of David and Billinder Pussell, 29 January 1683.

B. PUSSELL, DAVID son of David and Billinder Pussell, 20 June 1686.

B. PUSSELL, WILLIAM son of David and Billender Pussell, 25 August 1688.

B. PUSSELL, TOBIAS son of David and Billender Pussell, 23 December 1691.

B. PUSSELL, BILLENDER daughter of John and Sarah Pussell, 7 October 1719.

B. PUSSELL, KATHRINE daughter of Tobias and Margaret Pussell, __ Nov. 1721.

D. PUSSELL, TOMSIN 12 November 1721.

B. PUSSELL, WINNEFRED daughter of Tobias and Margaret Pussell, 22 March 1723/4.

B. PUSSELL, MARY daughter of John and Sarah Pussell, 1 July 1725.

D. PUSSELL, MARY 3 December 1725.

B. PUSSELL, DAVID son of John and Sarah Pussell, 10 March 1726.

B. PUSSELL, JOHN son of Tobias and Margaret Pussell, 17 January 1726/7.

B. PUSSELL, ELIZABETH daughter of Tobias and Margaret Pussell, 2 November 1730.

B. PURCELL, JUDA "a child baptized for Tobias Purcell," 2 July 1791 [L:29].

B. PURSSELL, LUCY daughter of Tobias and Rebeccah Pursell, 11 June 1792.

> [N.B. It appears that the above recording, together with the five
> immediately following, were recorded in the Lunenburg Parish
> Register, page 29, at the same time.]

B. PURSSELL, HANSFORD son of Tobias and Rebeccah Purssell, 17 May 1793.

B. PURSSELL, SAMUEL son of Tobias and Rebecah Purssell, 5 March 1795.

B. PURSSELL, REBECCA daughter of Tobias and Rebecah Purssell, 14 January 1797.

B. PURSSELL, RICHARD LAWSON son of Tobias and Rebecah Purssell, 17 Oct. 1798.

B. PURSSELL, FANNY daughter of Tobias and Rebecah Purssell, 8 February 1800.

PYCRAFT   SEE : PICRAFT PAGE 148

M. PYCRAFT, WINIFRED and Thomas Williams, 8 June 1732.

Q

B. QUIRK, ANNE and ALCE daughters of Thomas and Jane Quirk, 5 February 1724/5.

D. QUIRK, ANNE 19 March 1729.

R

D. RAINBOW, THOMAS RAWLINS bastard son of Mary Rainbow, 15 December 1750.

B. RAM, ABENEZER son of Abenezer and Elizabeth Ram, 12 June 1722.

M. RAMZE, ISABELL and Oliver Small, 11 June 1730.

M. RANDALL, THOMAS and Jane Davis, 4 October 1728.

M. RANDALL, MARY and Ely Reed, 20 August 1729.

D. RANN, JOHN 20 October 1725.

M. RAVEN, WILLIAM and Mary Nichols, 30 November 1738.

RAWLINGS : RAWLLINGS : RAWLINS : ROLENS

B. ROLENS, JOHN son of Thomas and Sarah Rolens, 23 August 1713.

B. ROLENS, THOMAS son of Thomas and Sarah Rolens, 25 March 1714.

B. ROLENS, MARY daughter of Thomas and Sarah Rolens, 7 April 1717.

B.   RAWLLINGS, JAMES son of Thomas and Sarah Rawllings, 20 April 1719.

D.   RAWLINS, SARAH 8 February 1719 [1719/20].

B.   RAWLLINGS, JUDITH daughter of Thomas and Elizabeth Rawllings, 22 April 1722.

B.   RAWLLINGS, SAMUEL son of Thomas and Elizabeth Rawllings, 8 April 1725.

D.   RAWLLINGS, ELIZABETH 14 February 1726.

M.   RAWLIN[G]S, THOMAS and Elizabeth Gibton, 2 March 1730/1.

B.   RAWLINGS, WINNEFRED daughter of Thomas and Elizabeth Rawlings, 24 Nov. 1731.

B.   RAWLINS, WILLIAM son of Thomas and Elizabeth Rawlins, 9 March 1736.

D.   RAWLINS, JOHN 25 November 1736.

B.   RAWLINS, JOHN son of Samuel and Elizabeth Rawlins, 13 January 1747.

B.   RAWLINS, RODAH son of Samuel and Elizabeth Rawlins, 27 April 1750.

B.   RAWLINS, VIOLETO daughter of Samuel and Elizabeth Rawlins, 12 June 1752.

B.   RAWLINS, NANNY daughter of Samuel and Elizabeth Rawlins, 3 March 1755.

B.   RAWLINS, SAMUEL son of Samuel and Elizabeth Rawlins, 2 May 1757.

D.   RAWLINS, GODFREY 20 September 1757.

B.   RAWLINS, RAWLEIGH son of Samuel and Elizabeth Rawlins, 23 August 1759.

     RAYNOLDS   SEE : REYNOLDS : RAYNOLDS   PAGE   156

M.   READ, MARY and David Burt. 19 October 1673.

D.   REASON, ELIZABETH 26 September 1723.

B.   REDMAN, SARAH daughter of Solomon and Mary Redman, 14 December 1720.

B.   REDMAN, WINNEFRED daughter of Solomon and Mary Redman, 28 July 1725.

B.   REDMAN, WILLIAM son of Richard and Rachell Redman, 12 September 1726.

B.   REDMAN, JOHN son of Solomon and Mary Redman, 2 January 1727.

M.   REDMAN, PRISCILLA and Stephen Wells, 21 August 1729.

B.   REDMAN, JOSEPH and BENJAMIN sons of Solomon and Mary Redman, 30 August 1730.

B.   REDMAN, LOUISA "a child baptized for Col. V. Redman," 19 June 1791 [L:33].

B. REDMAN, REBECCA "a child baptized for Col. V. Redman," 26 Sept. 1791 [L:33].

B. REED, WILLIAM son of Thomas and Catharine Reed, 1 October 1712.

D. REED, THOMAS 25 April 1719.

B. REED, THOMAS son of John and Elizabeth Reed, 11 July 1727.

M. REED, ELY and Mary Randall 20 August 1729.

M. REEVES, MARGARET and William Rolls 8 June 1674.

B. RENN, WILLIAM son of Thomas and Jane Renn, 16 March 1735.

REYNOLDS : RAYNOLDS

M. REYNOLDS, JOHN and Sarah Grimes 5 August 1674.

B. REYNOLDS, ELIZABETH daughter of Jeffery and Anne Reynolds, 28 March 1697.

B. REYNOLDS, DOMINICK son of Robert and Frances Reynolds, 21 May 1699. [sic]

B. REYNOLDS, DOMINICK son of Robert and Frances Reynolds, 7 December 1700.

D. RAYNOLDS, ROBERT 3 January 1719.

B. RAYNOLDS, REBECCAH daughter of Robert and Frances Raynolds, 15 March 1719.

D. RAYNOLDS, WILMOTH 29 February 1720.

M. RAYNOLDS, ANN and John Elmore 29 November 1728.

B. REYNOLDS, WILMOTH daughter of Robert and Ann Reynolds, 20 June 1738.

B. REYNOLDS, BETTY daughter of Robert and Ann Reynolds, 29 October 1740.

D. REYNOLDS, WILMOTH daughter of Robert and Ann Reynolds, 18 September 1746.

D. REYNOLDS, ELIZABETH daughter of Robert and Ann Reynolds, 25 September 1746.

D. REYNOLDS, JOHN son of Robert and Ann Reynolds, 28 September 1746.

B. REYNOLDS, GEORGE son of John and Betty Reynolds, 16 December 1752.

B. REYNOLDS, JOHN son of John and Betty Reynolds, 10 March 1754.

B. REYNOLDS, WILLIAM son of John and Betty Reynolds, 3 October 1755.

B. RAYNOLDS, ELIZABETH daughter of George and Frances Raynolds, 4 November 1777.

B. REYNOLDS, BETSEY daughter of Benjamin and Eleanor Reynolds, 30 November 1791 [L:33].

M. RIAN, DENNIS and Sarah Neives   24 October 1729.

B. RICE, SARAH daughter of William and Ruth Rice, 4 May 1777.

B. RICE, ELIZABETH DAVENPORT daughter of Charles and Sally Rice, 3 Feby 1778.

B. RICH, DAVID son of Mary Rich, a free mulatto, 2 January 1735.

B. RICH, WILMOTH daughter of Mary Rich, a free mulatto, 30 March 1742.

B. RICH, BOB son of Mary Rich, 22 April 1781.

B. RICH, DICK free Negro son of Mary Rich, 6 October 1782.

B. RICH, HANNAH [no parents entered], 26 April 1789.

B. RICH,-HANNAH B.D., daughter of Winney Rich, 15 July 1793.

B. RICH, GEORGE son of Criss Rich, 1 August 1793.

B. RICH, KENDAL son of Criss Rich, 12 October 1795.

B. RICH, NANCY daughter of Criss Rich, 25 October 1798.

B. RICH, ROBERT son of Criss Rich, 15 January 1799.

B. RICH, DANIEL son of Criss Rich, 8 May 1802.

B. RICH, THADDEUS son of Criss Rich, 30 August 1804.

B. RICH, J. BAS son of Criss Rich, 5 February 1807.

B. RICHARDS, WILLIAM son of Lewis and Jane Richards, 13 August 1691.

B. RICHARDSON, MARY daughter of William and Mary Richardson, 28 July 1688.

B. RICHARDSON, JOHN son of William and Mary Richardson, 13 November 1695.

D. RICHARDSON, JOHN 14 October 1720.

B. RICHARDSON, CHURCHILL a bastard son of Edward Willson and Molly Richardson, 23 May 1794 [L:43]; this couple were married 7 November 1796 [MRC., p.233].

B. RICHARS, ANNE daughter of William and Sarah Richars, 18 February 1715.

B. RICHARS, JANE daughter of William and Sarah Richars, 28 March 1721/2.

B. RICHARS, ELIZABETH daughter of William and Sarah Richars, 20 September 1723.

B. RICHARS, SARAH daughter of William and Sarah Richars, 1 February 1726.

B. RICHARS, JOHN son of William and Sarah Richars, 17 May 1728.

B. RICHARS, MARY daughter of William and Sarah Richars, 21 June 1729.

B. RICHARS, WILLIAM son of William and Sarah Richars, 22 December 1731.

B. RIDER, SIMEON son of John and Grace Rider, 14 March 1691.

B. RIDER, SARAH daughter of John and Grace Rider, 14 September 1695.

B. RIGHT, NANNY daughter of James and Eleanor Right, 7 April 1731.

M. ROBERSON, ANN and William Hastie, 17 September 1730. [See, ROBINSON below.]

D. ROBERTS, THOMAS 15 February 1716.

B. ROBERTSON, WILLIAM son of Anne Robertson, 18 January 1725.
[Major William Woodbridge (1668-1726) of Richmond County handsomely provid-
ed for this bastard child and his mother by his last will and Testament.
Richmond County WB#5, p.27; King George County DB 1-A, p. 279.]

B. ROBERTSON, MARY daughter of Margarett Robertson, 24 May 1731.

B. ROBINSON, ANNE daughter of William and Anne Robinson, 25 August 1679.

B. ROBINSON, ELIZABETH daughter of William and Anne Robinson, 4 December 1681.

B. ROBINSON, BARBARA daughter of William and Anne Robinson, 4 December 1683.

B. ROBINSON, FRANCES daughter of William and Anne Robinson, 10 November 1684.

B. ROBINSON, HANNAH daughter of Elias and Hannah Robinson, __ December 1688.

B. ROBINSON, ELIZABETH daughter of Elias and Hannah Robinson, 13 Sept. 1691.

M. ROBINSON, JAMES and Margaret Connelly 29 July 1739.

B. ROBINSON, MARY daughter of James and Margaret Robinson [Roberson], 5 September 1739.

B. ROBINSON, WILLIAM MARTIN son of James and Judith Robinson, 18 December 1772.

B. ROBINSON, THOMAS POPE son of James and Judith Robinson, 2 March 1774.

B. ROBINSON, JAMES son of James and Judith Robinson, 14 August 1776.

B. ROCK, THOMAS son of Francis and Judah Rock, 25 September 1784.

B. ROGERS, WILLIAM son of Mary Rogers, 20 January 1709.

D. ROGERS, [Christian name not entered] child of William Rogers, 1 Oct. 1741.

ROLENS SEE : RAWLINGS : RAWLLINGS : RAWLINS : ROLENS PAGE 154

B. ROLINGS, WILLIAM son of Nancy Rolings, 4 March 1778.

M. ROLLS, WILLIAM and Margaret Reeves, 8 June 1674.

B. ROOKER, GINNINGS son of John and Anne Rooker, 4 September 1725.

B. ROOKER, HANNAH daughter of Roger and Eleanor Rooker, 11 March 1729.

B. ROOKER, NANNY and HANNAH twins of Jinnings and Betty Rooker, 14 Oct. 1750.

B. ROOKER, WINNY daughter of Jennings and Betty Rooker, 20 March 1753.

B. ROOKER, JOHN son of Jennings and Betty Rooker, 12 March 1755.

B. ROS, VINCENT BARNETT a base born child, son of Elender Sisson, 22 April 1798 [L:35].

B. ROUT, SAMUEL son of Benjamin and Eleanor Rout, 20 February 1721; see RUST.

M. ROUT, JOHN and Winifred Sydnor 3 March 1731/2.

B. RUSS, JAMES a bastard child of Sally Yardley, 5 June 1792 [L:47].

M. RUSSELL, JOHN and Alicia Billington, 11 September 1673.

B. RUSSELL, CHARLES son of George and Elizabeth Russell, 26 August 1705.

B. RUSSELL, SAMUEL son of George and Rachell Russell, 4 November 1715.

B. RUSSELL, ELIZABETH daughter of John and Anne Russell, 4 October 1720.

B. RUSSELL, GEORGE son of George and Mary Russell, 30 November 1720.

B. RUSSELL, LUCY daughter of George and Mary Russell, 5 July 1723.

B. RUSSELL, JOSEPH son of Joseph and Sarah Russell, 13 January 1723/4.

B. RUSSELL, ANNE daughter of John and Anne Russell, 31 May 1725.

B. RUSSELL, LYDIA daughter of Joseph and Sarah Russell, 29 September 1726.

D. RUSSELL, SOLOMON 27 November 1726.

B. RUSSELL, BARBERY daughter of George and Mary Russell, 9 November 1727.

B. RUSSELL, SOLOMON son of Joseph and Sarah Russell, 22 February 1729.

B. RUSSELL, BETTY daughter of Thomas and Mary Ann Russell, 4 January 1764.

D. RUST, ELEANOR 10 November 1722.
[As Benjamin Rust and his first wife Eleanor Green (19 February 1702 - 10

November 1722) are known to have had an only child named Samuel Rust who d.s.p., it seems very certain from DB#7, p. 492, DB#11, p. 155 and MRC., p. 254, that the recording on p. 159 of the birth of Samuel Rout, son of Benjamin and Eleanor Rout, 20 February 1721, is an error and that this is actually the record of the birth of Samuel Rust who is mentioned in the above cited documents.]

B. RUST, JOHN son of Benjamin and Sarah Rust, 2 November 1725.

B. RUST, ANNE daughter of Benjamin and Sarah Rust, 4 October 1727.

B. RUST, METCALFE son of Benjamin and Sarah Rust, 12 September 1729.

B. RUST, SARAH daughter of Benjamin and Sarah Rust, 22 September 1731.

B. RUST, LEMUEL son of William and Ailce Rust, 29 April 1792 [L:33].

B. RUST, JAMES son of Samuel and Nancey Rust, 14 December 1798.

B. RYALS, JOHN son of William and Susanna Ryals, 3 February 1790 [L:33].

B. RYALS, ELLIOT son of William and Susanna Ryals, 4 December 1792 [L:33].

B. RYALS, COVINGTON son of William and Susanna Ryals, 19 August 1793 [L:33].

B. RYALS, SUSANNA daughter of William and Susanna Ryals, 7 Nov. 1796 [L:33].

D. RYLE, FRANCIS 1 May 1718.

B. RYLE, HENRY ALLIN son of James and Anney Ryle, 27 June 1797 [L:33].

S

B. SALLARD, SABRINA daughter of William and Ann Sallard, 23 February 1765.

SAMFORD   SEE : SANFORD PAGE 163

M. SAMFORD, MARY and John Webb, 14 July 1673.

B. SAMFORD, THOMAS son of Thomas and Mary Samford, "in the year 1674."

M. SAMFORD, ALICIA and William Fann, 23 January 1675. [The bridegroom's surname was Lunn, not Fann, as has been pointed out on pages 61 and 106. One segment of the descendants of Alicia Samford, seeking to perpetuate her surname, have altered the spelling to Sanford; see remarks by Colonel Brooke Payne in his book, The Paynes of Virginia (Richmond,Va., 1937), p. 228-230.]

B. SAMFORD, ANNE daughter of Thomas and Mary Samford, 16 April 1676.

B. SAMFORD, THOMAS son of Samuel and Elizabeth Samford, 20 March 1687.

B. SAMFORD, WILLIAM son of Samuel and Elizabeth Samford, 12 September 1692.

B. SAMFORD, GILES son of Samuel and Elizabeth Samford, 9 September 1699.

B. SAMFORD, ELIZABETH daughter of William and Elizabeth Samford, 1 October 1714.

B. SAMFORD, MARY daughter of William and Elizabeth Samford, 5 September 1716.

D. SAMFORD, ELIZABETH daughter of William and Elizabeth Samford, 16 Sept. 1717.

B. SAMFORD, ANNE daughter of William and Elizabeth Samford, 25 April 1721.

B. SAMFORD, WILLIAM son of William and Elizabeth Samford, 13 February 1722/3.

B. SAMFORD, ELIZABETH daughter of William and Elizabeth Samford, 12 Sept. 1725.

D. SAMFORD, ISABELL 29 November 1725.

D. SAMFORD, GILES 15 February 1726.

B. SAMFORD, SARAH daughter of William and Elizabeth Samford, 16 May 1727.

M. SAMFORD, ELIZABETH and Bennett Bogges, 27 December 1727.

M. SAMFORD, JAMES and Mary Barber, 20 September 1728.

B. SAMFORD, ANN daughter of James and Mary Samford, 25 November 1730.

B. SAMFORD, HANNAH daughter of William and Elizabeth Samford, 4 September 1731.

B. SAMFORD, JAMES son of James and Mary Samford, 19 January 1733.

B. SAMFORD, BETTY daughter of James and Mary Samford, 4 February 1734/5.

D. SAMFORD, JAMES 10 October 1735.

B. SAMFORD, GILES son of John and Sarah Samford, 24 July 1736.

D. SAMFORD, SAMUEL 15 August 1736.

B. SAMFORD, JESSE son of Samuel and Mary Samford, 23 February 1737.

B. SAMFORD, FRANCES daughter of James and Mary Samford, 15 April 1737.

B. SAMFORD, JAMES son of Thomas Samford, 10 May 1737.

B. SAMFORD, MARY daughter of Thomas Samford, 5 May 1739.

B. SAMFORD, WINNY daughter of James and Mary Samford, 15 July 1739.

B. SAMFORD, ANN daughter of John and Sarah Samford, 25 December 1739.

B. SAMFORD, THOMAS son of Thomas Samford, 12 April 1741.

M. SAMFORD, KEENE and Winny Dowden, 28 July 1742. [The full name of the bride-groom was William Keene Samford; he was born 13 February 1722/3. See p.161 and MRC., pages 177 and 261.]

B. SAMFORD, JAMES son of Keen and Winifred Samford, 15 July 1743.

D. SAMFORD, JAMES son of Keen and Winny Samford, 6 August 1743.

B. SAMFORD, ELIZABETH daughter of Thomas and Frances Samford, 26 November 1743.

B. SAMFORD, WILLIAM son of Keen and Winny Samford, 27 June 1745.

B. SAMFORD, JOHN AMISS son of Thomas Samford, 16 September 1746.

B. SAMFORD, SAMUEL son of Keen and Winny Samford, 3 February 1747.

B. SAMFORD, FRANCES daughter of Thomas and Frances Samford, 25 March 1750.

D. SAMFORD, FRANCES wife of Thomas Samford, 6 April 1750.

B. SAMFORD, JESSE son of Keen and Winny Samford, 13 October 1750.

B. SAMFORD, ASA son of Keen and Winny Samford, 1 March 1753.

B. SAMFORD, THOMAS son of Keen and Winny Samford, 1 October 1755.

B. SAMFORD, THOMAS son of Keen and Winny Samford, 7 March 1758.

B. SAMFORD, ELIZABETH daughter of Keen and Winny Samford, 24 August 1760.

B. SAMFORD, JOHN son of Giles and Mary Samford, 26 November 1761.

B. SAMFORD, THOMAS son of Giles and Mary Samford, 6 January 1771.

M. SAMFORD, JAMES and Rebecca McKenny, 3 April 1772.

B. SAMPSON, MARGARET daughter of Thomas and Mary Sampson, "in the year 1663."

B. SAMPSON, JOHN son of Thomas and Mary Sampson, "in the year 1674."

B. SAMPSON, WILLIAM son of Thomas and Mary Sampson, 29 February 1678.

B. SANDERS, GEORGE son of Edward and Magdalin Sanders, 9 October 1786.

B. SANDERS, SARAH daughter of Edward and Magdalin Sanders, 18 October 1788.

B. SANDERS, MISKELL son of Edwin (sis) and Magdalen Sanders, 30 March 1791.

B. SANDERS, THOMAS CONNOLLY son of Thomas and Nancey Saunders, 27 October 1791 [L:35].

B.   SANDERS, RACHEL daughter of James and Patty Sanders, 13 February 1792 [L:35].

B.   SANDERS, GRIFFIN son of Aleck and Ann Sanders, 22 September 1792 [L:35].

B.   SANDERS, SUCKEY daughter of Thomas and Katey Sanders, 27 Jany 1793 [L:35].

B.   SANDERS, JAMES son of William and Anne Sanders, 11 July 1793 [L:35].

B.   SANDERS, ALEXANDER GRIFFIN son of Aleck and Nancey Sanders, 30 July 1795 [L:35].

B.   SANDERS, ROBIN son of Aleck and Anne Sanders, 1 June 1798 [L:35].

B.   SANDY, THOMAS son of Thomas and Ann Sandy, 25 April 1798.

SANFORD   SEE : SAMFORD PAGES 160-162

B.   SANFORD, ANN daughter of John and Betty Sanford, 27 April 1788. [The surname should be SAMFORD; John A. Samford appears on the 1788 tax list.]

B.   SANFORD, WILLIAM HENRY son of Richard and Bethiah Sanford, 3 Nov. 1791 [L:35].

B.   SANFORD, CATY daughter of George and Jane Sanford, 14 February 1793 [L:35].

B.   SANFORD, BETHIA daughter of Joshua and Elizabeth Sanford, 26 Nov. 1795 [L:35].

SARGANT   :   SARGENT   :   SARGEANT

B.   SARGENT, KATHRINE daughter of John and Mary Sargent, 25 December 1718/9.

B.   SARGENT, ELIZABETH daughter of John and Mary Sargent, 23 September 1720.

B.   SARGANT, MARY ANN daughter of John and Mary Sargant, 21 October 1723.

B.   SARGANT, ALLIS daughter of John and Mary Sargant, 4 January 1725.

B.   SARGEANT, MARTHA daughter of John and Mary Sargeant, 14 May 1728.

D.   SARGEANT, MARY   21 November 1732.

B.   SAUNDERS, ELIZABETH daughter of John and Mary Saunders, 30 April 1711.

B.   SAUNDERS, GEORGE son of John and Mary Saunders, 10 May 1712.

B.   SAUNDERS, JOSEPH son of John and Mary Saunders, 25 September 1714.

B.   SAUNDERS, CHARLES son of John and Mary Saunders, 13 May 1716.

B.   SAUNDERS, JOHN and LISHA twins of Joseph and Elizabeth Saunders, 23 June 1735.

164

B. SAUNDERS, BETTY daughter of Joseph and Betty Saunders, 1 April 1737.

B. SAUNDERS, THOMAS WILLIAMS son of George and Mary Saunders, 24 December 1737.

B. SAUNDERS, WILLIAM son of Joseph and Betty Saunders, 1 June 1739.

B. SAUNDERS, KATHRINE daughter of George and Mary Saunders, 19 December 1739.

B. SAUNDERS, GEORGE son of George and Mary Saunders, 24 July 1742.

B. SAUNDERS, JOHN son of George and Mary Saunders, 11 January 1744.

B. SAUNDERS, JOSEPH son of George and Mary Saunders, 16 March 1746.

B. SAUNDERS, MARY daughter of George and Mary Saunders, 15 February 1749.

B. SAUNDERS, ELIZABETH daughter of George and Mary Saunders, 18 May 1753.

D. SAUNDERS, MARY 10 December 1755.

B. SAUNDERS, EDWARD son of George and Sarah Saunders, 23 December 1756.

B. SAUNDERS, SARAH daughter of George and Sarah Saunders, 8 May 1758.

B. SAUNDERS, MILDRED daughter of John and Licia Saunders, 18 May 1771.

B. SAUNDERS, BETTY daughter of John and Million Saunders, 16 September 1776.

B. SCATES, SALLY WHITE daughter of James and Peggy Scates, 15 October 1792 [L:35

B. SCATES, BILLEY BURCHEL son of James and Peggy Scates, 7 January 1794 [L:35].

B. SCATES, JAMES son of James and Peggy Scates, 7 January 1796 [L:35].

B. SCATES, WILLIAM son of Joseph and Patty Scates, 1 July 1798 [L:35].

B. SCATES, JOHN BARTLETT son of James and Peggy Scates, 14 November 1798 [L:35].

SCOFIELD ⌕ SCOFILL ⌕ SCHOFIELD

B. SCOFILL, ELIZABETH daughter of Robert and Elizabeth Scofill, 18 November 1719

B. SCOFIELD, JOHN son of Robert and Elizabeth Scofield, 24 May 1722.

D. SCHOFIELD, ROBERT 11 April 1737.

B. SCOTT, WILLIAM son of Joseph and Kathrine Scott, 14 February 1716.

D. SCOTT, SARAH 10 June 1719.

B. SCOTT, KATHRINE daughter of Joseph and Kathrine Scott, 6 October 1720.

D. SCOTT, KATHRINE 9 October 1720.

B. SCOTT, JOSEPH son of Joseph and Joanna Scott, 8 March 1723/4.

D. SCOTT, JOANNA 12 May 1724.

B. SCOTT, JAMES son of Charles Scott, 10 April 1779.

B. SCOTT, JOHN son of Thomas and Mary Scott, 10 October 1790 [L:35].

B. SCRIMSHER, _____ "a child baptized for William Scrimsher, no name mentioned," 6 January 1795.

B. SCRIMSHER, JAMES son of William and Fanney Scrimsher, 5 Jan. 1797 [L:35].

SCURLOCK SEE : SHERLOCK PAGE 166

B. SCURLOCK, ALEXANDER son of Thomas and Ann Scurlock, 22 June 1722.

B. SCURLOCK, THOMAS son of Thomas and Anne Scurlock, 11 June 1725.

M. SCURLOCK, MARY and James Howend [Howard], 7 November 1729.

M. SCURLOCK, MARGARET and Joseph Morrison, 9 December 1739.

D. SCURLOCK, ANN daughter of Thomas Scurlock, 25 April 1751.

D. SCURLOCK, THOMAS 14 March 1757.

B. SCURLOCK, SARAH daughter of George Scurlock, 2 May 1777.

SEAMAN : SEAMANS : SEAMAR : SEAMON : SEAMONS

B. SEAMAN, MARY daughter of John and Margaret Seaman, 5 November 1699.

B. SEAMAN, JOHN son of John and Abigall Seaman, 29 December 1699.

D. SEAMONS, ELIZABETH 20 February 1718/19.

B. SEAMONS, OBEDIAH son of Joseph and Charity Seamons, 10 April 1721.

B. SEAMONS, JEREMIAH son of Joseph and Charity Seamons, 11 June 1726.

D. SEAMONS, THOMAS 8 November 1726.

D. SEAMONS, JOHN 26 November 1726.

D. SEAMONS, ELIZABETH 11 March 1727.

M. SEAMONS, JOHN and Jane Hammock, 2 September 1727.

B. SEAMAR, WILLIAM son of John and Jane Seamar, 14 September 1728.

M. SEAMONS, JOHN and Katherine Foster, 17 July 1728.

D. SEAMONS, CHARITY 17 May 1729.

M. SEAMONS, JOHN and Elizabeth Jones, 30 November 1729.

B. SEAMANS, MARY daughter of John and Elizabeth Seamans, 16 December 1730.

B. SEBRE, RICHARD son of William and Jane Sebre, 27 May 1776.

B. SETTLE, FRANCIS son of John and Mary Settle, 6 December 1681.

B. SETTLE, JEMIMA daughter of Henry and Anne Settle, 19 June 1722.

B. SETTLE, KEZIA daughter of Henry and Anne Settle, 9 August 1726.

B. SETTLE, ANNE daughter of Henry and Anne Settle, 29 August 1728.

B. SETTLE, MARY daughter of Henry and Anne Settle, 3 November 1730.

M. SHAW, WILLIAM and Margaret Holland, 22 November 1680.

M. SHAW, CHRISTIAN and George Blackmore, 13 September 1729.

B. SHEARLY, THOMAS son of Joy Shearly, 23 August 1783.

B. SHEARLEY, THADDUS son of Peter and Hannah Shearley, 13 February 1794.

D. SHENROW, GEORGE [not entered] January, 1716.

SHERLOCK   SEE : SCURLOCK PAGE 165

M. SHERLOCK, DEBORAH and Andrew Morrow, 11 October 1728.

B. SHERLY, ARMSBY bastard child of Elizabeth Sherly, 17 May 1754.

SHEARMAN : SHERMAN

B. SHERMAN, MARTIN son of Qunctitian and Jean Sherman, 4 October 1673.

M. SHERMAN, JANE and Robert Fristow, 1 August 1675.

B. SHERMAN, BENJAMIN son of Martin and Mary Sherman, 7 September 1724.

D. SHEARMAN, MARY 10 March 1726.

D. SHEARMAN, MARTIN 15 March 1726.

B. SHEARMAN, EASTER daughter of Martin and Anne Shearman, 21 June 1730.

B. SHORT, ELEANOR daughter of Patrick and Ann Short, 5 June 1711.

B. SHORT, ANNE [names of parents omitted], 16 September 1713.

B. SHORT, PATRICK [names of parents omitted], 14 August 1715.

D. SHORT, ELIZABETH [not entered] September 1716.

D. SHORT, PATRICK [not entered] October 1716.

B. SHORT, PATRICK [names of parents omitted], 15 November 1716.

B. SHORT, ELIZABETH [names of parents omitted], 29 June 1718.

D. SHORT, WILLIAM 1 January 1726.

D. SHORT, PATRICK JUN^R 5 January 1726.   [These two dates must be 1726/7 as
                                               William and Patrick were mentioned
D. SHORT, PATRICK 14 August 1726.   in their father's will dated 14
                                               Aug. 1726 and proved 7 Sept. 1726.]
M. SHORT, ANN and Peter Smith 15 May 1727.

M. SHORT, ELEANOR and Henry Threkeld, 15 July 1728.

M. SHORT, CLARK and Mary Pendle, 2 March 1730/1.

B. SHORT, WILLIAM son of Clark and Mary Short, 30 August 1732.

B. SHORT, ANN daughter of Clark and Mary Short, 9 December 1734.

B. SHORT, VINSON son of Clark and Mary Short, 8 January 1741.

B. SHORT, [name omitted] a son of John Short, [not entered] December 1782.

B. SHORT, WILLIAM son of John [? and ?] Marthy Short, 10 September 1787.

B. SHORT, MARY DAVIS a bastard daughter of Winnifrit Short, 12 April 1788.

B. SHORT, NANCEY DAVIS "A B child," daughter of Winnefret Short, 8 Feby 1794.

D. SIAS, JOSEPH 1 January 1720.

B. SIMMONDS, BETTY daughter of Ephriam and Mary Simmonds, 18 July 1740.

B. SIMPSON, JOHN son of William and Elizabeth Simpson, 11 August 1736.

SINGER : SINGNER

B. SINGNER, ELIZABETH daughter of William and Sarah Singner, 3 June 1777.

B. SINGER, ANN daughter of William and Sarah Singer, 29 October 1779.

B. SINGLETON, SARAH daughter of Joshua and Anne Singleton, 3 August 1725.

B. SINGLETON, JOSHUA son of Joshua and Ann Singleton, 23 January 1727/8.

B. SINGLETON, ANNE daughter of Joshua and Ann Singleton, 27 August 1730.

D. SINGLETON, ANNE 15 November 1730.

B. SINGLETON, STANLY son of Joshua and Anne Singleton, 2 October 1731.

M. SINGLETON, ANN and James Hinds, 23 September 1739.

B. SINGLETON, ROBERT son of Joshua and Ann Singleton, 7 November 1750.

B. SINGLETON, JOSHUA son of Joshua and Ann Singleton, 20 December 1759.

B. SINGLETON, JAMES son of Joshua and Ann Singleton, 2 August 1762.

B. SINGLETON, JOHN son of Joshua and Ann Singleton, 3 January 1765.

B. SINGLETON, SAMUEL son of Joshua and Ann Singleton, 16 January 1767.

D. SINGLETON, JOSHUA 20 February 1773.

SISSON   SEE : TILSON PAGE 188

B. SISSON, MARY daughter of Robert and Abigal Sisson, 31 July 1692.

B. SISSON, GEORGE son of Robert and Abigall Sisson, 15 May 1695.

B. SISSON, SARAH daughter of Bryan and Anne Sisson, 6 October 1725.

B. SISSON, ANNE daughter of Henry and Anne Sisson, 30 May 1726.

M. SISSON, WILLIAM and Frances Gower, 31 August 1727.

B. SISSON, WILLIAM son of Bryan and Ann Sisson, 25 April 1728.

B. SISSON, STANLEY son of William and Frances Sisson, 19 June 1728.

B. SISSON, HANNAH daughter of George Sisson, 22 July 1783.

B. SISSON, WILLIAM ATWELL son of Richard Sisson and wife, 7 February 1791 [L:35].

B. SISSON, ORMON SMITH a bastard child of Mary Sisson, 30 November 1791 [L:35].

B. SISSON, JOHN BARNITT son of Henry Sisson and wife, 20 November 1793 [L:35].

B. SISSON, WILLIAM MYNN FRANKLIN a base born child, son of Hanner Sisson, 20 April 1798 [L:35].

B. SISSON, VINCENT BARNETT ROS a base born child, son of Elender Sisson, 22 April 1798 [L:35].

SKELLEY **:** SKELLY   SEE **:** KELLEY **:** KELLY PAGE 110

B. SKELLY, JAMES son of James and Elizabeth Skelly, 25 July 1714.

B. SKELLEY, JAMES son of James and Elizabeth Skelley, 1 March 1715.

B. SKELLY, THOMAS son of James and Elizabeth Skelly, 24 June 1716.

B. SKELLEY, KATHRINE daughter of James Skelley, 2 December 1718.

D. SKELLEY, THOMAS 10 October 1719.

D. SKELLEY, KATHRINE 15 November 1719.

B. SKELLEY, FRANCIS son of James and Elizabeth Skelley, 1 October 1720.

D. SKELLEY, JAMES 5 November 1726.

D. SKELLEY, ELIZABETH 16 December 1726.

D. SKELLEY, JOHN 18 December 1726.

B. SKELLY, MARGARET daughter of James and Kathrine Skelly, 15 July 1727.

M. SMALL, OLIVER and Isabell Ramze, 11 June 1730.

B. SMITH, JOHN son of William and Frances Smith, 11 March 1681.

B. SMITH, THOMAS son of William and Anne Smith, 30 October 1683.

B. SMITH, ELLIAS son of William and Frances Smith, 10 November 1683.

B. SMITH, WILLIAM son of William and Anne Smith, 13 May 1688.

B. SMITH, HANNAH BOWER daughter of Richard and Rachell Smith, ___ Nov. 1689.

B. SMITH, RICHARD son of Thomas and Mary Smith, 27 July 1690.

B. SMITH, ELIZABETH daughter of John and Mary Smith, 20 March 1691.

B. SMITH, GABRIEL son of William and Frances Smith, 10 March 1692.

B. SMITH, THOMAS son of Thomas and Mary Smith, [not entered] 1695.

B. SMITH, JOSEPH son of William and Frances Smith, 15 June 1695.

B. SMITH, SAMUEL son of William and Elizabeth Smith, 23 December 1713.

B. SMITH, ANNE daughter of Robert and Margaret Smith, 6 February 1715.

B. SMITH, ISAAC son of William and Elizabeth Smith, 2 July 1716.

B. SMITH, MARGARET daughter of Robert and Margaret Smith, 6 September 1718.

B. SMITH, JOHN son of John and Elizabeth Smith, 5 July 1719.

B. SMITH, DAVID son of William and Mary Smith, 26 February 1720.

B. SMITH, BENJAMIN son of William and Elizabeth Smith, 15 September 1720.

B. SMITH, ELIZABETH daughter of Robert and Margaret Smith, 28 January 1721.

B. SMITH, CATY daughter of Thomas and Jane Smith, 18 September 1721.

B. SMITH, ELIAS son of Elias and Elizabeth Smith, 25 September 1721.

D. SMITH, WILLIAM 6 February 1723/4.

B. SMITH, WILLIAM son of Robert and Margaret Smith, 16 May 1724.

B. SMITH, WILLIAM son of William and Mary Smith, 21 May 1724.

B. SMITH, THOMAS son of Thomas and Jane Smith, 10 February 1724/5.

D. SMITH, JUDITH 2 June 1725.

D. SMITH, JOSEPH 22 December 1725.

B. SMITH, ELIZABETH daughter of Elias and Elizabeth Smith, 8 January 1726.

M. SMITH, JOHN and Margaret Canterbery, 9 February 1725/6.

M. SMITH, KATHERINE and William Jones, 16 February 1725/6.

B. SMITH, THOMAS son of Robert and Margaret Smith, 18 July 1726.

B. SMITH, SAMUEL son of William and Mary Smith, 15 August 1726.

D. SMITH, WINIFRED 18 August 1726.

D. SMITH, ANNE 14 November 1726.

D. SMITH, ELIZABETH 20 November 1726.

D. SMITH, JOHN 22 November 1726.

D. SMITH, THOMAS 23 November 1726.

M. SMITH, FRANCES and Thomas Osborne, 11 February 1726/7.

D. SMITH, JANE 24 March 1726/7.

M. SMITH, FRANCES and Edward Bryant 6 April 1727.

M.   SMITH, PETER and Ann Short, 15 May 1727.

D.   SMITH, WILLIAM 1 September 1728.

B.   SMITH, JOHN son of Robert and Margaret Smith, 6 August 1729.

D.   SMITH, JOHN 10 December 1730.

M.   SMITH, WILLIAM and Sarah Truman, 5 July 1731.

M.   SMITH, WILLIAM and Agnes Baroh, 15 March 1731/2.

B.   SMITH, JOSEPH son of John and Mary Smith, 13 September 1734.

B.   SMITH, JOHN son of John and Mary Smith, 5 November 1735.

B.   SMITH, WILLIAM son of John and Mary Smith, 20 February 1737.

B.   SMITH, JESSE son of Thomas and Ann Smith, 24 July 1738.

B.   SMITH, SARAH daughter of John and Mary Smith, 23 January 1739.

B.   SMITH, EDWARD son of John and Mary Smith, 23 January 1741.

D.   SMITH, WILLIAM 7 January 1743.

B.   SMITH, MARY daughter of John and Mary Smith, 6 February 1743.

B.   SMITH, WILLIAM son of David and Ann Smith, 19 March 1743.

B.   SMITH, COLSTON son of John and Mary Smith, 2 March 1745.

B.   SMITH, MARY ANN daughter of Samuel and Sarah Smith, 22 August 1747.

B.   SMITH, BENJAMIN son of John and Mary Smith, 11 June 1748.

B.   SMITH, CATY daughter of Thomas and Ann Smith, 27 September 1750.

B.   SMITH, ANNE daughter of Thomas and Anne Smith, 28 May 1752.

B.   SMITH, THOMAS son of Thomas and Ann Smith, 28 April 1754.

M.   SMITH, SARAH and John Plummer, 7 May 1756.

B.   SMITH, CATY daughter of Thomas and Ann Smith, 6 October 1756.

B.   SMITH, JOHN son of Thomas and Ann Smith, 18 February 1759.

B.   SMITH, MARY COLSTON daughter of William and Mary Smith, 25 January 1761.

B.   SMITH, JOSEPH son of Thomas and Ann Smith, 27 March 1761.

B. SMITH, MARY daughter of John and Elizabeth Smith, 23 January 1762.

B. SMITH, BETTY daughter of Thomas and Ann Smith, 24 July 1763.

B. SMITH, NANNY daughter of John N. and Betty Smith, 15 December 1763.

B. SMITH, SARAH daughter of Edward and Fanny Smith, 13 January 1764.

B. SMITH, JOSEPH son of Edward and Fanny Smith, 13 October 1765.

B. SMITH, SALLY and MARY twins of Thomas and Ann Smith, 29 October 1768.

B. SMITH, CATHARINE GWIN daughter of William and Mary Smith, 9 February 1772.

B. SMITH, JOHN son of Benjamin and Elizabeth Smith, 3 November 1777.

B. SMITH, ORMON a bastard child of Mary Sisson, 30 November 1791 [L:35].

B. SMITH, MOLLY YATES daughter of William and Elizabeth Smith, 26 July 1792 [L:33].

B. SMITH, WILLIAM son of William and Elizabeth Smith, 17 May 1794 [L:35].

B. SMITH, WINIFRED HOW daughter of William and Elizabeth Smith, 24 April 1797.

B. SMITH, WINIFRED HOW daughter of William and Elizabeth Smith, 30 July 1799 [both of these entries, L:35].

SMITHER : SMITHERS

B. SMITHER, WILLIAM son of George and Mary Smither, 12 August 1709.

B. SMITHER, GEORGE son of George and Mary Smither, 4 April 1712 (sic).

B. SMITHER, GEORGE son of George and Mary Smither, 12 April 1712 (sic).

B. SMITHER, GABRIEL son of George and Mary Smither, 29 September 1717.

B. SMITHER, WINNY daughter of Gabriel and Wilmoth Smither, 20 November 1756.

B. SMITHER, LANCELOT son of Gabriel and Wilmoth Smither, 21 October 1758.

B. SMITHER, MARY daughter of Gabriel and Wilmoth Smither, 11 February 1761.

B. SMITHER, RICHARD son of Gabriel and Wilmoth Smither, 14 March 1763.

B. SMITHER, ELIZABETH daughter of Gabriel and Wilmoth Smither, 27 October 1765.

B. SMITHER, DEWANNA daughter of Gabriel and Wilmoth Smither, 10 October 1768.

B. SMITHER, SILLAH daughter of Gabriel and Wilmoth Smither, 8 February 1772.

B.   SMITHER, LUCY and ANN twins of Gabriel and Wilmoth Smither, 2 March 1774.

B.   SMITHERS, GABRIEL son of Gabriel and Willmuth Smithers, 14 November 1776.

B.   SMITHER, JOHN and WILLIAM sons of Gabriel and Wilmuth Smither, 29 May 1779.

B.   SMITHER, PEGGA FLEMING daughter of Launce L. and Nancy Smither, 5 December 1785.

B.   SMITHER, SAMUEL son of Launce L. and Nancey Smither, 5 September 1789.

B.   SMITHER, RICHARD son of Launce L. and Nancy Smither, 8 April 1792.

B.   SMITHER, RICHARD son of Richard and Sarah Smither, 13 February 1794.

B.   SMOOT, MARY daughter of William and Jane Smoot, 7 April 1693.

B.   SMOOT, ANNE daughter of William and Jane Smoot, 16 March 1698.

B.   SMOOT, ELIZABETH daughter of William and Jane Smoot, 16 March 1698.

D.   SMOOT, JANE 4 October 1726.

B.   SMOOT, ELEANOR daughter of William and Frances Smoot, 27 April 1750.

B.   SMOOT, SARAH daughter of William and Frances Smoot, 23 April 1756.

B.   SMOOT, THOMAS son of William and Frances Smoot, 26 July 1753.

B.   SMOOT, ANN daughter of William and Frances Smoot, 6 September 1761.

B.   SMOOT, JOHN son of William and Frances Smoot, 13 October 1764.

B.   SMOOT, BETTY daughter of William and Frances Smoot, 8 February 1771.

BAPT. SOLELEATHER, BETSY a daughter of Philip Soleleather, 8 years old, 23 February 1800 [L:34, Negro recordings].

B.   SOUTHERN, MARY daughter of William and Eleanor Southern, ____ August 1689.

B.   SOUTHERN, SUSANNA daughter of Thomas and Eleanor Southern, 19 March 1691.

B.   SOUTHERN, WINNIFRED daughter of Thomas and Eleanor Southern, 8 March 1693.

B.   SOUTHERN, THOMAS son of Thomas and Eleanor Southern, 4 December 1695.

B.   SPENCER, EDWARD son of Edward and Winnifred Spencer, 20 November 1710.

SPENDERGRASS   SEE : PENDERGRASS PAGE 145

B.   SPENDERGRASS, JOHN son of James and Mary Spendergrass, __ April 1697.

M. SPENDERGRASS, JOHN and Elizabeth Cribin, 2 December 1728.

B. SPENDERGRASS, ELEANOR daughter of James and Rebeccah Spendergrass, 15 May 1729.

B. SPENDERGRASS, JAMES son of John and Elizabeth Spendergrass, 23 November 1729.

B. SPENDERGRASS, JOHN son of Robert and Elizabeth Spendergrass, 10 December 1734.

BAPT. SPILLER, PATRICK son of Captain Spiller and wife, 31 July 1791 [L:35].

D. SPOONER, SARAH 15 July 1755.

B. SPRAG, MARY daughter of John and Frances Sprag, 24 July 1705.

D. SPRAGG, WILLIAM 1 August 1726.

M. SPRAGG, JOHN and Mary Edwards, 2 February 1726/7.

B. SPRIGGS, THOMAS BAKER son of Bridget Spriggs, 5 April 1741.

B. STANFIELD, BETTY daughter of Thomas and Mary Stanfield, 9 October 1723.

B. STANFIELD, MARMADUKE son of Thomas and Mary Stanfield, 4 February 1724/5.

M. STANFIELD, MARY and Jonathan Lyell, 16 October 1729.

D. STANFIELD, THOMAS 13 January 1730.

B. STANLY, NANNY daughter of John and Margaret Stanly, 17 August 1753.

B. STARKS, HENRY son of James and Eleanor Starks, 15 January 1705.

B. STARKS, ANNE daughter of James and Eleanor Starks, 19 February 1707.

B. STARKS, JANE daughter of James and Eleanor Starks, 1 April 1709.

B. STARKS, MARY daughter of James and Eleanor Starks, 1 March 1711.

B. STARKS, DORCAS daughter of James and Eleanor Starks, 14 August 1715.

B. STARKS, ELEANOR daughter of James and Eleanor Starks, 9 November 1718.

B. STARKS, WINIFRED daughter of James and Eleanor Starks, 13 August 1724.

D. STARKS, MARY 4 December 1726.

D. STARKS, JAMES 10 December 1726.

M. STARKS, JANE and John Alderson 4 July 1729.

M. STARKS, ELEANOR and William Abshone, 15 October 1729.

M. STARKS, DARKS and Simon Churchwell, 4 March 1730/1.

B. STEEL, SAMUEL son of Samuel and Jane Steel, 4 January 1690.

B. STEEL, MARGARET daughter of Samuel and Kathrine Steel, 29 May 1719.

B. STEEL, ELIZABETH daughter of Samuel and Kathrine Steel, 28 October 1721.

B. STEEL, AMBERAS son of Samuel and Kathrine Steel, 6 March 1724/5.

B. STEEL, KATHRINE daughter of Samuel and Kathrine Steel, 20 April 1727.

B. STEEL, SARAH daughter of Samuel and Kathrine Steel, 22 October 1729.

B. STEEL, SAMUEL son of Samuel and Kathrine Steel, 25 February 1731/2.

D. STEEL, AMBROSE 13 August 1735.

M. STEPHEN, DANIEL and Lucy Tarpley 20 October 1728.

B. STEVENS, ELIZABETH daughter of Tobias and Anne Stevens, 31 October 1679.

B. STEVENS, WILLIAM son of John and Frances Stevens, 17 June 1719.

D. STEVENS, DEBORAH 14 May 1720.

D. STEVENS, ROBERT 1 May 1729.

B. STEWART, MARGARET daughter of John and Judith Stewart, 20 August 1685.

B. STEWART, JOHN son of John and Judith Stewart, 15 March 1686.

B. STEWART, ANNE daughter of John and Judith Stewart, 10 August 1690.

B. STEWART, ELIZABETH daughter of John and Jane Stewart, 5 March 1692.

B. STEWART, ELIZABETH daughter of John and Judith Stewart, 27 December 1692.

B. STEWART, JAMES son of John and Judith Stewart, 15 February 1701.

D. STEWART, JANE 30 November 1730.

B. STEWART, JANE daughter of Robert and Elizabeth Stewart, 12 December 1746.

B. STONE, ASTIN son of Philip and Sarah Stone, 8 September 1700.

B. STONE, JUDITH daughter of Philip and Sarah Stone, 26 August 1702.

B. STONE, ANNE daughter of William and Elizabeth Stone, 5 March 1713.

B. STONE, MARGARET daughter of William and Elizabeth Stone, 5 January 1715.

B. STONE, PHILIP son of William and Elizabeth Stone, 10 January 1716.

B. STONE, JOSHUA son of Joshua and Mary Stone, 26 October 1716.

D. STONE, AUSTIN 12 December 1717.

D. STONE, JOSHUA 15 December 1717.

B. STONE, ELIZABETH daughter of William and Elizabeth Stone, 31 August 1719.

B. STONE, LUCY daughter of William and Elizabeth Stone, 29 October 1721.

B. STONE, JOANNA daughter of William and Elizabeth Stone, 11 April 1724.

D. STONE, JOANNA 11 December 1725.

B. STONE, HENRY son of William and Elizabeth Stone, 13 September 1726.

B. STONE, KATHRINE daughter of William and Elizabeth Stone, 16 January 1728.

M. STONE, SARAH and Thomas Penley, 30 January 1728/9.

B. STONE, SARAH daughter of William and Elizabeth Stone, 25 October 1731.

B. STONE, WILLIAM son of William and Elizabeth Stone, 1 March 1734.

M. STONE, JOSHUA and Wilmoth Bryant, 22 November 1738.

B. STONE, WILLIAM son of Joshua and Wilmoth Stone, 9 June 1740.

B. STONE, JOSHUA son of Joshua and Wilmoth Stone, 13 October 1744.

B. STONE, BENJAMIN son of Joshua and Wilmoth Stone, 26 September 1747.

B. STONE, THOMAS son of Joshua and Wilmoth Stone, 31 December 1750.

B. STONE, JOHN son of Joshua and Wilmoth Stone, 25 November 1754.

B. STONE, MOSES son of Joshua and Wilmoth Stone, 12 May 1758.

B. STONE, JOSHUA son of Thomas and Elizabeth Stone, 13 October 1775.

B. STONE, WILLIAM BRANNOM son of John P. Stone and wife, 15 September 1791 [L:35]

B. STONE, MOLLEY daughter of John and Martha Stone, 26 August 1793 [L:35].

B. STONE, ELIZABETH daughter of John and Martha Stone, 22 May 1795 [L:35].

B. STONE, MARTHEY daughter of John and Marthey Stone, 3 June 1797 [L:35].

B. STONUM, WILLIAM son of William and Sarah Stonum, 3 February 1718.

B. STONUM, SARAH daughter of William and Susanna Stonum, 3 April 1737.

B. STONUM, GEORGE son of William and Susanna Stonum, 24 October 1740.

B. STONUM, ANN daughter of William and Susanna Stonum, 22 June 1744.

B. STONUM, WILLIAM son of William and Susanna Stonum, 5 January 1752.

B. STONUM, FORTUNATUS son of William and Susanna Stonum, 20 February 1755.

B. STONUM, SUSANNA daughter of George and Mary Stonum, 21 January 1777.

B. STONUM, [Christian name omitted] daughter of George and Mary Stonum, 16 May 1778.

B. STONUM, NANCY daughter of George and Mary Stonum, 1 September 1781.

B. STONUM, ELLEN daughter of William Stonum, 2 June 1782.

B. STONUM, JOHN son of Lucy Dale, 12 November 1789.

B. STONUM, HENRY son of William and Frances Stonum, 8 March 1791.

B. STONUM, SAMUEL NORRIS son of William and Mary Stonum, 15 January 1801.

B. STOTT, JAMES son of John and Sarah Stott, 3 July 1775.

B. STOTT, MOLLY daughter of Robert and Elizabeth Stott, 10 July 1776.

B. STOTT, SALLY daughter of Eppy and Hannah Stott, 26 February 1779.

B. STOTT, ELEN daughter of LeRoy and Ann Stott, 2 December 1781.

B. STOTT, SALLY daughter of Oliver and Molly Stott, 19 January 1783.

B. STOTT, NANCY daughter of LeRoy and Ann Stott, 2 January 1788.

B. STOTT, SALLEY OLIVER daughter of John Stott, Junr, 20 April 1790.

B. STOWERS, JOHN son of John and Frances Stowers, 23 April 1708.

B. STOWERS, MARK son of John and Frances Stowers, 23 July 1711.

B. STOWERS, JOHN son of William and Ann Stowers, 4 April 1748.

B. STOWERS, FRANCES daughter of William and Ann Stowers, 16 March 1750.

B. STOWERS, CATY daughter of William and Ann Stowers, 30 October 1752.

B. STUCKE, GRIFFIN WARMOUTH daughter of Job Stucke, 5 April 1782.

B. STUCKEY, HANNAH daughter of Job and Mary Stuckey, 4 February 1781.

SUGGIT ; SUGGITT

B. SUGGITT, THOMAS son of John and Sarah Suggitt, 7 March 1677.

B. SUGGITT, ELIZABETH daughter of John and Elizabeth Suggitt, 29 October 1696.

B. SUGGIT, THOMAS son of Thomas and Rebeccah Suggit, 12 February 1708.

B. SUGGIT, EDGECOMB son of Edgecomb and Lucy Suggit, 3 March 1709.

B. SUGGIT, MARY daughter of Edgecomb and Lucy Sugitt, 13 October 1712.

B. SUGGIT, BERNIE daughter of James and Frances Suggit, 24 January 1714.

B. SUGGITT, JAMES son of James and Mary Suggitt, 18 April 1722.

M. SUGGITT, SARAH and William Hill, 3 March 1726/7.

D. SUGGITT, KATHRINE   28 July 1727.

M. SUGGETT, ELIZABETH and John Hill, 19 July 1728.

B. SUGGITT, LUCY daughter of Edgcomb and Elizabeth Suggitt, 25 November 1735.

B. SUGGITT, JOHN son of Edgcomb and Elizabeth Suggitt, 17 August 1737.

B. SUGGITT, ELIZABETH daughter of Edgecomb and Elizabeth Suggitt, 11 March 1741.

B. SUGGITT, SARAH daughter of Edgcomb and Elizabeth Suggitt, 13 May 1751.

B. SUGGITT, SUSANNA daughter of Edgcomb and Elizabeth Suggitt, 8 November 1752.

D. SUGGITT, EDGCOMB   9 January 1753.

B. SUGGITT, ELIZABETH daughter of John and Hannah Suggitt, 11 October 1768.

B. SUGGITT, JUDITH PANE daughter of John and Hannah Suggitt, 23 April 1770.

D. SUGGITT, JOHN   21 October 1771.

B. SUGGITT, JOHN son of John Suggitt (deceased) and Hannah, his wife, 1 August 1772.

B. SUTTON, RICHARD son of Richard and Fanney Sutton, 7 March 1798 [L:35].

M. SWAN, ALEXANDER and Judith Hinds, 15 November 1678.

B. SWAN, MARGARET daughter of Alexander and Judith Swan, [not entered], 1680.

B. SWAN, JOHN son of Alexander and Judith Swan, 22 January 1691.

B. SWAN, SALLEY daughter of Charles and Elizabeth Swan, 25 April 1800.

B. SWAN, JAMES son of Charles and Elizabeth Swan, 16 May 1803.

B. SWAN, CHARLES W. son of Charles and Elizabeth Swan, 7 December 1807.

B. SWAN, WILLIAM son of Charles and Elizabeth Swan, 7 August 1814.

D. SWELLAVENT, FRANCIS 25 November 1718.

B. SWINDALL, JOHN son of Timothy and Sarah Swindall, 20 March 1676.

D. SWINTON, FRANCIS [? FRANCES ?] 19 March 1724/5.

B. SYDNOR, WINIFRET daughter of Anthony and Elizabeth Sydnor, 6 February 1713/4.

B. SYDNOR, EPAPHRODITUS son of Anthony and Elizabeth Sydnor, 12 May 1715.

B. SYDNOR, BETTY daughter of Anthony and Elizabeth Sydnor, 23 February 1716/7.

B. SYDNOR, DUANNAH [DEWANNAH] daughter of Anthony and Elizabeth Sydnor, 9 January 1719.

B. SYDNOR, LUCY daughter of Anthony and Elizabeth Sydnor, 3 February 1722.

D. SYDNOR, WILLIAM 16 September 1722.

D. SYDNOR, JOHN 8 January 1726.

B. SYDNOR, RUTH daughter of Anthony and Elizabeth Sydnor, 15 March 1726.

B. SYDNOR, ANTHONY son of Anthony and Elizabeth Sydnor, 25 December 1726.

M. SYDNOR, JOHN and Elizabeth Heall, 27 May 1728.

B. SYDNOR, RUTH daughter of John and Elizabeth Sydnor, 4 May 1729.

B. SYDNOR, ANNE daughter of Anthony and Elizabeth Sydnor, 24 June 1729.

B. SYDNOR, SELAH [SILAH] daughter of Anthony and Elizabeth Sydnor, 6 July 1731.

M. SYDNOR, WINIFRED and John Rout, 3 March 1731/2.

B. SYDNOR, JOHN son of Epaphroditus and Mary Sydnor, 20 February 1736.

B. SYDNOR, WILLIAM son of Epaphroditus and Mary Sydnor, 24 February 1738.

B. SYDNOR, EPAPHRODITUS son of Epaphroditus and Mary Sydnor, 18 December 1742.

B. SYDNOR, ROBERT son of Anthony and Frances Sydnor, 23 January 1750.

B. SYDNOR, ANTHONY son of Epaphroditus and Mary Sydnor, 12 March 1752.

B. SYDNOR, ELIZABETH daughter of Anthony and Frances Sydnor, 25 November 1752.

B. SYDNOR, GILES son of Epaphroditus and Mary Sydnor, 8 August 1753.

B. SYDNOR, SUSANNA daughter of Anthony and Frances Sydnor, 28 April 1754.

D. SYDNOR, EPAPHRODITUS 15 March 1756.

B. SYDNOR, NANCY daughter of William and Judith Sydnor, 25 September 1764.

B. SYDNOR, JOHN son of William and Judith Sydnor, 3 September 1766.

B. SYDNOR, JAMES DOWNMAN son of Anthony and Elizabeth Sydnor, 12 December 1777.

B. SYDNOR, [not entered] a daughter of Jiles Sydnor, [not entered], 1783.

B. SYDNOR, HARRISON son of Epaphroditus and Milly Sydnor, 31 May 1789.

T

B. TAFF, CHARLES son of John Taff and Winifred Giffres, 10 April 1739.

B. TALBURT, MARY ANN daughter of Edward and Frances Talburt, 24 June 1726.

M. TALBURT, ELIZABETH and William Thornton, 10 August 1727.

B. TALBURT, KATHRINE daughter of Edward and Martha Talburt, 20 November 1731.

B. TARPLEY, JOHN son of James and Mary Tarpley, 21 February 1690.

B. TARPLEY, MARY daughter of James and Mary Tarpley, 1 February 1691.

B. TARPLEY, JAMES son of James and Mary Tarpley, 8 May 1692.

B. TARPLEY, WILLIAM son of James and Mary Tarpley, 16 March 1695.

B. TARPLEY, JOHN son of John and Elizabeth Tarpley, 16 July 1695.

B. TARPLEY, THOMAS son of James and Mary Tarpley, 28 February 1697.

B. TARPLEY, ELIZABETH daughter of James and Mary Tarpley, 2 February 1701.

B. TARPLEY, JOHN and BETTY son and daughter of John and Elizabeth Tarpley, 28 May 1720.

B. TARPLEY, MARY daughter of William and Mary Tarpley, 7 December 1723.

B. TARPLEY, EDWARD RIPPING son of John and Elizabeth Tarpley, 19 April 1727.

M. TARPLEY, LUCY and Daniel Stephen, 20 October 1728.

B. TARPLEY, ELIZABETH daughter of John and Elizabeth Tarpley, 4 March 1728/9.

B. TARPLEY, JOHN son of William and Mary Tarpley, 29 September 1729.

B. TARPLEY, JAMES son of William and Mary Tarpley, 8 December 1731.

B. TARPLEY, THOMAS son of James and Mary Tarpley, 28 October 1734.

B. TARPLEY, HANNAH daughter of William and Mary Tarpley, 6 January 1735.

B. TARPLEY, LUCY daughter of James and Mary Tarpley, 17 August 1736.

B. TARPLEY, BETTY daughter of Traverse and Betty Tarpley, 28 July 1738.

B. TARPLEY, SARAH daughter of James and Mary Tarpley, 13 September 1738.

B. TARPLEY, JOHN son of John and Ann Tarpley, 13 December 1738.

B. TARPLEY, ELIZABETH daughter of John and Ann Tarpley, 5 April 1740.

B. TARPLEY, MARY daughter of James and Mary Tarpley, 30 October 1740.

B. TARPLEY, WINIFRED daughter of Traverse and Betty Tarpley, 1 November 1740.

B. TARPLEY, ALICE daughter of John and Ann Tarpley, 24 November 1742.

B. TARPLEY, FANNY daughter of Traverse and Betty Tarpley, 2 July 1743.

B. TARPLEY, JAMES son of James and Mary Tarpley, 21 July 1743.

B. TARPLEY, WINNY daughter of John and Ann Tarpley, 16 September 1744.

B. TARPLEY, LUCY daughter of Traverse and Betty Tarpley, 7 January 1745.

B. TARPLEY, BETTY daughter of James and Mary Tarpley, 6 August 1746.

B. TARPLEY, TRAVERSE son of John and Ann Tarpley, 12 August 1746.

B. TARPLEY, THOMAS son of John and Ann Tarpley, 3 June 1748.

B. TARPLEY, SAMUEL TRAVERSE son of Traverse and Betty Tarpley, 15 December 1748.

B. TARPLEY, CATY daughter of John and Ann Tarpley, 13 April 1750.

B. TARPLEY, MILLY daughter of Traverse and Betty Tarpley, 28 September 1756.

B. TAVERNER, SARAH daughter of John and Elizabeth Taverner, 7 January 1679.

B. TAVERNER, ELIZABETH daughter of John and Elizabeth Taverner, 25 March 1681.

B. TAVERNER, JOHN son of John and Elizabeth Taverner, 7 March 1682/3.

B. TAVERNER, RICHARD son of John and Elizabeth Taverner, 30 July 1685.

   TAYLER   SEE : TAYLOR :   TAYLER   PAGES   182 - 183

B. TAYLOE, ELIZABETH daughter of William and Anne Tayloe, 26 July 1686.

B. TAYLOE, JOHN son of William and Anne Tayloe, 15 February 1687/8. [See notes under GWIN on page 76.]

   TAYLOR   :   TAYLER

B. TAYLOR, SARAH daughter of Simon and Elizabeth Taylor, 28 September 1692.

B. TAYLOR, PETER son of William and Mary Taylor, 26 November 1699.

B. TAYLOR, CATHARINE daughter of Charles and Anne Taylor, 2 July 1707.

D. TAYLOR, RICHARD 23 January 1716.

B. TAYLER, JOSEPH son of John and Catharine Tayler, 18 May 1717.

D. TAYLOR, SIMON 2 February 1718.

B. TAYLOR, ANNE daughter of Robert and Philadelphia Taylor, 14 January 1722.

B. TAYLOR, JOHN son of Robert and Philadelphia Taylor, 6 July 1725.

D. TAYLOR, THOMAS 20 March 1726.

D. TAYLOR, WILLIAM 2 November 1726.

D. TAYLOR, ELIZABETH 7 October 1727.

B. TAYLOR, WILLIAM son of Robert and Philadelphia Taylor, 6 March 1727/8.

B. TAYLOR, SIMON son of John and Hannah Taylor, 11 March 1728.

M. TAYLOR, KATHERINE and Joseph Bruce, 30 April 1728.

D. TAYLOR, SIMON 10 January 1728/9.

D. TAYLOR, THOMAS 9 January 1730.

M. TAYLOR, WILLIAM and Elizabeth Hendorson, 8 October 1730.

B. TAYLOR, ELIZABETH daughter of John and Hannah Taylor, 26 September 1731.

B. TAYLOR, SARAH daughter of Septimus and Bridget Taylor, 19 November 1733.

B. TAYLOR, ANN daughter of William and Elizabeth Taylor, 9 September 1734.

B.   TAYLOR, JAMES son of James and Alice Taylor, 13 December 1734.

B.   TAYLOR, HARRISON son of John and Hannah Taylor, 14 August 1735.

B.   TAYLOR, ANN daughter of Septimus and Bridget Taylor, 23 September 1735.

B.   TAYLOR, CHARLES son of Septimus and Bridget Taylor, 8 January 1737.

B.   TAYLER, RICHARD son of John and Hannah Tayler, 8 November 1738.

D.   TAYLER, JOHN   28 February 1740.

B.   TAYLER, KATHRINE daughter of Septimus and Bridget Tayler, 1 October 1740.

B.   TAYLER, WILLIAM son of George and Mary Tayler, 7 April 1741.

B.   TAYLOR, TARPLEY son of George and Mary Taylor, 24 February 1742.

B.   TAYLOR, JOHN son of Septimus and Bridget Taylor, 25 December 1742.

B.   TAYLOR, SIMON son of George and Mary Taylor, 9 March 1744.

B.   TAYLOR, SEPTIMUS son of Septimus and Bridget Taylor, 29 September 1745.

B.   TAYLOR, GEORGE son of George and Mary Taylor, 21 October 1747.

B.   TAYLOR, LUCY daughter of George and Mary Taylor, 19 February 1749.

D.   TAYLOR, GEORGE   25 October 1749.

B.   TAYLOR, WILLIAM DUDLEY a bastard child of Ann Taylor, 23 July 1755.

B.   TAYLOR, WILLIAM son of Charles and Caty Taylor, 30 September 1763.

B.   TERRANCE, THOMAS a mulatto belonging to John Tarpley, 16 December 1723.

D.   THACKOM, MARY   15 April 1721.

B.   THOMAS, RICHARD son of John Thomas, 8 August 1686.

B.   THOMAS, ELIZABETH daughter of Evan and Elizabeth Thomas, 17 March 1696.

B.   THOMAS, MARY daughter of Robert and Deborah Thomas, 15 June 1711.

D.   THOMAS, GEORGE   15 January 1726.

M.   THOMAS, ANN and Richard Hillman, 10 July 1729.

B.   THOMAS, JEREMIAH son of Mary Ann Thomas, 1 December 1732.

B.   THOMAS, NANCY daughter of Thomas and Winy Thomas, 30 December 1776.

B. THOMAS, BETSY daughter of Peter and Judith Thomas, 8 January 1778.

B. THOMAS, VINCENT BRAMHAM son of William Thomas, 9 May 1797 [L:37].

THOMPSON : THOMSON

B. THOMPSON, ELIZABETH daughter of Walter and Mary Thompson, 19 October 1680.

D. THOMPSON, ROBERT 6 October 1722.

M. THOMPSON, GEORGE and Katherine Phillips, 21 February 1725/6.

D. THOMPSON, ELIZABETH 1 October 1726.

D. THOMPSON, REBECCAH 1 September 1727.

B. THOMSON, WILLIAM son of George and Kathrine Thomson, 1 April 1728.

B. THOMPSON, ANN daughter of George and Kathrine Thompson, 29 August 1731.

THORN : THORNE

B. THORNE, SARAH daughter of Daniel and Joanna Thorne, 16 February 1715.

D. THORN, THOMAS 31 October 1717.

B. THORNE, HENRY son of Thomas and Jane Thorne, 20 November 1717.

D. THORNE, SUSANNA 14 March 1726/7.

B. THORN, JANE daughter of Merriman and Kathrine Thorn, 14 September 1740.

B. THORN, SUSANNA daughter of Merriman and Jane Thorn, 19 December 1741.

B. THORN, THOMAS son of Merryman and Kathrine Thorn, 4 March 1744.

B. THORN, ANN daughter of Merryman and Kathrine Thorn, 2 August 1746.

B. THORN, CATY daughter of Merryman and Kathrine Thorn, 29 October 1748.

B. THORN, BETTY daughter of Merryman and Caty Thorn, 22 July 1751.

B. THORN, MERRYMAN son of Merryman and Caty Thorn, 11 March 1754.

B. THORNBROUGH, FRANCIS son of Rowland and Marcey Thornbrough, 23 Sept. 1717.

B. THORNTON, ROGER son of Henry and Anne Thornton, 17 June 1686.

B. THORNTON, MARK son of Luke and Ann Thornton, 23 September 1686.

B. THORNTON, THOMAS son of Luke and Ann Thornton, 5 April 1688.

B. THORNTON, HENRY son of Roger and Isabel Thornton, 15 November 1709.

B. THORNTON, MARY daughter of Roger and Isabel Thornton, 5 July 1712.

B. THORNTON, JOHN son of Roger and Isabel Thornton, 25 June 1718.

B. THORNTON, ANNE daughter of Roger and Isabel Thornton, 9 February 1720.

B. THORNTON, ROBERT son of Robert and Mary Thornton, 20 October 1722.

B. THORNTON, WILLIAM son of Roger and Isabel Thornton, 14 March 1722/3.

B. THORNTON, BRIDGET daughter of Robert and Mary Thornton, 28 May 1724.

B. THORNTON, MARY daughter of James and Anne Thornton, 13 March 1725.

B. THORNTON, ROGER son of Robert and Isabella Thornton, 14 June 1725.

D. THORNTON, WILLIAM 14 November 1726.

D. THORNTON, BRIDGET 26 November 1726.

B. THORNTON, JOHN son of Robert and Mary Thornton, 9 April 1727.

M. THORNTON, WILLIAM and Elizabeth Talburt, 10 August 1727.

M. THORNTON, MARGARET and Robert Boston, 14 September 1727.

M. THORNTON, LUKE and Millisent Longworth, 2 January 1727/8.

M. THORNTON, ELLEN and Alvin Mountjoy, 3 May 1728.

B. THORNTON, WILLIAM son of Roger and Elizabeth Thornton, 17 June 1728.

B. THORNTON, WILLIAM son of James and Anne Thornton, 2 August 1728.

D. THORNTON, MATTHEW 10 February 1730.

B. THORNTON, JAMES son of James and Ann Thornton, 8 August 1731.

B. THORNTON, DAVID son of Robert and Frances Thornton, 24 March 1788.

B. THORNTON, SHARLOTT daughter of Robert and Frances Thornton, 29 November 1791 [L:37].

THRELKELD : THRELKILL

M. THRELKELD, HENRY and Eleanor Short, 15 July 1728.

B. THRELKILL, GEORGE son of Henry and Eleanor Threlkill, 24 March 1729/30.

D. THRELKILL, HENRY 11 March 1731.

B. THRIFT, WILLIAM son of Nathaniel and Elizabeth Thrift, 30 January 1675.

M. THRIFT, ELIZABETH and William Davis, 23 April 1677.

B. THRIFT, REBECCAH daughter of Nathaniel and Rebeccah Thrift, 4 April 1696.

B. THRIFT, WILLIAM son of Nathaniel and Elizabeth Thrift, 20 September 1699,

B. THRIFT, NATHANIEL son of Nathaniel and Elizabeth Thrift, 27 July 1704.

B. THRIFT, JANE daughter of Nathaniel and Elizabeth Thrift, 29 October 1706.

B. THRIFT, JOB son of Nathaniel and Elizabeth Thrift, 29 October 1708.

B. THRIFT, JEREMIAH son of Nathaniel and Elizabeth Thrift, 24 December 1719.

B. THRIFT, ESTHER daughter of William and Ann Thrift, 6 February 1724/5,

D. THRIFT, ESTHER 29 June 1725.

B. THRIFT, ESTHER daughter of William and Anne Thrift, 1 September 1725.

B. THRIFT, ESTHER daughter of William and Ann Thrift, 1 September 1726.

D. THRIFT, ESTHER 9 September 1726.

B. THRIFT, WINNEY daughter of William and Anne Thrift, 25 May 1731.

B. THRIFT, NATHANIEL son of John and Massy Thrift, 26 April 1744.

B. THRIFT, MERRYMAN son of John and Massey Thrift, 16 February 1746,

D. THRIFT, AMADINE daughter of John and Massey Thrift, 27 March 1749,

B. THRIFT, AMADINE daughter of John and Massie Thrift, 1 July 1752.

B. THRIFT, MASSIE daughter of John and Massie Thrift, 20 April 1755, -

B. THRIFT, SAMUEL son of John and Massie Thrift, 5 March 1759.

B. THRIFT, WILLIAM son of Meriman Thrift, 18 August 1782.

B. THRIFT, SAMUEL son of Nathaniel and Elizabeth Thrift, 11 July 1788.

B. TIGNOR, CATEY SMITH daughter of Thomas and Salley Tignor, 30 May 1794.

B. TIGNOR, WILLIAM JOHNSON son of Thomas and Sally Tignor, 1 September 1796.

B. TIGNOR, NANCEY WOOLLARD daughter of Thomas and Sally Tignor, 30 Nov. 1798.

B. TIGNOR, THOMAS SMITH son of Thomas and Salley Tignor, 21 January 1802.

M. TILLERY, HENRY and Mary Wascole, 7 November 1675.

B. TILLERY, HENRY son of Henry and Mary Tillery, 12 November 1679.

B. TILLERY, MARY daughter of Henry and Mary Tillery, 23 November 1685.

B. TILLERY, RICHARD son of Charles and Eleanor Tillery, 12 August 1688.

B. TILLERY, JOB son of Thomas and Priscilla Tillery, 6 December 1695.

B. TILLERY, JOB son of Job and Mary Tillery, 3 March 1705.

B. TILLERY, GEORGE son of John and Margaret Tillery, 8 August 1715.

B. TILLERY, BETTY daughter of John and Margaret Tillery, 10 February 1717.

B. TILLERY, THOMAS son of Richard and Elizabeth Tillery, 25 March 1718.

B. TILLERY, JOHN son of Richard and Elizabeth Tillery, 2 August 1720.

B. TILLERY, MARY ANN daughter of John and Margaret Tillery, 16 November 1720.

B. TILLERY, MARY daughter of Job and Mary Tillery, 28 April 1721.

D. TILLERY, JOHN 26 August 1721.

B. TILLERY, ANNE daughter of Richard and Elizabeth Tillery, 18 August 1722.

B. TILLERY, JOHN son of Samuel and Winnefred Tillery, 6 August 1724.

B. TILLERY, JOANNA daughter of John and Margaret Tillery, 17 February 1725.

B. TILLERY, WILLOUGHBY son of Richard and Elizabeth Tillery, 7 April 1725.

D. TILLERY, THOMAS 16 February 1726.

D. TILLERY, ANNE 18 December 1729.

D. TILLERY, JOB 21 April 1730.

D. TILLERY, MARY 21 April 1730.

M. TILLERY, JOAB and Elizabeth Mackgyer, 27 August 1730.

B. TILLERY, THOMAS son of Job and Elizabeth Tillery, 13 June 1731.

B. TILLERY, JOB son of Job and Elizabeth Tillery, 1 January 1732.

B. TILLERY, ANN daughter of Richard and Ann Tillery, 27 July 1733.

D. TILLERY, THOMAS 9 January 1734.

D. TILLERY, ANN 6 February 1735.

B. TILLERY, JOHN son of Job and Elizabeth Tillery, 20 September 1735.

B. TILLERY, BETTY daughter of Job and Elizabeth Tillery, 5 April 1739.

B. TILLERY, ELIZABETH daughter of George and Judith Tillery, 29 May 1739.

D. TILLERY, JOHN son of Job and Elizabeth Tillery, 5 August 1739.

B. TILLERY, JOYCE daughter of Job and Elizabeth Tillery, 14 March 1741.

B. TILLERY, WILLIAM son of Job and Elizabeth Tillery, 14 March 1744.

D. TILLERY, ELIZABETH 13 June 1745.

D. TILLERY, GEORGE 18 January 1750.

B. TILLERY, JOHN son of George Tillery, deceased, and Judith, his wife, 26 January 1750.

B. TILLERY, WILLIAM son of Willoughby and Margaret Tillery, 14 July 1754.

B. TILLERY, JOHN son of Willoughby and Margaret Tillery, 1 May 1757.

B. TILLERY, ELIZABETH daughter of Willoughby and Margaret Tillery, 12 June 1760.

B. TILLERY, KATHRINE daughter of Willoughby and Margaret Tillery, 7 June 1766.

B. TILLERY, JUDITH CONWAY daughter of Eppey and Violet Tillery, 10 Sept. 1775.

B. TILLERY, [not entered] daughter of Eppy and Vilot Tillery, 26 November 1777.

TILSON   SEE : SISSON PAGE 168

B. TILSON, SARAH daughter of Bryan and Anne Tilson, 3 October 1725.

M. TODD, CORNELIUS and Mary Jones, 17 December 1739.

B. TOMBLIN, ESTER daughter of Robert and Ester Tomblin, 27 June 1688.

B. TOMLIN, WILLIAM son of William and Anne Tomlin, 13 July 1694.

BAPT. TOMLIN, WILLIAMSON BALL son of Walker and Sylla Tomlin, 27 February 1792 [L:37].

B. TRASSE, NANCY daughter of John and Susanna Trasse, 31 December 1777.

B. TRAVERSE, REBECCAH daughter of Samuel and Frances Traverse, 15 October 1692.

B.   TRAVERSE, FRANCES daughter of Samuel and Frances Traverse, 20 August 1697.

M.   TRAVERSE, WINIFRED and Daniel Hornby, 28 November 1741.

B.   TROCK, MARY daughter of John and Sarah Trock, 29 May 1681.

M.   TRUMAN, SARAH and William Smith, 5 July 1731.

M.   TUNE, JAMES and Mary Jackman, 6 September 1680.

B.   TUNE, ANNE daughter of Mark and Elizabeth Tune, 18 May 1710.

B.   TUNE, ELIZABETH daughter of Mark and Elizabeth Tune, 10 April 1712.

D.   TUNE, JAMES 10 December 1717.

B.   TUNE, JOHN son of John and Phebe Tune, 6 October 1719.

B.   TUNE, HARRIS son of John and Phebe Tune, 6 August 1721.

B.   TUNE, ANTHONY son of John and Phebe Tune, 17 September 1723.

B.   TUNE, RAWLEIGH son of William and Joanna Tune, 6 January 1726.

D.   TUNE, MARK 23 November 1726.

M.   TUNE, THOMAS and Ann Harris, 24 July 1727.

B.   TUNE, ELIZABETH daughter of Thomas and Ann Tune, 19 April 1729.

B.   TUNE, ELIZABETH daughter of William and Joanna Tune, 19 April 1729.

B.   TUNE, MARY daughter of John and Phebe Tune, 26 April 1729.

B.   TUNE, SAMUEL son of William and Joanna Tune, 25 January 1731.

B.   TUNE, JOSEPH son of John and Phebe Tune, 1 May 1731.

B.   TUNE, TRAVERSE son of Thomas and Ann Tune, 15 February 1731/2.

B.   TUNE, RICHARD bastard son of James Tune and Ann Allgood, 2 November 1732.

D.   TUNE, JOSEPH 17 September 1733.

B.   TUNE, THOMAS son of Thomas and Ann Tune, 28 March 1734.

B.   TUNE, NANNY daughter of John and Phebe Tune, 14 June 1734.

B.   TUNE, HENRY son of William and Joanna Tune, 28 July 1734.

D.   TUNE, BETTY 13 November 1734.

D. TUNE, THOMAS 24 November 1734.

B. TUNE, JOHN son of John and Phebe Tune, 23 December 1735.

B. TUNE, SARAH daughter of Thomas and Ann Tune, 23 December 1735.

B. TUNE, ANN daughter of Thomas and Ann Tune, 1 March 1737.

B. TUNE, WILLIAM son of William and Joanna Tune, 20 February 1738.

B. TUNE, TARPLEY son of William and Joanna Tune, 24 February 1741.

D. TUNE, JOHN 28 August 1742.

B. TUNE, DUANNAH daughter of Thomas and Ann Tune, 28 November 1743.

B. TUNE, LEANNA daughter of William and Joanna Tune, 16 April 1745.

B. TUNE, ANTHONY son of Anthony and Dorcas Tune, 31 October 1750.

B. TUNE, JOHN son of Anthony and Dorcas Tune, 16 May 1752.

D. TUNE, WILLIAM 20 May 1755.

B. TUNE, WILLIAM son of Samuel and Sarah Tune, 31 October 1757.

B. TUNE, BETTY ANN daughter of Anthony and Dorcas Tune, 7 July 1759.

B. TUNE, WINNY daughter of Samuel and Sarah Tune, 6 March 1760.

B. TUNE, JAMES son of Samuel and Sarah Tune, 30 June 1762.

B. TUNE, THOMAS son of Samuel and Sarah Tune, 25 March 1765.

B. TUNE, NANSY daughter of Samuel and Sarah Tune, 17 May 1767.

B. TUNE, JESSE son of Anthony and Dorcas Tune, 31 October 1768.

B. TUNE, SAMUEL son of Samuel and Sarah Tune, 12 January 1770.

B. TUNE, THOMAS son of Castor and Elizabeth Tune, 2 January 1771.

B. TUNE, HENRY son of Samuel and Sarah Tune, 1 December 1775.

B. TUNE, CATY daughter of Castor and Elizabeth Tune, 4 November 1776.

B. TUNE, LEWIS son of Samuel and Sarah Tune, 1 March 1777.

B. TUNE, GEORGE son of Castor and Betty Tune, 28 January 1781.

B. TUNE, GEORGE DAVENPORT son of Kestor Tune, [not entered] February 1781.
[N.B. As there was only one man by the name of Castor/Kestor Tune in Rich-

mond County in 1781, it seems certain that the two entries next above concern the same person. Probably George Davenport Tune was born 28 January 1781 and baptized in February following.]

B. TUNE, MARY daughter of Samuel and Sarah Tune, 5 January 1782.

B. TOON, TRAVERSE son of Kestor and Elizabeth Toon, 12 April 1783.

B. TUNE, SAMUEL son of Anthony and Nancey Tune, 26 December 1796.

B. TUNNER, NANSY daughter of John and Lettice Tunner, 2 August 1754.

M. TURNER, HEZEKIAH and Elizabeth Hugell, 8 June 1674.

D. TWINNY, THOMAS 1 January 1744.

U

M. UNDERWOOD, ALICE and Thomas Warring, 5 October 1673.

B. UNDERWOOD, MARY daughter of Thomas and Sarah Underwood, 22 October 1687.

B. UNDERWOOD, WILLIAM son of Mooto and Anne Underwood, 6 January 1726.

B. UNDERWOOD, SETH son of Mooto and Anne Underwood, 1 May 1729.

B. UNGWIN, RACHELL daughter of Shadrack and Mary Ungwin, 23 September 1679.

V

D. VENNEN, PHILLIP 13 September 1728.

B. VENUS, RICHARD son of Milley Venus a free mulatto, 8 August 1790.

B. VERNON, BERIAH son of Ephraim and Anne Vernon, 10 September 1724.

D. VINSON, GRACE 22 December 1726.

D. VITCH [? VRTCH ?], WILLIAM 21 December 1719.

VANLANDINHAM : VANLANDINGHAM

B. VANLANDINGHAM, MARY daughter of William and Sarah Vanlandingham, 15 October 1720.

B. VANLANDINHAM, LEROY son of John and Sarah Vanlandinham, 14 September 1753.

B. VANLANDINHAM, WILLIAM son of John and Sarah Ann Vanlandinham, 1 December 1755.

B. VANLANDINHAM, JOHN son of John and Sarah Ann Vanlandinham, 23 January 1758.

B. VANLANDINHAM, JUDITH daughter of John and Sarah Ann Vanlandinham, 24 August 1760.

B. VANLANDINGHAM, MOLLY daughter of J. Vanlandingham, 20 June 1787.

B. VANLANDINGHAM, SALLY daughter of John and Nancey Vanlandingham, 24 May 1798.

D. VRTCH [? VITCH ?], WILLIAM 21 December 1719.

W

WADE : WAID

M. WADE, JEAN and Simon Polling, 19 October 1673.

B. WADE, JOSEPH son of John and Jane Wade, 17 December 1711.

D. WAID, JOHN 10 August 1734.

D. WADE, JOSEPH 16 December 1743.

D. WADE, JANE 14 February 1745.

D. WADE, JOHN 4 October 1750.

WAID : WADE SEE WADE : WAID PAGE 192

D. WAIT, WILLIAM 2 November 1722.

WALD SEE WALL PAGE 193

B. WALD, NANCY daughter of Edward and Peggy Wald, 27 April 1777.

B. WALKER, ELIZABETH daughter of Thomas and Anne Walker, 8 November 1679.

B. WALKER, ANNE daughter of Thomas and Anne Walker, 4 November 1681.

B. WALKER, MARY daughter of Thomas and Anne Walker, 28 December 1683.

B. WALKER, SARAH daughter of Thomas and Anne Walker, 15 February 1685.

B. WALKER, RACHELL daughter of Thomas and Anne Walker, 5 August 1688.

B. WALKER, ELIZABETH daughter of Charles and Sarah Walker, 29 October 1691.

B. WALKER, WILLIAM son of Thomas and Anne Walker, 9 August 1696.

B. WALKER, WILLIAM son of William and Jane Walker, 23 September 1722.

B. WALKER, ELIZABETH daughter of William and Jane Walker, 24 March 1724/5.

B. WALKER, BETTY daughter of William and Hannah Walker, 10 April 1725.

B. WALKER, THOMAS son of William and Jane Walker, 22 July 1727.

B. WALKER, GEORGE son of Thomas and Elizabeth Walker, 20 June 1728.

B. WALKER, JOHN son of William and Hannah Walker, 6 October 1728.

B. WALKER, SARAH daughter of Thomas and Elizabeth Walker, 25 March 1729.

B. WALKER, SOLOMON son of William and Jane Walker, 31 August 1729.

B. WALKER, SAMUEL son of William and Jane Walker, 30 August 1731.

B. WALKER, MAGDALENE daughter of John Walker, 30 August 1735.

B. WALKER, FRANCES daughter of John and Esther Walker, 13 August 1738.

B. WALKER, RANDOLPH son of John and Alice Walker, 15 September 1741.

B. WALKER, ANN daughter of John and Alice Walker, 27 July 1744.

B. WALKER, SALLEY daughter of William and Kathrine Walker, 6 August 1746.

B. WALKER, VINCENT son of William and Kathrine Walker, 18 April 1748.

D. WALKER, WILLIAM 9 January 1750.

B. WALKER, RACHEL daughter of John and Anne Walker, 5 June 1751.

B. WALKER, ELIZABETH daughter of John and Anne Walker, 20 October 1757.

B. WALKER, JEREMIAH son of David and Magdaline Walker, 26 June 1768.

B. WALKER, NANCY daughter of Thomas and Elenor Walker, 23 July 1778.

WALL   SEE :   WALD   PAGE   192

B. WALL, JAMES son of Edward and Margaret Wall, 19 September 1775.

WALLACE   :   WALLIS

B. WALLACE, GEORGE son of Walter and Margaret Wallace, 2 April 1737.

B. WALLACE, ELIZABETH daughter of Walter and Margaret Wallace, 4 November 1739.

B. WALLIS, ELIZABETH daughter of Walter and Margaret Wallis, 15 September 1751.

WARMOTH : WORMOTH

B. WORMOTH, ANN daughter of Thomas and Kathrine Wormoth, 4 February 1738.

B. WARMOTH, KATHRINE daughter of Thomas and Catherine Warmoth, 7 April 1741.

B. WARMOTH, ELIZABETH daughter of Thomas and Kathrine Warmoth, 22 Dec. 1744.

B. WARMOTH, MARY daughter of Thomas and Betty Warmoth, 13 February 1756.

B. WARMOTH, PATIENCE daughter of Thomas and Betty Warmoth, 18 October 1757.

B. WARMOTH, BETTY daughter of Thomas and Betty Warmoth, 21 October 1757 (sic).

B. WARMOTH, WILLIAM son of Thomas and Betty Warmoth, 29 February 1759.

B. WARMOTH, THOMAS son of John and Sarah Warmoth, 8 January 1760.

B. WARMOTH, WILLIAM son of Thomas and Betty Warmoth, 2 September 1778.

B. WARMOTH, CATY daughter of Thomas and Betty Warmoth, 9 January 1782.

B. WARNER, SARAH daughter of William and Betty Warner, 30 April 1760.

B. WARNER, WILLIAM son of William and Betty Ann Warner, 2 April 1778.

B. WARRIN, ROBERT son of Catherine Warrin, 23 November 1742.

M. WARRING, THOMAS and Alice Underwood, 5 October 1673.

M. WASCOLE, MARY and Henry Tillery, 7 November 1675.

B. WASHINGTON, JAMES WINDER son of William and Elizabeth Washington, 26 June 1798 [L:43].

B. WATERS, WARING daughter of John and Hannah Waters, 1 April 1718.

B. WATERS, JOSHUA son of John and Hannah Waters, 23 March 1721.

B. WATERS, PRUDENCE daughter of John and Hannah Waters, 16 November 1724.

D. WATSON, DAVID 15 August 1722.

M. WATSON, JOHN and Mary Huntly, 7 June 1730.

M. WATTS, JOHN and Mary Alverson, 9 January 1729/30.

B. WATTS, WILLIAM son of Spencer and Catharine Watts, 24 December 1753.

WEATHERS : WITHERS

B. **WITHERS, ANNE** daughters of Samuel and Elizabeth Withers, 15 August 1717.

B. WEATHERS, THOMAS son of Samuel and Elizabeth Withers, 15 November 1719.

B. WEATHERS, SAMUEL son of Samuel and Elizabeth Weathers, 30 August 1722.

B. WEATHERS, JOHN son of Samuel and Elizabeth Weathers, 24 January 1724/5.

B. WEATHERS, SUSANNA daughter of Samuel and Elizabeth Weathers, 16 Oct. 1728.

D. WEATHERS, SAMUEL   25 January 1728/9.

D. WEATHERS, SUSANNA   23 August 1732.

M. WEBB, JOHN and Mary Samford, 14 July 1673.

B. WEBB, JAMES son of John and Mary Webb, 9 August 1673.

B. WEBB, GILES son of John and Mary Webb, 15 April 1677.

M. WEBB, ISAAC and Mary Bedwell, 6 April 1678.

B. WEBB, ISAAC son of John and Mary Webb, 18 December 1681.

B. WEBB, JOHN SPAN son of Giles and Elizabeth Webb, 9 October 1705.

B. WEBB, ISAAC son of Giles and Elizabeth Webb, 25 September 1709.

B. WEBB, BETTY daughter of Giles and Elizabeth Webb, 1 February 1711.

B. WEBB, GILES son of Giles and Elizabeth Webb, 4 August 1714.

B. WEBB, MARY daughter of Giles and Elizabeth Webb, 11 November 1717.

B. WEBB, CUTHBERTH son of Giles and Elizabeth Webb, 3 March 1718/19.

B. WEBB, WINNEFRED daughter of Giles and Elizabeth Webb, [date not entered; probably circa 1720].

B. WEBB, WILLIAM son of Jane (sic) and Barbara Webb, 10 May 1720.

D. WEBB, TABITHA 9 February 1722.

B. WEBB, TABITHA daughter of Giles and Elizabeth Webb, 9 October 1722.

B. WEBB, JAMES son of Barbery Webb, 12 June 1729.

B. WEBB, PETER bastard son of Elizabeth Webb, 17 November 1731.

B.   WEBB, JOHN son of Isaac and Frances Webb, 1 February 1737.

B.   WEBB, THOMAS son of Ann Webb, 28 March 1738.

B.   WEBB, ISAAC son of Isaac and Frances Webb, 30 October 1739.

D.   WEBB, ISAAC son of Isaac and Frances Webb, 15 November 1740.

B.   WEBB, GILES son of Isaac and Frances Webb, 9 November 1741.

B.   WEBB, WILLIAM son of John Spann and Sarah Webb, 25 May 1742.

B.   WEBB, JAMES son of Isaac and Frances Webb, 11 September 1743.

B.   WEBB, CUTHBERT son of Isaac and Frances Webb, 1 June 1745.

B.   WEBB, WINNY daughter of Isaac and Frances Webb, 20 March 1750.

D.   WEBB, JAMES 10 May 1750.

D.   WEBB, JAMES HANKS son of James and Anne Webb, 20 November 1750.

B.   WEBB, ANNE daughter of Isaac and Frances Webb, 22 January 1753.

B.   WEBB, PRISCILLA daughter of Isaac and Frances Webb, 6 June 1754.

D.   WEBB, SARAH   25 August 1754.

D.   WEBB, FRANCES daughter of Isaac and Frances Webb, 6 February 1755.

B.   WEBB, GILES son of Isaac and Frances Webb, 25 January 1756 (sic).

B.   WEBB, CHARLES son of Isaac and Frances Webb, 27 April 1756 (sic).

D.   WEBB, JOHN   3 May 1756.

B.   WEBB, ISAAC son of Isaac and Frances Webb, 19 November 1758.

B.   WEBB, SARAH daughter of John and Clarahman Webb, 20 October 1761.

B.   WEBB, JOHN son of Isaac and Elizabeth Webb, 16 December 1790 [L:43].

B.   WEBB, NANCEY daughter of Isaac and Elizabeth Webb, 23 May 1793 [L:43].

B.   WEBB, CAROLINE daughter of Richard and Elizabeth Webb, 21 November 1798.

B.   WEBB, PHILIP a free Negro, son of Roger Webb a free Negro, 23 June 1799 [L:42].

B.   WEBSTER, AARON son of Henry and Charity Webster, 7 April 1687.

B. WEBSTER, WINNEFRED daughter of Henry and Elizabeth Webb, 19 February 1711.

B. WEBSTER, WINNEFRED daughter of Aaron and Elizabeth Webb, 19 February 1711.

B. WEBSTER, NATHANIEL son of Henry and Elizabeth Webster, 29 November 1713.

B. WEBSTER, GEORGE LEASURE son of Henry and Elizabeth Webster, 13 Feby 1714.

B. WEBSTER, NATHANIEL son of Aaron and Elizabeth Webster, 29 November 1714.

B. WEBSTER, HENRY son of Moses Webster, 25 October 1716.

B. WEBSTER, GEORGE son of Aaron and Elizabeth Webster, 13 December 1716.

D. WEBSTER, JOHN 17 January 1719.

B. WEBSTER, ELIZABETH daughter of Aaron and Elizabeth Webster, 4 Sept. 1719.

B. WEBSTER, JUDITH daughter of Henry and Elizabeth Webster, 12 December 1719.

B. WEBSTER, MORRIS son of Morris and Leah Webster, 29 December 1719.

D. WEBSTER, HENRY 14 January 1720.

D. WEBSTER, ELIZABETH 21 November 1726.

M. WEBSTER, HENRY and Mary Ann Collins, 15 September 1730.

M. WEBSTER, THOMAS and Katherine English, 11 September 1739.

B. WEBSTER, ANN daughter of Nathaniel and Margaret Webster, 19 February 1740.

B. WELCH, WILLIAM son of Thomas and Elizabeth Welch, 14 December 1715.

B. WELCH, MARGARET daughter of Thomas and Elizabeth Welch, 14 September 1718.

B. WELCH, JANE daughter of Thomas and Elizabeth Welch, 20 January 1720.

D. WELCH, THOMAS 12 May 1720.

D. WELCH, ESTHER 29 January 1721/2.

B. WELCH, MARGARET 5 September 1723 [no parents entered].

B. WELCH, JANE daughter of Thomas and Elizabeth Welch, 14 August 1726.

M. WELLDON, JOHN and Winifred Hobs, 7 July 1729.

M. WELLS, STEPHEN and Alice Howard, 3 December 1677.

M. WELLS, STEPHEN and Priscilla Redman, 21 August 1729.

B.   WELLS, BETTY daughter of Stephen and Priscilla Wells, 30 May 1730.

   WEYMOTH   SEE :   WARMOTH   :   WORMOTH   PAGE   194

B.   WHARTON, SAMUEL son of Samuel and Anne Wharton, 19 November 1684.

B.   WHARTON, JOHN son of Samuel and Anne Wharton, 24 December 1686.

B.   WHITE, SARAH daughter of Walter and Mary White, 27 December 1698.

B.   WHITE, THOMAS son of Walter and Mary White, 29 May 1704.

D.   WHITE, LEROY 20 February 1718.

D.   WHITE, THOMAS 21 February 1718.

D.   WHITE, BARTHOLOMEW 10 October 1720.

B.   WHITE, THOMAS son of William and Kathrine White, 1 December 1726.

B.   WHITE, SUSANNA daughter of William and Kathrine White, 22 December 1729.

B.   WHITE, SALLEY WALKER MORRIS daughter of Abraham and Caty White, 19 March
     1798 [L:43].

B.   WHITE, WILLIAM son of Abram and Caty White, 2 April 1799 [L:43].

M.   WIDDILOW, MARY and Patrick Connelly, 28 July 1728.

   WILCOCKS   :   WILLCOCKS

B.   WILLCOCKS, WINIFRED daughter of Godfrey and Elizabeth Willcocks, 9 January
     1741.

B.   WILCOCKS, JOHN son of Godfrey and Elizabeth Wilcocks, 29 April 1742.

B.   WILCOCKS, WILLIAM son of Godfrey and Elizabeth Wilcocks, 9 August 1755.

B.   WILCOCKS, NANNY daughter of Godfrey and Elizabeth Wilcocks, 19 Feby 1757.

B.   WILCOCKS, JOHN son of George and Hannah Wilcocks, 5 July 1776.

M.   WILCOX, JOHN and Ann Jenings, 2 March 1729/30.

   WILDEN   :   WILDER   :   WILDY   &c.

B.   WILDY, SIDWELL daughter of Michael and Susanna Wildy, 12 December 1721.

B.   WILDER, JONATHAN son of Michael and Susanna Wilder, 18 January 1728/9.

B.   WILLDAY, ROSANNA daughter of Michael and Susanna Willday, 9 January 1730/1.

B. WILDEN, WINIFRED daughter of Jonathan and Mary Wilden, 29 December 1761.

B. WILDEN, JOHN son of William and Sarah Wilden, 31 May 1765.

B. WILDEN, WILLIAM son of William and Sarah Wilden, 5 December 1766.

B. WILDEN, DANGERFIELD son of William and Sarah Wilden, 10 January 1769.

D. WILKINS, JANE   28 August 1722.

B. WILKINS, MARY daughter of James and Frances Wilkins, 23 April 1751.

B. WILKINS, ROBERT son of James and Frances Wilkins, 10 September 1753.

B. WILKINS, GEORGE son of James and Frances Wilkins, 24 October 1756.

B. WILKINS, ELIZABETH daughter of James and Frances Wilkins, 14 December 1758.

B. WILKINS, JOHN son of James and Frances Wilkins, 30 December 1760.

B. WILKINS, JAMES son of James and Frances Wilkins, 16 January 1763.

WILKINSON : WILKERSON

B. WILKERSON, ELIZABETH daughter of Charles and Jane Wilkerson, 23 Sept. 1711.

B. WILKINSON, JANE daughter of Charles and Jane Wilkinson, 10 March 1715.

B. WILKINSON, BRIDGETT daughter of Charles and Jane Wilkinson, 10 April 1719.

B. WILKINSON, PICKRILL son of Charles and Jane Wilkinson, 5 December 1721.

M. WILKERSON, JANE and Owin Jones, 19 January 1730/31.

B. WILLIAMS, SHADRACK son of Roger and Jean Williams, 1 February 1673.

B. WILLIAMS, REBECCAH daughter of Roger and Jane Williams, 20 June 1675.

B. WILLIAMS, LUKE son of Luke and Anne Williams, 13 May 1692.

B. WILLIAMS, JOHN son of Luke and Mary Williams, 15 September 1701.

B. WILLIAMS, JANE daughter of Henry and Lettice Williams, 26 November 1702.

B. WILLIAMS, THOMAS son of David and Mary Williams, 12 January 1707.

B. WILLIAMS, JANE daughter of David and Mary Williams, 19 August 1709.

B. WILLIAMS, OWING son of David and Mary Williams, 22 September 1712.

B. WILLIAMS, DAVID son of David and Mary Williams, 22 April 1714.

B. WILLIAMS, MARY daughter of Charles and Catharine Williams, 29 January 1716.

D. WILLIAMS, ANNE 22 September 1717.

B. WILLIAMS, ANNE daughter of David and Mary Williams, 28 December 1718.

B. WILLIAMS, SHADRACK son of Roger and Mary Williams, 20 October 1720.

D. WILLIAMS, WINIFRED 5 June 1721.

B. WILLIAMS, MARY ANN daughter of David and Mary Williams, 12 August 1721.

B. WILLIAMS, LUKE and SARAH twins of John and Jane Williams, 15 March 1722.

D. WILLIAMS, JANE 12 October 1722.

D. WILLIAMS, SHADRICK 28 January 1723/4.

B. WILLIAMS, THOMAS son of John and Jane Williams, 12 April 1724.

B. WILLIAMS, ELIZABETH daughter of Roger and Mary Williams, 13 February 1724/5.

B. WILLIAMS, JANE daughter of John and Jane Williams, __ February 1725.

M. WILLIAMS, THOMAS and Sarah Audley, 2 October 1726.

M. WILLIAMS, HENRY and Susanna Gower, 22 December 1726.

D. WILLIAMS, MARY 11 October 1727.

M. WILLIAMS, ANN and Roger Williams, 5 August 1728.

M. WILLIAMS, ROGER and Ann Williams, 5 August 1728.

B. WILLIAMS, SAMUEL son of John and Jane Williams, 4 September 1728.

B. WILLIAMS, JOHN son of Roger and Mary Williams, 3 December 1729.

B. WILLIAMS, JOHN son of Roger and Ann Williams, 9 December 1729.

M. WILLIAMS, HENRY and Priscilla Oldham, 22 January 1729/30.

B. WILLIAMS, SARAH daughter of Henry and Priscilla Williams, 11 December 1730.

D. WILLIAMS, ALCE 29 January 1731.

D. WILLIAMS, SARAH 8 January 1731/2.

B. WILLIAMS, GEORGE son of Roger and Ann Williams, 28 March 1732.

M. WILLIAMS, THOMAS and Winifred Pycraft, 8 June 1732.

B. WILLIAMS, JOHN son of Henry and Priscilla Williams, 20 June 1733.

B. WILLIAMS, GEORGE son of Roger and Ann Williams, 30 January 1734.

D. WILLIAMS, ELIZABETH 8 March 1735.

D. WILLIAMS, ELIZABETH 27 May 1735.

B. WILLIAMS, ISAAC son of Henry and Priscilla Williams, 28 December 1735.

D. WILLIAMS, SUSANNAH 9 January 1736.

B. WILLIAMS, MOSES son of John and Sarah Williams, 4 June 1736.

B. WILLIAMS, LUKE son of Roger and Ann Williams, 22 November 1738.

B. WILLIAMS, ANN daughter of John and Elizabeth Williams, 17 August 1739.

B. WILLIAMS, JOHN son of Henry and Ann Williams, 2 June 1740.

D. WILLIAMS, JOHN son of Henry and Ann Williams, 6 June 1740.

B. WILLIAMS, HUKEY [?] son of Roger and Ann Williams, 12 December 1740.

B. WILLIAMS, ABRAHAM son of Henry and Ann Williams, 20 December 1741.

B. WILLIAMS, LUCY daughter of John and Elizabeth Williams, 22 September 1742.

D. WILLIAMS, ANN 23 January 1743.

B. WILLIAMS, JUDITH daughter of Henry and Ann Williams, 31 October 1743.

B. WILLIAMS, CILLA and MENAS daughter and son of Henry and Priscilla Williams, 7 March 1744.

B. WILLIAMS, SARAH daughter of Roger and Ann Williams, 18 November 1744.

D. WILLIAMS, ANN wife of Roger Williams, 31 December 1744.

B. WILLIAMS, JONATHAN son of John and Elizabeth Williams, 28 April 1745.

B. WILLIAMS, WILLIAM son of Luke and Lucy Williams, 8 March 1745/6.

B. WILLIAMS, BETTY daughter of John and Betty Williams, 10 March 1747.

B. WILLIAMS, EDWARD son of Thomas and Winifred Williams, 7 December 1747.

B. WILLIAMS, ANN daughter of Luke and Lucy Williams, 16 January 1747/8.

B. WILLIAMS, SAMUEL son of Luke and Lucy Williams, 1 March 1749.

D. WILLIAMS, JOHN SEN.^{R} 15 March 1750.

B. WILLIAMS, JESSE son of Thomas and Winifred Williams, 8 September 1750.

B. WILLIAMS, JANE daughter of John and Elizabeth Williams, 28 September 1750.

B. WILLIAMS, JUDITH daughter of Luke and Lucy Williams, 13 January 1751.

B. WILLIAMS, WINIFRED daughter of Samuel and Betty Williams, 30 March 1752.

B. WILLIAMS, NANNY daughter of John and Sarah Williams, 19 August 1752.

B. WILLIAMS, BUTLER son of Luke and Lucy Williams, 30 November 1753.

B. WILLIAMS, SARAH SUGGITT daughter of Samuel and Betty Williams, 12 March 1754.

B. WILLIAMS, RAWLEIGH son of John and Elizabeth Williams, 18 March 1754.

B. WILLIAMS, BETTY daughter of John and Sarah Williams, 5 May 1754.

B. WILLIAMS, THOMAS son of Luke and Lucy Williams, [not entered] 1756.

B. WILLIAMS, WINNY daughter of John and Sarah Williams, 31 August 1756.

B. WILLIAMS, THADDEUS son of Samuel and Betty Ann Williams, 18 September 1756.

B. WILLIAMS, SHADRACH son of John and Sarah Williams, 28 August 1758.

B. WILLIAMS, SUSANNA daughter of Thomas and Winny Williams, 11 September 1758.

B. WILLIAMS, SAMUEL son of Samuel and Betty Ann Williams, 13 May 1759.

D. WILLIAMS, ELIZABETH wife of Roger Williams, 25 October 1759.

B. WILLIAMS, JOANNA and SARAH twins of Luke and Lucy Williams, 9 May 1760.

B. WILLIAMS, THOMAS PLUMMER son of Thomas and Winny Williams, 1 October 1761.

B. WILLIAMS, DAVID son of Samuel and Betty Ann Williams, 24 March 1762.

B. WILLIAMS, CYRUS son of Samuel and Betty Ann Williams, 19 July 1765.

B. WILLIAMS, TABITHA daughter of George and Caty Williams, 20 February 1766.

B. WILLIAMS, BETTY ANN daughter of Samuel and Betty Ann Williams, 19 April 1769.

D. WILLIAMS, CYRUS son of Samuel and Betty Ann Williams, 17 December 1770.

B. WILLIAMS, REBECKIAH daughter of Samuel and Betty Ann Williams, 14 March 1774.

D. WILLIAMS, REBECKIAH daughter of Samuel and Betty Ann Williams, 14 Sept. 1774.

B. WILLIAMS, LUKE son of Butler and Anne Williams, 29 January 1776.

B. WILLIAMS, CATHARINE daughter of Thomas and Rachel Williams, 19 May 1777.

B. WILLIAMS, SAMUEL son of Butler and Ann Williams, 16 August 1778.

B. WILLIAMS, BETSY CORRIE daughter of Thaddeus and Caty Williams, 22 June 1788.

B. WILLIAMS, CATY daughter of Thaddeus and Caty Williams, 8 September 1790.

WILLSON : WILSON

B. WILSON, THOMAS son of Henry and Sarah Wilson, 2 May 1674.

B. WILSON, THOMAS son of Charles and Isabella Wilson, 1 November 1678.

B. WILSON, HENRY son of Charles and Isabella Wilson, 1 July 1681.

B. WILLSON, JAMES son of James and Mary Willson, 16 October 1703.

B. WILLSON, SARAH daughter of John and Margaret Willson, 6 November 1703.

B. WILLSON, ANNE daughter of James and Mary Willson, 15 March 1707.

B. WILLSON, JOHN son of James and Mary Willson, 15 July 1710.

B. WILSON, EDWARD son of John and Judah Wilson, 15 July 1781.

B. WILLSON, JAMES son of Daniel and Mary Willson, 16 August 1784 [L:43].

B. WILLSON, HANNAH daughter of Daniel and Mary Willson, 8 December 1791 [L:43].

B. WILLSON, HENRY MUSE son of Daniel and Mary Willson, 17 August 1793 [L:43].

B. WILLSON, CHURCHILL a bastard son of Edward Willson and Molly Richardson, 23 May 1794 [L:43]. [This couple were married per bond 7 November 1796; MRC, p. 233].

B. WILLSON, NANCEY MARKS daughter of Daniel and Mary Willson, 2 September 1796 [L:43].

B. WILLSON, ALVIN EIDSON son of Edward and Molley Willson, 6 January 1797 [L:43; see notation above in regard to this couple's marriage].

M. WIN, JUDITH and Luke Demeritt, 13 February 1728/9.

B. WINN, MARY daughter of John and Betty Winn, 13 July 1739.

WINTER : WINTERS   SEE : WINTOR PAGE 204

B. WINTERS, RICHARD son of Richard and Mary Winters, 5 October 1722.

B. WINTER, HENRY son of Richard and Mary Winter, 6 February 1730.

D. WINTER, RICHARD 4 February 1735.

D. WINTERS, JOHN 27 June 1743.

B. WINTERS, WILLIAM son of free Nancey, formerly the property of Dr. Moore Fauntleroy, 20 February 1793 [L:10].

WINTOR   SEE : WINTER : WINTERS   PAGE   203

D. WINTOR, HENRY 3 September 1729.

WITHERS   SEE : WEATHERS : WITHERS PAGE 195

B. WOOD, THOMAS son of Robert and Mary Wood, 15 November 1673.

B. WOOD, ROBERT son of Robert and Mary Wood, 25 September 1679.

B. WOOD, THOMAS son of Thomas and Anne Wood, 2 February 1700.

B. WOOD, JOHN son of Thomas and Anne Wood, 30 November 1712.

B. WOOD, MARY ANN daughter of Thomas and Elizabeth Wood, 12 October 1725.

D. WOOD, THOMAS 1 February 1726.

B. WOOD, CHARLES son of Charlotte Wood, 29 June 1795.

B. WOODBRIDGE, WILLIAM son of Paul and Bridget Woodbridge, 14 July 1668.

B. WOODBRIDGE, ELIZABETH daughter of Paul and Bridget Woodbridge, 24 December 1677 [see MRC, pgs. 126, 202].

B. WOODBRIDGE, JOHN son of William and Sarah Woodbridge, 24 November 1706.

B. WOODBRIDGE, ELIZABETH daughter of William and Sarah Woodbridge, 6 July 1709.

B. WOODBRIDGE, SARAH daughter of William and Sarah Woodbridge, 18 November 1714.

D. WOODBRIDGE, WILLIAM 14 November 1727. [There must be some error here as the will of Major William Woodbridge (1668-1726/7) was dated 16 November 1726 and recorded 1 February 1726/7 in Will Book #5, page 27.]

B. WOODCOCK, JOANNA daughter of William and Elizabeth Woodcock, 19 March 1718.

B. WOODCOCK, MARY daughter of William and Elizabeth Woodcock, 12 November 1722.

D. WOODCOCK, SUSANNA 31 January 1726.

D. WOODCOCK, JOANNA 3 February 1726.

B. WOODCOCK, JOHN SHEARMAN son of William and Elizabeth Woodcock, 24 Jan.ʸ 1734.

D. WOODCOCK, WILLIAM 13 February 1734.

B. WOOLLARD, MARY daughter of John and Mary Woollard, 1 October 1682.

B. WOOLLARD, JOHN son of John and Mary Woollard, 14 April 1685.

B. WOOLLARD, REBECCAH daughter of John and Mary Woollard, 9 September 1687.

B. WOOLLARD, RICHARD son of John and Mary Woollard, 22 October 1691.

B. WOOLLARD, ELLING daughter of John and Mary Woollard, 31 March 1696.

B. WOOLLARD, JOHN son of Richard and Sarah Woollard, 17 June 1716.

B. WOOLLARD, MARY daughter of Richard and Sarah Woollard, 6 January 1718.

B. WOOLLARD, ISAAC son of John and Anne Woollard, 5 August 1720.

B. WOOLLARD, SUSANNA daughter of Richard and Sarah Woollard, 17 September 1721.

B. WOOLLARD, SARAH daughter of Richard and Sarah Woollard, 30 July 1724.

B. WOOLLARD, JOHN son of John and Ann Woollard, 25 April 1725.

D. WOOLLARD, MARY 20 January 1726.

B. WOOLLARD, JOSEPH son of John and Ann Woollard, 29 January 1726.

B. WOOLLARD, ELEANOR daughter of Richard and Sarah Woollard, 26 March 1727.

B. WOOLLARD, WILLIAM son of John and Ann Woollard, 10 October 1729.

B. WOOLLARD, RICHARD son of Richard and Sarah Woollard, 12 November 1729.

B. WOOLLARD, ANN daughter of John and Ann Woollard, 15 August 1732.

B. WOOLLARD, WILLIAM son of Richard and Sarah Woollard, 4 October 1732.

B. WOOLLARD, SAMUEL son of John and Ann Woollard, 25 December 1735.

B. WOOLLARD, ELISHA and BETTY ANN daughters (sic) [? twins ?] of Richard and Sarah Woollard, 1 April 1736.

D. WOOLLARD, JOHN JUN^{R}. 27 September 1738.

B. WOOLLARD, ESAW son of Isaac and Cathrine Woollard, 15 November 1747.

B. WOOLLARD, WILLIAM son of William and Mary Woollard, 20 January 1749.

D. WOOLLARD, CATY 24 February 1749.

B. WOOLLARD, WILLIAM son of John and Sarah Woollard, 1 November 1751.

D. WOOLLARD, WILLIAM 6 November 1751.

B. WOOLLARD, JOHN son of John and Sarah Woollard, 7 January 1752.

B. WOOLLARD, WINIFRED daughter of Richard and Elizabeth Woollard, 14 April 1755.

B. WOOLLARD, JOSEPH son of Richard and Elizabeth Woollard, 25 February 1758.

B. WOOLLARD, JOHN son of Samuel and Mary Ann Woollard, 28 July 1763.

B. WOOLLARD, ELIZABETH daughter of Samuel and Mary Ann Woollard, 4 Oct. 1765.

B. WOOLLARD, RICHARD son of Richard and Elizabeth Woollard, 6 October 1766.

B. WOOLLARD, ANN daughter of Samuel and Mary Ann Woollard, 9 November 1769.

B. WOOLLARD, JOHN son of Joseph and Winnefred Woollard, 4 February 1782.

B. WOOLLARD, CATHERINE WILLIAMS daughter of Joseph and Winney Woollard, 20 October 1792.

WORMOTH   SEE :   WARMOTH :   WORMOTH   PAGE   194

B. WORSDELL, MARY daughter of Richard and Sarah Worsdell, 12 October 1720.

B. WREN, JOHN son of Thomas and Jane Wren, 4 October 1737.

B. WREN, BETTY daughter of Thomas and Jane Wren, 4 November 1739.

WRIGHT   SEE :   RIGHT   PAGE   158

D. WRIGHT, HUGH   23 October 1719.

B. WRIGHT, MARGARET daughter of James and Eleanor Wright, 14 April 1721.

B. WRIGHT, JOHN son of Jane (sic) and Eleanor Wright, 17 February 1722/3.

B. WRIGHT, BETTY daughter of James and Eleanor Wright, 13 February 1726.

B. WRIGHT, JAMES son of Roger and Eleanor Wright, 18 February 1728/9.

B. WYET, WILLIAM son of James and Bethelem Wyet, 26 September 1746.

X

Y

B.   YARDLEY, JAMES RUSS a bastard child of Sally Yardley, 5 June 1792 [L:47].

B.   YEATES, PRISCILLA daughter of Ellias and Mary Yeates, 9 February 1681.

B.   YEATES, DOROTHY daughter of Thomas and Mary Yeates, 31 October 1686.

B.   YEATES, WILLIAM son of Thomas and Mary Yeates, 15 March 1689.

B.   YEATES, RICHARD son of Thomas and Mary Yeates, 31 October 1693.

B.   YEATES, ANNE daughter of William and Elizabeth Yeates, 14 November 1695.

B.   YEATES, THOMAS son of Thomas and Mary Yeates, 14 June 1699.

B.   YEATES, PHILLIS daughter of Thomas and Mary Yeates, 23 March 1702.

M.   YEATES, JUDITH and John Hammond, 21 February 1725/6.

D.   YEATES, ELIZABETH 7 January 1726.

D.   YEATES, JOHN 1 February 1726.

B.   YEATMAN, SARAH daughter of John and Hannah Yeatman, 28 March 1727.

B.   YEATMAN, MARTHA daughter of John and Hannah Yeatman, 6 June 1729.

B.   YEATMAN, MARTHA daughter of Thomas and Elizabeth Yeatman, 17 Oct. 1795 [L:47].

B.   YEATMAN, NELLEY THORNTON daughter of Thomas and Elizabeth Yeatman, 18 September 1797 [L:47].

B.   YERBY, MARY RUST daughter of George Yerby, 7 June 1791.

D.   YEWELL, DAVID 18 August 1721.

Z

FINIS

For reasons which will be apparent
to some persons, I have included in
the aforegoing arrangement certain
entries pertaining to mulattoes,
free born persons of color, and a
few others.

All mulattoes, free born Negroes of
light complexion, and some others
who may have been legally emancipat-
ed, did not remain status quo in
their ancestral domains and when
they migrated northward and westward
they sometimes attained "white"
status and intermarried with persons
of the Caucasian race.

BOTH REGISTERS abound with Negro birth recordings and since it would be impracticable to detail these, I have made an alphabetical arrangement of the Negro slave owners. However, it must not be overlooked that there is ample evidence in the court records that many persons purchased slaves from the masters of slave ships as they arrived in Virginia and others from Virginia planters and oftentimes they brought these Negro slaves into court to have their ages adjudged and thus it was certified they were their property. Thus they do not appear in the parish registers and consequently the names which follow by no means represent a full recording of all the parties who were slave holders in Richmond County during the period covered by these two parish registers. This list is designed simply to give an insight into the Negro recordings in these two parish registers and those who wish further information may consult the manuscript volumes.

The names followed by the capital letter "L" will be found in the Lunenburg Parish Register on the page indicated while those names with no further designation will be found in North Farnham Parish Register. The date following the name is the earliest date I have noted a party of this name mentioned as the proprietor of a Negro slave.

ALDERSON, James		1780
John		1790
ALLOWAY, Alexander		1747
Gabriel		1726
ASHTON, Colonel		1729
BAILEY, Charles		1781
Estate of Samuel		1727
Samuel		1745
BAKER, William		1727
BALL, George		1778
William		1729
Williamson [L:2]		1792
Estate of Williamson		
	[:36]	1793
BARBER, Thomas		1750
William		1775
BARNES, Charles		1781
Richard [L:2]		1791

BEALE, Richard		1780
Thomas [L:2]		1791
Thomas		1722
William		1731
BECHWITH, Jennings [L:2]		1788
Jonathan Sr. [L:2]		1791
Marmaduke		1718
Richard M. [L:44]		1800
BELFIELD, John Sr. [L:2]		1791
John [L:44]		1798
Sydnor [L:2]		1792
Thomas [L:2]		1791
BENNEHAM, Dominick		1772
Dudley		1740
George		1787
Richard		1796
BERNARD, William [L:2]		1791
BLACKERBY, James		1729
Leannah		1775

BLUETT, Thomas	1740	
BOOTH, James	1777	
John	1781	
BRADY, Owen	1754	
BRAGG, Charles [L:44]	1799	
Est. of Moore [L:44]	1796	
William [L: 2]	1791	
BRAMHAM, Benjamin [L: 2]	1792	
Benjamin Sr. [L:44]	1797	
BRANHAM, John	1730	
Richard	1726	
BRENT, Sinah	1783	
BRERETON, Elizabeth	1728	
BROCKENBROUGH, Champe [L:4]	1796	
Dr. John [L:2]	1792	
Moore [L:22]	1791	
Estate of		
Moore [L:2]	1791	
Newman	1710	
Estate of		
Newman	1754	
Newman [L:44]	1800	
Thomas [L:2]	1792	
William	1756	
BROOME, Thomas	1738	
BROWN, Eleanor [Ellen]	1774	
Marthy	1796	
Richard	1747	
Thomas	1766	
Vincent	1777	
BRUCE, Bettey [L:44]	1797	
BRYANT, Alexander	1762	
CARTER, Charles Esq.r	1727	
Charles of Corotoman	1771	
John Esq.r	1737	
Col. Robert Esq.	1729	
Estate of Col.		
Robert Esqr	1732	

CHAPROON, John	1729	
CHINN, Rawleigh	1728	
CHRISTIAN, Francis H.	1770	
CLARK, Alexander	1730	
Thomas [L:4]	1791	
William	1747	
CLARKE, Susanna [L:4]	1800	
CLAYTOR, Mary [L:4]	1793	
COLSTON, Charles	1726	
Lucy	1781	
Est. of Travers	1731	
William	1777	
CONNELL, Michell	1713	
CONNELLEE, George [L:4]	1800	
CONNOLLY, George [L:4]	1797	
James	1777	
CONWAY, Judith	1776	
Thomas	1777	
CORBIN, Hannah	1776	
COX, Mary	1778	
CRAWLEY, John	1728	
CREWDSON, William [L:4]	1799	
CROUCHER, Richard	1725	
DALE, Elizabeth	1796	
Hannah	1775	
Joseph	1789	
DAVENPORT, Elizabeth	1783	
Fortunatus	1775	
George	1789	
Joseph	1790	
Opey	1787	
William	1733	

DAVIS, George	1775	EFFORD, John	1747
John	1773		
		EIDSON, Edward [L:8]	1792
DEATLY, Christopher	1789	Estate of Edward "	1796
DEEK, Elizabeth	1724	ELMORE, John	1726
Katherine	1730		
Sarah	1727	ERRESKIEN, William	1744
DEGGES, William	1730	EVERETT, Daniel	1757
		William	1738
DICKENSON, Metcalfe	1733		
		FAUNTLEROY, Griffin M.	1789
DIGMAN, James [L:6]	1794	John	1782
		John [L:10]	1793
DOBYNS, Abner	1782	Moore	1727
Abner Sr.	1800	Moore	1777
Charles	1733	Robert [L:10]	1794
Daniel	1790	William [L:10]	1791
Edward	1774		
Griffin	1746	FAWCETT, John [L:10]	1792
Estate of Griffin	1753		
Henry	1777	FLEMMING, William	1731
Rebecca	1798		
Estate of Samuel	1782	FLOOD, Elizabeth	1781
Thomas	1771	Nicholas	1746
William	1774		
		FORRESTER, Bridget	1788
DODSON, Charles	1788	Robert	1784
David	1735	William	1744
James B.	1794	Est. of William	1773
Thomas	1726		
		FRANKS, Henry [L:10]	1791
DONAWAY, Samuel	1777		
DOWNMAN, Elizabeth	1775		
James	1745	GALBRATH, Robert	1741
Rawleigh	1771		
Robert	1735	GALLOWAY, John	1776
Estate of Robert			
Porteus	1782	GARLAND, George [L:12]	1793
Travers	1748	Griffin [L:12]	1791
William	1727	Mary [L:12]	1799
		Sarah [L:12]	1799
DUCHER, John	1740		
		GARNETT, Thomas	1788
DURHAM, Mary	1735		
Thomas	1730	GIBSON, Betty	1782
		Priscilla	1776
EDWARDS, George	1776		

GLASCOCK, Ann	1771	
George	1730	
George Jr.	1790	
John	1741	
Estate of John	1796	
Judith	1750	
Million	1727	
Milton S.	1788	
Thomas	1734	
William	1728	
William Sr.	1754	
William Jr.	1754	
GOODRIDGE, Richard	1775	
GOWER, Elizabeth	1728	
Standley	1726	
GREENHAM, Jeremiah	1730	
GRIFFIN, Elizabeth	1753	
Judith	1776	
LeRoy	1735	
Thomas B.	1776	
GRYMES, Charles	1726	
GWIN, Kathrine	1726	
Maximilian	1726	
HACKNEY, Benjamin	1788	
HALL, Richard	[L:14]	1796
HAMES, William	1739	
HAMMOCK, Robert	1757	
HAMMOND, Charles	1745	
Job	1753	
John	1770	
Lewis	1782	
William	1741	
HARDWICK, John	1776	
Mary	1773	
HARRIS, Hugh	1781	
John	1759	
Sarah	1776	

HARRISON, Mathew	1762	
HASTIE, William	1734	
HAYNIE, Holland	1782	
HAZARD, Henry	1774	
Zach:	1771	
HEAIL, Captain George	1730	
HEAL, George	1728	
HIGHTOWER, Chaloner	1740	
John	1729	
HILL, Francis	[L:14]	1796
John		1737
Thomas Suggitt		1768
HINDS, John	1773	
HIPKINS, Samuel		1733
Samuel	[L:14]	1798
HODGKINSON, William	1727	
HORNBY, Daniel	1731	
HOWARD, Spencer	1777	
Thomas	1781	
HUGHLETT, John	1729	
HUGHS, Reubin	[L:14]	1792
HUNT, George	1733	
HUNTON, Alexander	1776	
John	1775	
JACKSON, Thaddeus		1772
Vincent		1778
Vincent	[L:16]	1791
William	[L:16]	1793
Estate of Wm.	[L:16]	1796
JENKINS, Thomas	1801	
JESPER, Caty		1798
Daniel		1777
Thomas		1743

JONES, Barbary 1779
    Estate of Charles [L:16] 1795
    Edward 1729
    John 1789

KELLY, Captain James [L:18] 1797
    John [L:18] 1792
    John (joiner) [L:18] 1799
    John Senior [L:18] 1794

KELSICK, Samuel 1771
    Samuel [L:18] 1792

KENNAN, Estate of John 1782
    William 1752

LAMBERT, Hugh 1734

LAWSON, Christopher 1745
    Estate of Christopher 1773
    Daniel [L:20] 1794
    John 1732
    Sarah 1777

LEE, Francis L. [L:20] 179?

LEWIS, Edward 1738
    James 1776
    Thomas 1726
    William 1787

LOYD'S Estate 1726

LYELL, Estate of John 1739
    Jonathan 1728

MC CALL, Archibald 1791

MC CARTY, Ann 1746
    Bartholomew 1790
    Billington 1729
    Estate of Billington 1755
    Charles 1776
    Charles T. [L:22] 1796
    Elizabeth 1775
    Mary 1778

MC GINNIS, Richard [L:22] 1797

MC KAY, William 1746
    Rev. William 1763

MC KENNY, Elizabeth [L:22] 1795

MANTON, William 1776

MARKS, Estate of John [L:22] 1791

MARMADUKE, Daniel [L:22] 1795

MARSHALL, Caty [L:22] 1792

MARTIN, Hannah 1788
    Hannah [L:22] 1790
    William 1783

MASON, Nathaniel 1741

MEEKS, Richard 1726

METCALFE, Gilbert 1726

MILLNER, John 1755
    Luke 1736
    Mary 1747

MISKELL, George 1755
    Henry 1739
    Magdalen 1781
    Newman 1768
    William 1761

MITCHELL, Ann 1790
    James 1787
    Mary 1744
    Richard 1725
    Robert 1747
    Robert [L:22] 1793

MONTAGUE, Hannah 1787
    James 1775

MOORE, Garland [L:22] 1792

MORGAN, Frances/ [Francis] 1772

MORRIS, Edward 1735
    Elizabeth 1776
    John [L:22] 1799
    William [L:22] 1794

SINGLETON, Drusilla	1782	TEBBS, Elizabeth [L:36]	1792
Joshua	1730		
Est. of Joshua	1777	THRELKALD, Henry	1729
Robert	1773		
Samuel	1782	TILLERY, John	1787
SISSON, George	1777	TOMLIN, Catharine [L:36]	1798
Henry	1726	Robert	1726
		Robert [L:36]	1792
SMITH, Charles	1790	Robert (deceased) "	1797
John	1735	Susanna "	1797
Colonel John	1775	Walker	1787
Joseph W.	1783	Walker [L:36]	1791
Robert	1725		
Thomas	1726	TUNE, Anthony	1777
Estate of Thomas	1783	Caster [Castor, Kestor]	1783
William	1723		
Estate of William	1790	TURBERVILLE, George Lee [L:36]	1791
SMITHER, Gabriel	1748		
Estate of Gabriel	1789	WEBB, Betty	1755
		Charles	1782
STONE, William	1738	Cuthbert	1780
		Elizabeth	1759
STONUM, William	1773	Frances [Francis]	1779
		Francis	1776
STOTT, Elizabeth	1771	Isaac	1730
		James [L:42]	1800
SUGGITT, Edgcombe	1724	John Spann	1733
Elizabeth	1765		
James	1724	WELDON, John [L:42]	1799
SYDNOR, Anthony	1724	WHELDON, John [L:42]	1796
Dewanna	1777		
Elizabeth	1777	WHITE, Thomas	1727
Epaphroditus	1737	Zachariah [L:42]	1792
Giles [Jiles]	1777		
John	1775	WILLIAMS, Abraham	1771
Mildred	1777	Betty	1777
		Betty Ann	1781
TARPLEY, John	1723	Caty (an infant)	1802
John Sr.	1727	Elizabeth G.	1791
Travers	1745	Henry	1726
William	1728	John	1724
		John Jr.	1745
TAYLOE, John	1726	John Sr.	1745
John [L:36]	1792	Rawleigh	1776
		Richard	1732
TAYLOR, George	1729	Roger	1731
Hannah	1741	Samuel	1772
John	1726		

WILLIAMS, Estate of Thaddeus		1795
Thomas		1727
WILLSON, Daniel	[L:42]	1792
Elias	[L:42]	1792
Morton	[L:42]	1792
WOODBRIDGE, John		1726
WOOLLARD, Isaac		1745
John		1749
Samuel		1772
WREN, Thomas		1738
WRIGHT, John	[L:42]	1791
WROE, John		1789
YEATES, John		1727
YEATMAN, John		1729
YERBY, George		1770
John		1770
Thomas		1775

Not to know what came to
pass before you were born,
is always to remain a child.
                    Cicero

The study of genealogy, like
charity, should begin at home.
                    [Anonymous]

I N D E X

AS THE REGISTERS OF NORTH FARNHAM PARISH 1663 - 1814
AND LUNENBURG PARISH 1783 - 1800 ARE ARRANGED ALPHA-
BETICALLY BY SURNAMES IN CHRONOLOGICAL ORDER ON PAGES
1 - 207, THESE ENTRIES ARE NOT CARRIED IN THE FOLLOW-
ING INDEX

---

* See note on page 208

```
        ******
         *****
          ***
           *
```

"I cannot tell how the truth may be;
I say the tale as 't was said to me."

[Sir Walter Scott, The Lay of the Last Minstrel]